T0323416

Caught in the Cultural Preference Net

Caught in the Cultural Preference Net

Three Generations of Employment Choices in Six Capitalist Democracies

MICHAEL J. CAMASSO
RADHA JAGANNATHAN

OXFORD
UNIVERSITY PRESS

OXFORD
UNIVERSITY PRESS

Oxford University Press is a department of the University of Oxford. It furthers
the University's objective of excellence in research, scholarship, and education
by publishing worldwide. Oxford is a registered trade mark of Oxford University
Press in the UK and certain other countries.

Published in the United States of America by Oxford University Press
198 Madison Avenue, New York, NY 10016, United States of America.

Library of Congress Cataloging-in-Publication Data
Names: Camasso, Michael J., author. | Jagannathan, Radha, author.
Title: Caught in the cultural preference net : three generations of employment choices
in six capitalist democracies / Michael J. Camasso, Radha Jagannathan.
Description: New York : Oxford University Press, 2021. |
Includes bibliographical references and index.
Identifiers: LCCN 2020033771 (print) | LCCN 2020033772 (ebook) |
ISBN 9780190672782 (hardback) | ISBN 9780190672805 (epub) | ISBN 9780190672812
Subjects: LCSH: Labor market—Developed countries—Social aspects—Case studies. |
Job vacancies—Developed countries—Case studies. |
Generations—Developed countries—Case studies.
Classification: LCC HD5706 .C246 2021 (print) | LCC HD5706 (ebook) | DDC 331.1—dc23
LC record available at https://lccn.loc.gov/2020033771
LC ebook record available at https://lccn.loc.gov/2020033772

DOI: 10.1093/oso/9780190672782.001.0001

1 3 5 7 9 8 6 4 2

Printed by Integrated Books International, United States of America

For Carol Ann who passed on much too soon but whose life on this earth endures uninterrupted in our thoughts

Contents

Preface

As the title of this book suggests, we focus our attention on the role that culture—the amalgam of values, beliefs, preferences, and attitudes responsible for national identities—has played and continues to exert on individuals' decisions to participate in the labor market. At a time when millennials face many employment challenges and Generation Z can be expected to encounter even more, a clearer understanding of the ways cultural transmission could facilitate or hinder productive and rewarding work would appear to be both useful and well-timed.

The book's title conveys our aim to determine if work-related intentions and preferences have remained stable across generations in six democracies or if they have been altered by changing economic conditions. While millennials serve as the anchoring point for much of our discussion and analyses, we do not neglect the significance that their parents from Generation X (b. 1965–1982) and grandparents from the baby boom (b. 1945–1964) have had in their socialization.

One of our principal methods for isolating the effects of cultural and cultural transmission is what is referred to as the stated choice experiment. We conducted a stated preference experiment with family members from each of these three generations with the purpose of identifying the type(s) of employment that maximizes individual utility (values) for engaging in work. We expand our examination of intergenerational variation by placing it in a comparative context; for example, we replicate our experiment in six countries selected to maximize variation in the social and governmental conditions under which a market economy operates. In selecting countries we drew heavily upon Gosta Esping-Andersen's (1990, 2002) typology of welfare capitalism with Sweden providing our representative of social democratic capitalism; Germany, the model for corporatist ordoliberalism; Italy and Spain, countries where the market economy is backstopped by family; and the United States and India, examples of free market liberalism. By nesting cross-generational experiences within a cross-national context, we believe we have significantly increased our capacity to disentangle cultural determinants from the economic causes of employment preference.

Our cross-generational experiments in each of these countries are augmented with survey data detailing respondents' work attitudes, beliefs around individual achievement, risk-taking, trust and cooperation, and redistributive justice. These data, together with qualitative information we have gathered from face-to-face interviews and other "deep culture" analyses, help us provide the reader with texture and a richness we feel are often missing in large-scale values studies. How successful we have been in conveying this detail, however, waits on the judgment of the reader.

While our incursion into the controversial field known as "cultural economics" is far from the first nor is it likely to be the last, it is quite unique. We believe we are the first social scientists to have conducted a multigenerational, multination preference experiment. If readers view our findings as useful in gaining a better understanding of the importance of culture in economic transactions that occur in the labor market, we will have achieved a good deal of our purpose for writing this book. If, in addition, readers recognize that capitalism is a social process that can unfold with economic efficiency or inefficiency as well as with cultural legitimacy or illegitimacy, then we will have achieved a good deal more.

Acknowledgments

There are a great number of individuals who helped make this book possible. In Sweden, we are especially grateful to Annika and Johnny Hansen and Ewa Satermo; in Germany, Christine Tolksdorf and Cecilia Kaltz; in Italy, Roberta Celia and Professor Maurizio Caserta; in Spain, Irene Herranz-Vazquez and Professor Jose Arco-Tirado; in the United States, Sheridan Quarless Kingsberry and Anne E. Camasso; and in India, Rajalaksmi Sadagopan. We would also like to thank the 60 three-generation family members who agreed to share their beliefs, attitudes, preferences, and knowledge with us. The technical assistance of Chet Jagannathan was critical at several junctures in the manuscript preparation process as was the editorial assistance of Jessica Varela and Rachel Towlen-Yepez. Ms. Towlen-Yepez's work on the book's cover design was exceptional. Dana Bliss, our editor at Oxford, showed the patience of Job, and this is greatly appreciated.

Notwithstanding the help we received from these individuals and the encouragement from our colleagues at Rutgers, we alone are responsible for any errors that remain and for the conclusions we draw.

Michael J. Camasso
Radha Jagannathan

1

Cultural Orientations and Economic Outcomes

Nations like Human Beings are influenced by realities, by practical considerations as to what constitutes self-interest, but they are also influenced by their value codes, by their national characteristics.
—David C McClelland, *The Roots of Consciousness*
(1964, p. 90)

There has been a great deal written in the economics literature on the impact of economic institutions, monetary, and labor policy and individual economic capital on outcomes ranging from labor force participation and unemployment to private sector business growth, entrepreneurial activity, and human productivity. With respect to youth and their success in the labor market, the subject of this book, the typical culprits implicated in the problem of unemployment include supply-side factors like skill obsolescence, lower returns to employment than unemployment, skill mismatch (i.e., situations where skill supply and demand diverge due to economic shocks, business cycles, etc.; Layard, 1982; Borjas, 2008; CEDEFOP, 2018a), or insufficient labor demand because of a slow or no-growth economy, excessive taxes or regulations leading to labor market rigidity, and global trade and job exportation (Barlett and Steele, 1996; Crisp and Powell, 2017; Borjas, 2008). Minimum wage policies have also been implicated in employers' decisions to hire youth (Card and Kruger, 1995; Layard, 1982; Piketty, 2014) with higher wages thought to lower demand.

The economic remedies that have been prescribed for unemployment due to both equilibrium factors (labor supply) and disequilibrium factors (labor demand) depend greatly on the school of economic thought that the prescription writer attended. Classical and neoclassical economists from Adam Smith (1776/2000), the often-called "father of modern economics," and Leon Walras (1900), the founder of general equilibrium theory, to Nobel laureates like Milton Friedman (1962) and Paul Samuelson (Samuelson and

Caught in the Cultural Preference Net. Michael J. Camasso and Radha Jagannathan, Oxford University Press (2021).
© Oxford University Press. DOI: 10.1093/oso/9780190672782.003.0001

Norhaus, 2010) favor market mechanisms like market expansion, efficient labor pricing, competition, and innovation to address the problem. On the other hand, John Maynard Keynes (1936) and his many devotees (see, e.g., Galbraith, 1973; Lucas, 2002) point to the cyclical nature of unemployment in capitalist economies that calls for government interventions in the forms of tariffs, jobs programs, expanded money supply, and other regulatory actions. Finally, Marxists (Marx, 1894/1967; Kautsky, 1959; Sweezy, 1972), who view as immoral any economic system (capitalism) that requires an "industrial reserve army" of unemployed to keep the system running, consider market tinkering as ineffectual and the dissolution of labor markets that alienate workers from the wealth they produce as the only responsible course of action.

No matter the school of thought, economic theories around unemployment are framed around the idea of choices—be they the choices of employers, actual and prospective employees, the government, or other interested parties. As James Duesenberry (1960) once quipped, "Economics is all about choices while sociology is about why people have no choices" (p. 233). Duesenberry may be overstating the case a bit inasmuch as many of the economists we have already listed have discussed limited choices or even no choices (here we would also place some of the work emanating from the Austrian School; e.g., Hayek, 1967; Schumpeter, 1966). Choices, moreover, are rooted in an individual's preferences, a neoclassical concept that means whenever individuals in a marketplace are presented with a choice they will select one bundle of goods/services over another by attempting to maximize their utility (i.e., their satisfaction; Becker, 1996; McFadden, 1986; Phillips et al., 2002) with the choice. Individuals here are typically portrayed as rational actors whose choices and marginal utilities are the consequences of personal experiences, past consumption behaviors, and psychological motivations. An individual, for example, may choose to remain unemployed even if a surplus of jobs is available if she concludes that her current status as a part-time student (with the training that accompanies this status) offers future earnings that will substantially outweigh wages she could earn in the current labor market.

With this emphasis on the individual, rational actor, neoclassical models of choice have come under scrutiny and criticism for not realistically describing how decisions are made (Kahneman et al., 1999; Coleman, 1990; Bourdieu, 2005). Kahneman et al. (1999), as an example of this critique, assert that preferences, as typically conceived in economics, are simply expressions of attitudes measured on a dollar scale. Coleman (1990) argues that individual choices are subject not only to an individual's re-source constraints but also to the pressures of social relationships and group cultures. Many neoclassical trained economists respond to these critiques of emotionality and group pressure by advocating for the elabora-tion and extension of the core preference principle through the inclusion of relevant psychological and sociological factors. There is a caveat, however, summed up succinctly by Gary Becker (1996): "Some anthropologists and sociologists go too far when they claim cultures so dominate behavior there is little room for individual choice" (p. 17). Douglas and Wildavsky (1982) make the same point when they observe that individuals make lifestyle choices all the time, often without group pressure and without succumbing to irrationality.

Culture and Economic Preferences

Arguably, the embedding of rational choices and preferences within the am-bience of noneconomic factors began with the observations of the econo-mist, Max Weber (1904/1958). Weber notes:

> A glance at the occupational statistics of any country of mixed religious composition brings to light with remarkable frequency a situation which has several times provoked discussion in the Catholic press and in Catholic Congresses in Germany, namely, the fact that business leaders and owners of capital, as well as the higher grades of skilled labour, and even more the higher technically trained personnel of modern enterprises, are over-whelmingly Protestant. (p. 35)

Thus begins Weber's disquisition into the genesis of modern capitalism in the 17th century where Puritans, an offshoot of Calvinism, developed a rational, morally sanctified business culture (pp. 53–55). Weber finds the shibboleth for this new way of conducting business in the Christian Bible "Seest thou a man diligent in his business? He shall stand before kings" (Proverbs 22:29). Business conducted virtuously (i.e., with honesty, frugality, modesty, and industry) had utility not only because it facilitated credit, contract enforce-ment, and trade but also because it guided an individual on a path of right-eousness, a calling, leading to eternal salvation. Other work on the power of religious and cultural values and beliefs to impact economic choices, preferences, and behaviors quickly followed (Sombart, 1911; Tawney, 1922).

Before we proceed with our discussion of culture and economic outcomes, this might be a good place to define terms like *culture, values*, and the like, which appear throughout this book. Many of these terms have been employed interchangeably, resulting in a substantial amount of confusion. First, among the literally hundreds of definitions that appear in the literature, we follow Gary Becker (1996) and consider *culture* as shared values and preferences handed down from one generation to another through families, peer groups, ethnic and religious groups, etc. (p. 16). Becker sees culture as a set of control mechanisms—plans, recipes, rules, and instructions—that provide an orientation for behaviors, are not easily altered, and have a very small depreciation rate. Note Becker's acknowledgment of small depreciation rate. The principal components of this definition are often shared in the economics literature (see e.g., Mokyr, 2019; Casson, 2006; Guiso, Sapienza, and Zingales, 2006) and remain true to earlier descriptions that appear primarily in anthropology (Kluckhohn, 1951; Kroeber and Kluckhohn, 1952; Schein, 1984).[1]

Our definition of values is the same as that provided by the anthropologist Clyde Kluckhohn (1951): "A value is a conception, explicit or implicit, distinctive of an individual or characteristic of a group, of the desirable which influences the selection from available modes, means and ends of action" (p. 395). Kluckhohn goes on to identify the inherent endogeneity of cultural values (i.e., values produce future actions, and these actions, in turn, may cause modifications to a society's values). Kluckhohn also makes the point that concepts of the desirable can often exhibit a stubborn persistence.

Two additional terms that are too frequently used as substitutes for values are beliefs and attitudes (Kraaykamp, Cemalcilar, and Tosun, 2019; Schwartz, 2012). We do not ascribe to the convertibility of these concepts; instead, we embrace the distinctions proposed by Fishbein and Ajzen (1975) in their classic text on consumer behavior and reasoned action. Whereas values identify desired states of reality, beliefs according to Fishbein and Ajzen represent the information an individual possesses and holds to be true about some

---

[1] Lest the reader express dismay over what could be construed as a reliance on late-arriving economists to the definition of culture, we provide a more typical definition that appears in the culture of economics literature; namely, culture is a choice of equilibrium strategies in a game of multiple equilibria and standard preferences. Here the heterogeneity lies in the expectations over the strategies that will be played in equilibrium (Fernandes, 2008). From this vantage point, it would appear that our adopted definition of culture is a rationality tempered by broader social science.

person, object, event, or situation. Hence, beliefs have a rational (cognitive) basis that, in principle, can be altered when an individual encounters new information that runs contrary to already held convictions. Attitudes, on the other hand, are defined as "a person's favorable or unfavorable evaluation of a person, object, etc." (p. 72). Fishbein and Ajzen equate evaluative with affective predispositions, emotional intentions, and behavioral responses. As we have already noted, some prominent social scientists (Kahneman et al., 1999; Bourdieu, 2005) see little downside with the conflation of attitudes and preferences. We will continue to follow the more common convention of treating these concepts as distinctive. Attitudes, throughout this book, will be measured and discussed as individuals' favorable or unfavorable responses to questions constructed with simple ranking or rating scales while preferences will be measured as the responses of individuals to choice sets (i.e., opportunities for respondents to demonstrate how they would maximize their utilities (satisfaction) under resource constraints). Analysis of the former allows us to examine characteristics of the decision-making individual that might influence current and past employment status. The latter modeling of choice sets permits the economic analysis of the actual decisions made by individuals, which, we believe, brings us closer to an understanding of the youth employment problem that is our focus (for more on this distinction, see Hoffman and Duncan, 1988; Camasso and Jagannathan, 2001). We will have a good deal more to say about the different statistical modeling strategies for attitudes and beliefs, on the one hand, and preferences, on the other, in Chapters 6 and 7 of this volume.

Challenges to Cultural Analyses

For many years after Weber's seminal work on the economic consequences of cultural values and beliefs, economists, on the whole, appeared to have been content to limit their investigations of individual preferences and other economic matters to economic causes and consequences like income and prices. The admonition offered by Nobel laureate Robert Solow (1970) was emblematic of the hazards awaiting economists who dare employ culture and noneconomic factors in their analyses. Solow warned these researchers they ran the high risk of "ending up in a blaze of amateur sociology" (p. 102). But there are worse risks than being called a sociologist, and that is the risk that discussions of culture could pose to career and livelihood. As David Landes

(2002) declared, "culture in the sense of inner values and attitudes that guide a population, frightens scholars. It has a sulfuric odor of race and inheritance, an air of immutability" (p. 32). When Solow penned his famous quote, social scientists in the United States and Europe were still in the process of trying to digest the findings of the Moynihan Report (Rainwater and Yancey, 1967) and the Coleman Report (Mosteller and Moynihan, 1972). While neither report was authored by an economist, both reports described in vivid detail the educational and economic deprivation that seemed to follow cultural deprivation, measured as racial differences. The personal attacks on Patrick Moynihan and James Coleman were both constant and long-lasting with redemption given only grudgingly and only recently (Hill, 2017; Massey and Sampson, 2009).

It is a 2001 article that appeared in the *Quarterly Journal of Economics*, co-authored by an economist, that would seem to make Landes's point brilliantly. Entitled "The Impact of Legalized Abortion on Crime," Donohue and Levitt (2001) provided evidence indicating that abortion increases made possible by legislation under the *Roe v. Wade* U.S. Supreme Court decision in 1973 were responsible for the dramatic drop in crime rates in the early through mid-1990s. A careful reading of the article, however, reveals that it is not abortions per se that are the precipitating factor but abortions among Black women that really appear to be responsible. When race entered the analyses, so did a torrent of controversy (Joyce, 2004; Camasso, 2007) that is perhaps best reprised in *The Economist* article "Oops-nomics: Did Steven Levitt, Author of Freakonomics Get His Most Notorious Paper Wrong?" ("Oops-nomics," 2005).

As Landes (2002) remarks, the issue goes beyond race and extends to any measures of cultural values and preferences that are perceived by politicians, the general media, and a broad swath of academia as intimating permanency, particularly if this permanency is for the worse. Gannon and Pillai (2016) note that there can be a fine and fuzzy line that separates what social scientists call a stereotype of a society or group's values, preferences, and behaviors, on one hand, and solid empirical evidence regarding these elements, on the other. Stereotypes are commonly defined in the sociological and psychology literature as group descriptions with low fact content and high levels of caricature, exaggeration, and overgeneralization. What complicates attempts to distinguish unequivocally negative stereotyping from accurate, real-world portrayals of a society or group is the amount of fact contained in the stereotype. Researchers including Jussim et al. (2009) and Simpson and

Yinger (1985), among others, maintain that negative fact content can often be quite high in a culture. We will have a good bit more to say about this contention in Chapter 2 of this volume.

Our Research Questions

Notwithstanding the risks of hectoring and name calling, a sizeable number of economists have bravely entered into a subfield called *cultural economics* (Fernandez, 2008). Within this subfield, researchers have explored a myriad of topics ranging from fertility and terrorism to artistic output and transportation choices. What interests us in this book are three lines of inquiry that have the potential to help students of both culture and economics gain a better understanding of youth unemployment and labor force attachment.

1. Do some national cultures possess value orientations that are more successful than others in promoting economic opportunity?
2. Does the transmission of these value orientations demonstrate a persistence irrespective of economic conditions, or are they simply the results of these conditions?
3. If a nation's value orientation does indeed impact economic opportunity, does it do so by influencing an individual's preferences?

What we know about the answers to these questions is suggestive but far from settled science.

A perusal through any of the rankings of gross domestic product (GDP), per capita income or business activity authored by the World Bank, the International Monetary Fund, the United Nations or the OECD could be viewed as prima facie evidence that some nations possess a set of traits or characteristics contributing to high levels of economic activity that other nations do not possess. A country's comparative or competitive advantage has been traced to favorable geography and insulation from major wars (Kennedy, 1989), natural disasters, and the lack of natural resources (OECD, 2011; Brunnschweiler and Bulte, 2008) and to too many natural resources (Lindsay, 2000; Sachs and Warner, 2001). None of these explanations, however, account for more than a small portion in the variance extant in these rankings. A much larger literature examines the hypothesis that country rankings are the consequence of differences in cultural values, especially whether the national culture promulgates individualist or collectivistic values (Franke, Hofstede, and Bond, 2002; Dietrich and Moller, 2016; Triandis, 2002; Hauff and Kirchner, 2015). Often, however, these culture studies devolve into simple (or complex) econometric analysis where GDP or other measure of economic activity is regressed on a variable designating the name of the country and the reader is left to ponder the choices and marginal utilities (preferences) of real individuals—the proximate economic actions—that are responsible for any correlation between country and size of GDP. Without identifying the value orientations responsible for a nation's economic activity, Question 1 remains, at best, only partially answered.

With respect to the transmission of cultural values across and within societies, several research themes have emerged. One is the apparent resilience of cultural values and preferences, both helpful and harmful to economic development, that have come to define nation-states. Sowell (1996), for example, uses the term "cultural capital" to describe the relative significance that nation-states attach to thrift, intellect, time, knowledge, art, and other features of living that make human existence possible (p. 379). Sowell considers six cultures—German, Italian, Jewish, Chinese, Japanese, and Indian—where values toward work and risk-taking allow individuals to excel in economic endeavors, not only in their native countries but in countries to where they immigrate. Easterly (2006), conversely, documents the persistence of cultures of mistrust and corruption found in many developing countries in Africa and South America. He observes that in countries where you can only trust family members the size of companies is limited by the size of family (p. 51). The resilience of mistrust and corruption in southern Italy is often pointed to as the reason that this region lags behind the rest of the country in economic prosperity (Guiso, Sapienza, and Zingales, 2006; Bigoni et al., 2018). Deaton (2013, 2018) argues that the persistence of corruption in many developing countries dooms foreign aid as an investment tool leading only to failure.

The pessimism surrounding persistence—of both "good" and "bad" values—has been countered to some degree by economists who see cultural factors as temporary barriers to the diffusion of social development and economic growth (The Economist, the Uncultured Science, 2019). Mokyr (2019) traces industrialization and the reality of sustained economic growth to the humanistic approach to scientific inquiry founded in 17th-century England. As linguistic and other communication barriers in Europe were overcome, this belief in Puritan science and technology spread rapidly throughout the continent. Spolaore and Wacziarg (2009, 2018) likewise, dispel some of the doom and gloom of immutability by providing analyses that find that a society's ancestral distance from a dominant technological frontier (the United States in this case) acts as only a temporary barrier to the diffusion of development and per capita income. McCloskey's (2006) work on the creation of business-respecting culture and its effect on social class distances is another instance of eventual cultural mutation. Suffice it to say that at this point the question of intact versus modifiable cultural transmission remains a topic of much interest and of significant disagreement.

Answering Question 2 is essential for legitimizing any role that culture-based employment policies can expect to play in addressing youth unemployment. The sociologist Pierre Bourdieu (1986) provides one answer, and it can be summarized in what has been termed the Bourdieu paradox: while an economic calculation lies behind every action, every action cannot be reduced to an economic calculation (p. 253). Hence, from this perspective preferences and behavioral intentions can be the results of "playing the economic game" with symbolic as well as economic interests coming into play. For Bourdieu, individuals invest time and money in the economic system not only for the prospect of economic gain but also because cultural and symbolic capital are realized. The purchase of a Peugeot by a Frenchman instead of a BMW can be a source of national or regional pride that has utility that can eclipse cost, technology, or efficiency considerations. Quite a different answer to Question 2 is offered by the economist Gary Becker (Becker, 1996; Stigler and Becker, 1977) who maintains that it is technology and costs that constrain preference choices, with culture exerting a stabilizing effect on meta-preferences only (1996, p. 132)—what we have called here *value orientations*—but exerting substantially less influence on transactional preferences or behavioral intentions. These day-in and day-out choices are viewed by Becker (1996) as the result of price, incomes, wages, and economic opportunities (p. 35). Bourdieu and Becker in essence extend the Weber–Marx quarrel to the origins of personal tastes.

To answer Question 2 with some degree of confidence, it is necessary to solve the endogeneity problem that has confronted cultural economics from its inception. In a nutshell, the problem that must be solved is one of causal direction: Are cultural values responsible for economic outcomes like labor force attachment or economic prosperity, or is the reverse also true? In attempts to solve this problem, economists are on the lookout for a suitable instrumental variable, a stand-in for culture that is related to culture and is not directly related to economic outcomes but is indirectly correlated with any economic outcomes through culture.[2] A few examples of the creative use of instruments will help the reader better understand the concept. Guiso, Sapienza, and Zingales (2006) examine whether values of trust impact the probability of becoming an entrepreneur. Rather than simply use a measure of trust gleaned directly from individuals' responses to an attitude survey, the authors use a measure of trust that is correlated with type and level of religiosity. The logic here is that trust, emanating from religious values, occurs prior to entrepreneurial decisions and outcomes. In another instance, these authors use an individual's current residence, identified as a city in Italy that was governed as an independent city-state 500 years in the past or was ruled by a foreign king, on investment and lending practices (Guiso, Sapienza, and Zingales, 2008). Spolaore and Wacziarg (2017) use genetic markers (blood group systems) as instruments for the cultural values responsible for economic activity and national prosperity. In their own words, "the underlying idea was that populations at greater distance (genetically) from each other had more time to diverge in terms of intergenerationally transmitted traits, such as cultural norms, values, beliefs, habits, language and religion" (p. 750). This ancestral distance from a technological frontier (e.g., 17th-century England vs. 20th-century United States) acts as a barrier to the spread of innovations and economic development.

One of the most common practices for addressing the endogeneity issue is to employ an intergenerational, cultural transmission model. The assumption here is that while economic conditions like prices, wages, costs, technology, and product supply/demand change overtime (especially in a capitalist society), cultural values and preferences change more slowly (Fernandez, 2008; Bisin and Verdier, 2011; Twenge et al., 2010). Bisin and Verdier (2011) provide a theoretical justification for this assumption, which they refer to as "imperfect empathy." They note that there is a fundamental friction in parental altruism, which sustains cultural transmission by biasing parents toward their own cultural traits. While parents generally want the best for their children (altruism), they evaluate their choices using their own and not their children's

---

[2] A good instrumental variable has three qualities. First, it has relevance (i.e., instrument Z affects X the independent variable). In Spolaore and Wacziarg (2017) genetic blood groups are transmitted (Z) while transmitting culture (X). Second, it affects Y the dependent variable only through X. This is called the exclusion condition. One would not expect blood group, per se, to impact per capita income; if it has an effect, the effect works through culture. Third, it has no common cause with Y. This is the independence criterion. See Angrist and Pischke (2015) for an excellent discussion of instrumental variables.

preferences (p. 341). In a similar fashion, Guiso, Sapienza, and Zingales (2008) describe a dynamic where parents do not weigh future and current benefits exactly the same way children do because parents internalize more of the costs of their children's mistakes when they are still at home. These economists show that the transmission tends to be biased toward excessively conservative priors. Societies with prior value orientations that stress cooperation, trust, and optimism tend to operate economically in a state of high-trust, high-trade equilibrium; those that stress pessimism languish in more sluggish economies, stuck in a low-trust, low-trade equilibrium.

The approach we use in this book to address the culture–economic activity endogeneity problem can be termed the *overlapping generations/transmission of culture* model. Controlling for country differences in Sweden, Germany, Italy, Spain, the United States, and India, we examine whether the preferences, attitudes, and beliefs of millennials, their parents, and their grandparents exhibit intergenerational stability or change. Our analyses also allow us to assess if country differences in preferences, attitudes, and beliefs persist notwithstanding any generational differences. How successful we have been in establishing an independent impact of culture can be judged by our readers in the analyses we perform in Chapters 6 and 7. We are reminded here of Tawney's (1922) critique of Max Weber and his groundbreaking examination of the *Spirit of Capitalism*. Tawney queries:

> Is it not a little artificial to suggest as Weber appears to imply, that capital enterprise had to wait till religious changes had provided a capitalist spirit? Would it not be equally plausible, and equally one sided, to argue that the religious changes were themselves merely the result of economic movements? (p. 262)

We think Tawney seriously undervalues the cultural instruments Weber provided to his readers, and it is in that spirit we offer ours.

Our answers to Question 3 appear in the empirical analyses we conduct in Chapters 6 and 7. Chapter 6 tests eight attitudes and beliefs that have been conceptually and/or empirically linked to the intention to engage in economic activity. These beliefs and attitudes operationalize culture at the day-to-day transaction level, and their stability or variance across nations and generations can give us added insights into the culture–economy relationship. Chapter 7 tests the national and generational stability or variance in preferences for employment directly. We do this by conducting a stated preference experiment that allows us to observe choice behaviors directly.

Preferences in our modeling are viewed as the critical linchpin in value orientations that link culture to market behavior (McFadden, 1975).

Our Conceptual Framework and Plan of this Book

In this book we examine how the values, preferences, and attitudes of grandparents (born mid-1940s–1964) and parents (born 1965–1982) compared with the labor force attachment, achievement, and risk-taking preferences and work values of their grandchildren and children (born 1983–2000). These three generations have been identified by demographers as members of the traditionalist baby boom generation, Generation X, and millennials (Kalleberg and Marsden, 2013; Settersten, Furstenberg, and Rumbaut, 2008). We conduct a series of discrete choice experiments (DCEs) with members of all three generations. In this application, the DCEs are a quantitative method for measuring the utilities that influence individual employment choices, specifically choice of a job type. We augment these experiments with survey data that provide us with information on an individual's attitudes and beliefs around eight important components of economic activity: trust, personal achievement, cooperation, risk-taking, redistributive justice, development of economic capital through education and training, and the values of work centrality and labor force attachment. These beliefs and attitudes have been linked to the intention to seek or avoid employment. By *intention* here we mean, as does Fishbein and Ajzen (1975), the probability of acting on belief, attitude, or preference. We illustrate the architecture of our modeling in Figure 1.1.

Figure 1.1 reflects several substantial intellectual debts. We acknowledge the influence of Kluckhohn (1951), Kroeber and Kluckhohn (1952), and Schein (1984) on the distinction we make on deeper value orientations, which are difficult to measure, and more visible beliefs and attitudes that can signal intentions and behavior patterns. Our inclusion of eight beliefs and attitudes linked to economic activity is the result of a distillation of a broad body of work in cultural economics that we shall elaborate upon in Chapter 2. The modeling of observable preferences and behavioral intentions as the culture stimuli responsible for updated value orientations owes a great deal to the work of Guiso, Sapienza, and Zingales (2004, 2006, 2008), Bisin and Verdier (2011), Tabellini (2008a, 2008b), and Fernandez (2008).

While the focus of nearly all our analyses is on how preferences and the constellation of the eight indicators of cultural intentions are manifest in the

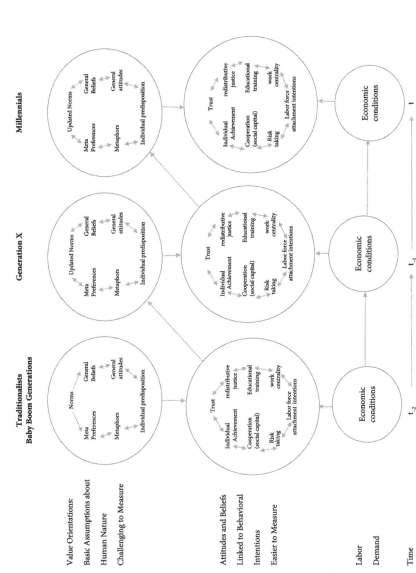

Figure 1.1 Conceptual model used to organize the book's arguments and analyses.

baby boom, Generation X, and millennial generations, we make an additional effort to evaluate the usefulness of a component of basic value orientations we label *metaphors*. Gannon (2009) defines a cultural metaphor as "any activity, phenomenon or institution which all or most members of an ethnic or national culture consider important and with which they identify both intellectually and emotionally" (p. 275). Metaphors in this context do not simply mean the exercise of some rhetorical or literary device; rather, they succinctly capture and transfer a culture's norms, preferences, beliefs, etc., using analogical expression to provide vivid, compact, and realistic summaries of cultural orientation (Lakoff and Johnson, 1980; Ortony, 2001). Long a tool in the qualitative research performed by anthropologists (Kroeber and Kluckhohn, 1952; Geertz, 1991), we subject the cultural metaphors that have often been used to characterize nation-states (e.g., the symphony that is Germany, the opera that is Italy) to quantitative analysis with the objective of determining if they indeed serve as a shorthand definition of a nation's cultural identity. As the reader has doubtlessly observed this book's title is metaphorical: it likens culture and its relationship to economic activities to the experiences of being ensnared in a meshed fabric that, if not constructed properly or if punctured, can open up choice alternatives well beyond the confines of the net.

There is one last feature of our model that needs to be addressed before proceeding any further in our discussion. We study the impact of culture on youth employment in six countries. The countries, Sweden, Germany, Italy, Spain, India, and the United States, were selected to maximize differences in economic conditions within capitalist democracies and to maximize distinctions between neoclassical and interventionist approaches to labor market regulation. We have relied on the typology of welfare capitalism developed by Gosta Esping-Andersen (1990, 2002). Esping-Andersen has identified four approaches to world capitalism, which he distinguishes as social democratic, conservative-corporatist, southern European, and classic liberalism. Sweden, with the importance it attaches to government policy, is widely seen as an exemplar of the social-democratic model (Gabel and Kamerman, 2006; UNICEF Innocenti Research Center, 2000, 2005, 2012, 2016). Germany, with its rigid labor markets and work-related welfare benefits system, illustrates what has been termed the "corporatist approach" to capitalism while Italy and Spain provide prime examples of the family-centered approach. Lastly, the United States and India (with its historical ties to the United Kingdom) populate Esping-Andersen's often-maligned classic liberalism category where markets determine the depth and breadth of the cultural safety net. The Esping-Andersen typology has exerted a substantial influence on subsequent efforts by social scientists outside of economics to distinguish distinctive varieties of operational capitalism (see, e.g., Hall and Sorskice, 2001; Hancke, Rhodes, and Thatcher, 2007).

Over the next three chapters, we will explore the three major hypotheses that have been advanced as possible explanations for youth employment patterns. In Chapter 2, we detail cultural arguments that have figured prominently in the debates over differences in economic activity, both between countries and across generations. Here we will examine a variety of qualitative as well as quantitative research efforts including the utility of cultural metaphors in bridging the qualitative–quantitative divide.

In Chapters 3 and 4, we examine conditions in the labor market affecting youth employment—supply factors first and then demand conditions. In Chapter 3, we take an in-depth look at a set of labor market conditions that have been criticized for constructing inefficient labor supply including overskilling and academization, the maintenance of obsolete skill sets, and the creation of skill mismatches that leave young people underemployed (i.e., doing jobs where they are overqualified) or cause them to decline work offers entirely. The chapter on demand shifts the focus to factors that affect employer decisions to hire and include the strength of economic activity in a country or region and government efforts to stimulate demand through unemployment benefits, work programs, and minimum wage policies.

In Chapter 5, we lay out our research design and the overlapping generations/transmission of culture model that underpins the design. Here we describe our sampling methods and the communities in Sweden, Germany, Italy, Spain, India, and the United States where our three-generation respondent interviews took place. We detail the development and administration of our interview schedule and the items used to measure the beliefs, attitudes, preferences, and metaphors shown in Figure 1.1.

Chapter 6 contains our statistical analyses of beliefs and attitudes with descriptive and qualitative results preceding the multivariate econometric analyses that comprise the bulk of the chapter's content. In Chapter 7, we provide details about the construction of the DCE and the statistical methods we use in the analyses of these data. In Chapter 8, we offer the reader a discussion and set of conclusions that we believe could lead to a more thorough understanding of the roles that national cultures and the intergenerational transmission of those cultures play in the structure, operations, and health of the youth labor markets.

2

The Prominence of Culture
in Economic Decisions

*I think the perception of there being a deep gulf between science and
the humanities is false.*
—Clifford Geertz, *On Ethnography and Social Construction* (1991)

When culture and cultural value orientations have entered into our discourse
on things economic they have done so through pathways ranging from
poetry and novels to sophisticated statistical analysis and the construction of
observation-based typologies. One has to look no further than Max Weber
(1904/1958) and his heavy reliance on the aphorisms of Benjamin Franklin
describing the "Spirit of Capitalism" to see clearly how anecdote and data are
blended for maximum effect. In this chapter we will first examine how case
studies, documenting the lives of the fictional and actual, have influenced
our thinking about national cultures, and the relative lethargy and productivity of country inhabitants. We then turn to etic (quantitative) and emic
(qualitative) typologies used to empirically classify countries on a range of
cultural values, beliefs, and preferences, some of which have been employed
in economic analyses.

Culture as Deep Description

Many of the most poignant analysis of culture's consequences have not
come from those in the mainstream culture field (i.e., anthropologists and
sociologists), but from journalists, historians, psychologists, novelists, and
others who see themselves as merely eyewitnesses to the human condition.
As one instance consider the observations of Henry Kissinger (1986) in an
essay he wrote for the *Washington Post* newspaper entitled "Soccer Imitates

Caught in the Cultural Preference Net. Michael J. Camasso and Radha Jagannathan, Oxford University Press (2021).
© Oxford University Press. DOI: 10.1093/oso/9780190672782.003.0002

Life." In recounting the exploits of perennial soccer power Germany, no doubt leavened by his personal experiences growing up near Nuremberg, Germany, Kissinger declares:

> The German National team plays soccer the way its General Staff prepares for a war; its games are meticulously planned, each play is skilled in both attack and defense. . . . Anything achievable by human foresight, careful preparation and hard work are accounted for. . . . [Yet] the impression is unavoidable that the German's often outstanding national soccer team has not brought a proportionate amount of joy to the people that may in its heart of hearts believe that joy is not its national destiny. (p. 31)

His assessment of another power, Italy, is equally illuminating:

> The Italian style of soccer reflects the national conviction forged by the vicissitudes of an ancient history that the grim struggle must be based on a careful husbanding of energy for the main task. It presupposes a correct assessment of the character of the opponent, paired with an unostentatious and matter-of-fact perseverance that obscures the many intricate levels on which the competition takes place. (p. 31)

The German as the precise, highly productive pessimist and the Italian as the dissembling protagonist in a prolonged quarrel are images that are difficult to escape.

Both Germany and Italy have been subject to (seemingly) countless efforts to capture and distill the essence of what it means to be a German, an Italian. Mueller (2012) in his book on olive oil culture portrays the two countries as adversaries in the battle between animal fat (butter) and the sacred oleum, a battle that rages to this very day. Hofstede (1977), in a Machiavellian twist, classifies Germany as a culture of foxes and Italy as one of lions although both cultures are keen to avoid uncertainty in any social sphere.

Deep descriptions of German culture generally tend to paint a very dark picture. Lynn Payor (1988) notes the while English fairy tales end with "and they lived happily ever after" and the French add "and they had lots of children," German fairy tales end with "and if they have not yet died they are still living" (p. 77). Payor remarks that there is no word for "happy end" in German and in circumstances where they believe the concept is needed, they borrow the English term and speak of "das Happy End" (see also McClelland's, 1961, analysis of children's books.)

But when someone wants to take a deep dive into the German culture abyss, they invariably surface with J. W. von Goethe's (1963) play *Faust*. Readers will recall from their high school literature classes that Heinrich Faust, a German scholar, traded his soul to the devil in exchange for knowledge without limit. Carl Jung (1945, 1957) asserts that "nobody but a German could ever have devised such a figure, it is so intrinsically, so infinitely German; In Faust we see the same hungering for the infinite born of inner contradictions and dichotomy, the same eschatological expectation of the Great Fulfillment" (p. 207). Gibson (2007), drawing upon Faust's lament of having two souls, one striving to abandon the other, writes, "The thread running through all things German is obsessive quest for the authentic—the authentic German, the authentic emotion, the authentic philosophy, the authentic esthetic, the authentic faith. Germans want to know where the truth is to be found and they will risk anything and betray anyone, even themselves, to get it" (p. 120). Books by Michael Lewis (2011) and Mark Reiff (2015) discuss how internal contradictions that so conflicted Faust were responsible for Germany's response to its suffering European Union partners during the financial crisis of 2008.

While the Germans search for the truth, deep descriptions of the Italians document an eternal struggle with deception, treachery, and the fatalistic philosophy that both these beliefs help propagate. The debate within Italy seems to be, Are these beliefs and philosophy endemic to the entire country or are they limited to the south: that is, Abruzzi, Puglia, Basilicata, Calabria, Campania, and the islands of Sicily and Sardinia? Banfield and Fasano's (1958) famous ethnography, *The Moral Basis of a Backward Society*, was based on field work undertaken in one village in Basilicata, but the imagery conveyed by the authors soon became the symbol of Italy. The authors stated that the villagers lived their lives by following one rule: maximize the material and the short-run advantage of the nuclear family; assume that all others will do likewise. Banfield went on to label people whose behavior was consistent with the rule "amoral familist" (p. 85) and to question their commitment to community and governmental institutions.

Italian suspicions of extra-family economic and social groupings have a long history, perhaps going as far as the 11th century. One can readily conclude from a reading of Machiavelli (1513/1975) or more recent Italian scholars like the economist Vilfredo Pareto (1935/1963) or political scientist

Gaetano Mosca (1939/1959) that government is largely a circulation of elites where citizens are confronted with the Hobson's choice of "rule by force" or "rule by fraud" (see Pareto, especially Volume 3 of *Mind and Society*).

Beginning with the work of Putnam (Putnam, Leonardi, and Raffaella, 1993) the general trend in deep cultural descriptions of Italy is to embrace the tale of two Italys, the economically prosperous North and the benighted and economically struggling South. Putman traces the origins of these differences in economic performance to the Middle Ages when the northern sections of the country were governed as independent city-states while the South was subject to a series of authoritarian rulers like the Normans. In what is apparently a remarkable testament to the persistence of cultural value orientations, a number of recent research studies conducted by economists (Bigoni et al., 2016; Tabellini, 2008a; Guiso, Sapienza, and Zingales, 2006, 2008) find that economic preferences in northern Italian regions remain strong for conditional cooperation, optimism regarding contacts with external groups (what Putnam has termed "bridging capital"), and the favorable benefits-to-cost ratios of commerce, all which were values essential to the economic prosperity of the city-states. In the South, obversely, the choices for economic action remain rooted in the preference of betrayal aversion (Bigoni et al., 2018), "warm glow" transactions (Andreoni, 1990; Tabellini, 2008b),[1] and pessimism toward trade and investment. These result in a "no trust—no trade" equilibrium (Guiso, Sapienza, and Zingales, 2008) that continues to depress the economy.

To bolster their econometric analyses of North–South economic differences Guiso et al. (2008) offer as evidence two Italian novels written in the 19th century: *The Betrothal* by Alessandro Manzoni (a northerner) and *I Malavoglia* by Giovanni Verga (a southerner). The plot of *The Betrothal* depicts a young couple of humble origin who fight against a powerful nobleman who tries to stop their marriage. Optimism exudes from the lovers, and there is no doubt that their love will conquer all, which it ultimately does. *Malavoglia*, on the other hand, conveys life where tragedy begets only more tragedy. A family decides to use their fishing boat to engage in trade but cannot find anyone to share the enterprise's risk or to insure against loss. While returning with their cargo, the crew encounters a terrible storm; they lose the boat, the cargo, and also their home which they provided as collateral for the cargo's

---

[1] The authors refer to this phenomenon as a seemingly altruist act that provides the donor with personal gain. In this sense, it is an example of a norm of "limited morality," which in the extreme can morph into Banfield's "amoral familism."

purchase (p. 317). In our opinion, two novels are not necessary to distinguish the regions' values when one, *Il Gattopardo* by Di Lampedusa (1960), performs the task equally well. Considered one of the greatest historical novels ever written and an all-time best seller in Italy, *The Leopard* is set in 19th-century Sicily and is peppered with references to Sicilian intransigence to northern incursions.

Here is one example:

> The Cardinal of Palermo (from North of Italy) had tried to leaven with Northern activity the inert and heavy dough of the island's spiritual life in general and the clergy's in particular. But soon he had to realize he was, as it were, firing into cotton wool, the little hole made at the moment was covered after a few seconds by thousands of tiny fibers, and all remained as before, the only additions being cost of powder, ridicule at useless effect and deterioration of material. Like everyone who in those days wanted to change anything in the Sicilian character, he had acquired the reputation of being a fool. (pp. 315–316)

Another country that has been subjected to perpetual deep description of its core values is the United States. Beginning with Alexis de Tocqueville's (1840/1945) masterpiece, *Democracy in America*, the United States has been judged to be the exceptional capitalist democracy founded on the values of egalitarianism, liberty, individualism, and laissez-faire economics (Lipset, 1967). De Tocqueville traces this exceptionalism to its "Puritanical origin," its good fortune to exploit a European knowledge base without "laboring to amass this treasure" and a geographical location and natural resources that facilitated boundless economic expansion (de Tocqueville 1840/1945, pp. 37–40; also see de Tocqueville's Chapter 19 on what causes almost all Americans to follow industrial callings). De Tocqueville also heaped praise on Americans for their pragmatism, their orientation toward action, values that limited the appetite for intellectualism as an end in itself, and their honor for labor and making money, noting that even the president of the United States works for pay (pp. 161–162).

A component of America's value orientation that held special intrigue for de Tocqueville and that continues to puzzle many even today is how a nation of individuals can function as a cohesive society. He identifies the secret as the "principle of self-interest rightly understood" (see de Tocqueville 1840/1945, Chapter 8). Referred to also as the altruism of self-interest, this principle guides Americans by stressing the utility—indeed, the virtue—of "an enlightened regard for themselves" as the motivation for helping others. De Tocqueville contrasts this approach to ensuring the public welfare with that of the European elites who are facile with the idea of self-sacrifice, "incessantly talking of the beauties of virtue" given without expectation of reward, but whose actions belie such abnegations (p. 130). The principle in all likelihood accounts for some of the stark differences in civilian terror that distinguished the American Revolution from the exceedingly bloody events that took place in France and elsewhere in Europe (Lefebvre, 1962; Brinton 1965; Lipset, 1967).

David McClelland (1961, 1964), in his deep dive into American's culture and psyche a little more than 100 years after de Tocqueville, outlines a set of values that had changed very little. He describes the "American Value Formula" as a combination of (a) free choice according to one's wishes and desire, (b) action over contemplation, and (c) the need for achievement and other-directedness (p. 73). McClelland, too, identified the principle of obligation to self as the necessary condition for obligation to society.

More recent examinations of American values have focused a great deal more on the vices of a society based on self-interest, even if that self-interest is enlightened. Critics of U.S. culture have honed in on values that they assert results in racial discrimination and persistent poverty. For example, after a two-week visit to the United States in December 2017, the special rapporteur to the Human Rights Council (2018) of the United Nations issued a report condemning the United States for the failure to address the persistent discrimination of Black and Hispanic minorities, a job market that is extraordinarily limited, one of the highest poverty rates in the OECD and the highest rate of income equality among western countries.[2] While the rapporteur places the blame for these problems at the feet of insensitive governmental tax, employment, criminal justice, and welfare policies, more thoughtful observers see America's shortcomings as emanating from a more complex mix of cultural, economic, and governmental pressures.

Recall our rather brief discussion of the Moynihan Report in Chapter 1 of this book. In what has been termed the most famous piece of social scientific analysis *never* published (Massey and Sampson, 2009; Small, Harding, and Lamont, 2010), Moynihan found the cause of the vast difference in economic

[2] The Unites States announced its withdrawal from the U.N. Human Rights Council in June 2018 citing the dubious human rights records of many council members (Venezuela, China, and Saudi Arabia, among others) and anti-Israeli and U.S. bias.

outcomes between White and Black Americans to reside in the latter's matriarchal family structure and the "cultural influences" this structure signaled, fueling a "tangle of pathology" (Rainwater and Yancey, 1967, p. 29). This thesis of a linkage between one race and a culture of poor economic outcomes suggested what was unthinkable for many social scientists, government officials, and politicians (e.g., change your culture, adopt the values of White America, and your economic conditions will improve; Small, Harding, and Lamont, 2010; Haskins, 2009). When a sort of renaissance of the Moynihan thesis emerged about 10 years ago (see especially Wilson, 2009), the response was predictable and swift. In a *New York Times* piece, Cohen (2010) observes, "For more than 40 years, social scientists investigating the causes of poverty have tended to treat cultural explanations like Lord Voldemort: That Which Must Not Be Named." Stephen Steinberg (2011), writing in the *Boston Review*, strikes a more strident tone when he complains that the problem with Moynihan and the new crop of culturalists who have resurrected him is that they have inverted cause and effect and, in effect, have blamed the victim. Steinberg says that by regarding Black culture as an independent and self-sustaining determinant of their economic woes, these social scientists are giving intellectual cover to the racism of employers, bankers, realtors, and others responsible for the functioning economy in America.

Tracing achievement differences in the Unites States to cultural (and sometimes racial) origins remains unpopular and controversial. If the reader has doubts about this contention, she or he has only to examine reaction to books like *The Triple Package* (Chua and Rubenfeld, 2014), *Race and Culture* (Sowell, 1994), or *More Than Just Race* (Wilson, 2009) or even newspaper columns like "The Limits of Policy" by David Brooks (2010) of the *New York Times* or "Culture Explains Asians' Educational Success" by Jason Riley (2019) of the *Wall Street Journal*.

It is quite another matter, however, when it comes to comparing American culture with other democratic, capitalist countries, especially those in western Europe. Such comparisons remain exceedingly popular, more often than not showing the United States as coming up short. Was the United Nation's rapporteur (Human Rights Council, 2018), introduced earlier, correct to vouchsafe the United States the dubious title of an OECD member with one of the highest child poverty rates? Measured as the percentage of children living in a household where the income is less than 50 percent of the national median, the Unites States percentage continues to hover around 22 percent over the past 20 years according to OECD (UNICEF Innocenti

Research Centre 2000, 2005, 2012; UNICEF Office of Research, 2016) with the OECD country average around 13 percent. Certainly the child poverty rate is too high in the United States, around 18 percent, but it is falling according to Anne E. Casey Foundation (2019). But is the rate higher than OECD countries like Mexico or Turkey, which the UNICEF reports suggest? Inasmuch as the United States has a much higher median income than either Mexico or Turkey, the higher rate may simply be an artifact of OECD's measurement approach.

The United States fares poorly in many cross-national comparisons of students' achievement at the primary (elementary school) and secondary (high school) levels. Recent reports from Programme for International Student Assessment administered by the OECD rank American students as 30th in mathematics and 19th in science proficiency (OECD, 2017; DeSilver, 2017). Moreover, these disappointing results comport clearly with scores reported in recent releases of the National Assessment of Educational Progress administered to American students by the U.S. Department of Education.

If you believe it is America's poor treatment of its children that raises the most outrage among European and American critics, you would be incorrect. This ignominy is reserved for the nation's failure to address the problem of income inequality (Guillaud, 2013; Brooks, 2013; Burtless, 2007). There are several ways of measuring the inequality of an income or wealth distribution in a country's population but the most widely used (by OECD, the International Monetary Fund, and the World Bank) is the GINI coefficient.[3] The coefficient ranges from zero (perfect equality with income distributed equally across society) to 1 (perfect inequality with income or wealth held by very few individuals). Among the six countries we discuss in this book, the net income GINI coefficients for 2018 look like this: Sweden, 25.7; Germany, 29.0; Italy, 33.3; Spain, 34.3; United States, 37.8; and India, 47.9 ("Wealth Distribution," 2019). In 2000, the coefficient for United States was 36.8, indicating a bit more concentration over the last two decades. The position of OECD is that growing income inequalities can undermine the foundation of

---

[3] The computation of the GINI coefficient (or index as it is sometimes called) is a relatively simple matter:

GINI coefficient = ([area under perfect equality Lorenz curve – area under actual Lorenz curve] / area under perfect equality Lorenz curve), where the perfect curve area is defined by a theoretical income (or wealth) distribution where income accumulation in the bottom quintile of earners is the same as the income accruals in all the other quintiles and the actual curve area is defined by quintile income accumulation observed in a population of real-world earners. If these income distributions are identical, the value of GINI is zero. If they differ, the GINI coefficient can be calculated with a bit of integral calculus using the quintile rule (see Borjas, 2008).

capitalist economies by weakening the incentive to invest, increasing barriers to opportunity, and slowing social mobility while admitting that the evidence supporting these contentions remain thin and conflicting (Causa, De Serres, and Ruiz, 2014; Naguib, 2015). It should be noted that over the last decade in the U.S. increases in income inequality have been associated with higher gross domestic product (GDP) levels, and as Brooks (2013) astutely points out, the policies of meritocracy favored by both liberals and conservatives in America only serve to accelerate any existing income disparities.

In the early years of the U.S. republic and continuing through the late 1950s, the American economic and social order was often contrasted with those of France and Great Britain; contemporary comparisons highlighting American vices and virtues now favor Sweden as the frame of reference (e.g., see Gabel and Kamerman, 2006). It is easy to see why: Sweden outperforms the United States on measures of child poverty, academic achievement, infant mortality, income equality, and a host of other quality of life measures. In point of fact, Sweden outperforms virtually all OECD member countries as well. During the 2016 U.S. presidential campaign, it was not uncommon for candidates (usually Democratic Party candidates) to proclaim "We need to be more like Sweden," and this is happening once again in the 2020 U.S. presidential campaign.

But is it possible to alter a value orientation framed around "self-interest rightly understood" with one of "balanced group interest" that characterizes Sweden and other Nordic countries? Esping-Andersen (1985) describes the unique historical context that produced the social democracy and managed capitalism of Sweden. Unlike many other countries including Norway and Denmark, Sweden adopted a revisionist version of socialism that (a) rejected the breakdown of capitalist argument, (b) committed to the idea that an organized and planned capitalism could advance the socialist cause, and (c) recognized that class collaboration among liberal farmers, a tiny bourgeoisie, and the socialist working class could advance the economic interest of all, better than class warfare (pp. 8–9). For reasons we will suggest in Chapter 4, Americans seeking to adopt "Swedish socialism" might be getting more (or less) than what they are bargaining for. Schumpeter (1962) hints at the potential transfer problems by calling attention to the cultural origins of socialism, noting, "It is absurd for other nations to copy Swedish examples; the only effective way to do so would be to import the Swedes and to put them in charge" (p. 335). On the other hand, Swedish and American capitalism may have more in common than we think possible. As we have seen, the net income GINI coefficients for the two countries indicate a significant differ-ence in salaries and wages. However, when the wealth GINI indices are cal-culated for each nation and the combination of wages/salaries, investments, property, and other assets are taken into consideration, differences narrow substantially, with the United States at 85.9 and Sweden at 83.4 ("Wealth Distribution," 2019).

Thus far we have offered examples of some deep culture descriptions in four of the six countries where we concentrate our research activity. Of course, these descriptions also exist in profusion in Spain and India as well with the caveat that the cultural fractures in the two countries make it more difficult to encapsulate a Spanish or Indian experience, economic or other-wise. The regional cleavages in Spain—Castilla vis-a-vis Catalonia, Andalusia against the North, the Basque, and everyone else—have long historical and economical roots. Lowe's (2014) *Fear and Loathing in La Liga* captures this tension between Castilla and Catalonia masterfully in the fierce soccer ri-valry between Barcelona and Real Madrid, which has clear overtones of anti- and pro-Franco sentiments. More subtly, Morris (2008) makes the point in descriptions of Salamanca, Avila, Segovia, and Toledo. The beautiful but poor economic areas of Andalucía, which Morris does not visit, have become a flashpoint for contretemps around dissolution and regional independence.

Although Francisco Franco died in 1975, his ghost and mass graves continue to haunt the memories of older citizens and the culture of subse-quent generations too. Treglown (2013), for example, provides a myriad of instances, in art, literature, etc., where the dictator's loathing of socialism, which he regarded as a hereditary form of degeneracy (p. 16), suffuses the country's culture, preventing the flame of the Spanish Civil War from being extinguished altogether.

In the world's largest democracy India, religious differences often signal significant disparities in life chances and economic prosperity. While Hindus comprise the religious majority in India, their path toward economic self-sufficiency is typically not through entrepreneurship given the proscrip-tion of material pursuits advocated by their religious tenets (Singer, 1966). A thriving caste system further dictates legitimacy through generational occupational pursuits such as the Brahmins pursuing scholarly activities or the Vaishyas establishing business enterprises (Audretsch, Boente, and Tamvada, 2007) ranging from neighborhood grocery stores to multinational conglomerates. It is the religious minorities in India—the Muslims at 14 per-cent and Christians at 2.5 percent—who have a higher propensity toward entrepreneurship. For example, Muslims have traditionally dominated conventional businesses like brass work in Moradabad, leather processing in Kanpur, carpet making in Mirzapur and Bhadohi, lock-making in Aligarh, and manufacturing of low-quality cigarettes called Beedis. This is not to say that educational and social backwardness has not kept a substantial proportion of Muslims from attaining economic prosperity, perhaps as partially exemplified by the few and far between forays of the community into the technology-driven businesses and production lines.

Comparatively, Christians, a sizeable majority of whom occupy the south-western parts of India (e.g., Kerala), have done much better economically, with the community abounding in entrepreneurs promoting businesses big and small, right from the local village store to financial behemoths. Due to their predominance in several localities, Christians have, in the last couple of centuries, flourished in Kerala, setting up educational institutions, hospitals, community centers, malls, industries, etc. Factors determining entrepreneurial emergence such as education, experience, sound economic background, etc. are found in a larger measure among Christians than among the Hindus or Muslims of Kerala. A predisposition to risk-taking, a tradition of promoting and developing agriculture, industry, and commerce and adequacy of resources—financial and otherwise—has served this community well and produced entrepreneurs in large numbers.

Culture's Components and Dimensions

Inferences about a nation's culture drawn from historical analysis or from the accounts given by novelists and journalists often have a richness and poignancy that is difficult to match in the social science research literatures. Yet while deep description by Weber, de Tocqueville, Di Lampedusa, or Payor might be worth 100 factor analysis or 1,000 regressions, they share a characteristic—the amplification of difference—which can easily leave impressions of culture hyperbole and/or negative stereotypes. As we discussed earlier, the promulgation of any cultural values that may be judged deplorable and immutable (i.e., the authentic German, the suspicious Italian, the money-hungry American) are also values that make social scientists uncomfortable. The working hypothesis among those queasy about the idea of enduring values is that cultures share as many common values, beliefs, and preferences as they have values that divide them, with the likelihood that the former far outnumber the latter.

In the fields of cultural anthropology, sociology, and social psychology when national cultures are examined, the notion of cultural dimensionality has come to dominate conversations about the probabilities of similarities and differences. Here the research by the psychological and management consultant Geert Hofstede and his colleagues is perhaps the most well-known (Hofstede, 1978, 2001; Hofstede, Hofstede, and Minkov, 2010). In the late 1960s, Hofstede was given access by IBM to its managerial database containing over 100,000 employees from 72 countries. The Hofstede team administered a questionnaire to these employees asking them to rate their values and attitudes on a large number of Likert-scaled items. Some examples of these questions are as follows:

Managers should make most decisions without consulting subordinates.
Managers expect workers to closely follow instructions and procedures.
Group welfare is more important than individual rewards.

Employee responses to the items were subjected to a series of exploratory factor analyses,[4] which isolated six value dimensions: (a) employees prefer either high or low power distance (i.e., a paternalistic or collaborative management style); (b) they prefer individualism and the primacy of individual interests or they value group/collective interests more; (c) they value masculine reward (extrinsic recompense like salary and advancement) or feminine rewards like (intrinsic recompense like good working relationships; (d) employees either avoid uncertainty and the anxiety it invokes or they are readily confronted; (e) employees express a long-term orientation or they seek more immediate gratification; and (f) employees are indulgent and accept a variety of viewpoints readily or they are closed to their acceptance. By aggregating individual responses and cross-classifying any group level patterns by country, Hofstede turned a corporation's interest on promoting culturally sensitive management styles into an international discourse on national character.

---

[4] Factor analysis in its exploratory form is a data reduction technique that assumes that the observed variables are linear combinations of some underlying hypothetical or unobservable variables. Some of these factors are assumed to be common to two or more variables and some are assumed to be unique to each observed variable. In confirmatory factor analysis the researcher imposes substantively motivated constraints on which observed variables are affected by which specific underlying factor. See, for example, Long, 1983 and Kim and Mueller, 1978.

Taking only the individualism–collectivism dimension into consideration and applying Hofstede's factor scoring method to the six countries that we have built this employment preference study around, we get the following ranking measured on a scale of zero to 100: United States, 93; Italy, 74; Sweden, 70; Germany, 60; Spain, 50; and India, 47.[5] As expected, the United States has the highest values around self-interest, and India, the lowest; however, the ranking of the other four countries might raise some questions.

As might be expected, Hofstede's national rankings and the methodology that is responsible for generating them have come under some rather harsh criticism (Javidan et al., 2006; Hofstede, 2006; McSweeney, 2002). Without getting into the methodological weeds, there are three issues that stand out. The first is, Do Hofstede's dimensions possess construct validity? In other words, are there really six dimensions that define a nation's culture? In various iterations of Hofstede's own analyses, he has reported five and even four dimensions. Second, is a managerial database tantamount to a citizen level database? It could be possible that such a set of data truncates response variation and covers up subcultures within a nation. Finally, does the classification have criterion validity; that is, can it be useful in predicting economic or social outcomes?

Notwithstanding the criticisms of Hofstede's work, dimensional analysis and country classification of those dimensions remain popular. In a cross-nation research project nearly as impressive as Hofstede's body of work, Robert House and his team (House et al., 2004) sent questionnaires similar to those of Hofstede to over 17,000 middle managers from 92 companies in 62 nations. Employing both explanatory and confirmatory factor analysis of questionnaire responses, The Globe Study uncovered nine value dimensions. Four of the dimensions closely parallel those reported with the IBM data: future orientation, gender egalitarianism, power distance, and uncertainty avoidance. Individualism–collectivism is now captured by two separate dimensions—in-group and institutional—and new factors measuring assertiveness, humane orientation, and performance motivation are distinguished. Predictably, Hofstede (2006) disagrees. On the dimension of institutional collectivism (mean: 4.25), our six countries score as follows: Sweden, 5.22; India, 4.38; the United States, 4.20; Spain, 3.85; Germany, 3.79; and Italy, 3.68. It would be expected that Sweden would rank highest and Italy would rank lowest in their trust of institutions;

[5] For a complete listing of the Hofstede rankings, see Hofstede, Hofstede, and Minkov (2010).

however, the levels of collectivism reported for India and the United States could be legitimately questioned.

A third large scale effort to isolate distinctive component of culture is the values theory approach pioneered by Shalom Schwartz (Schwartz, 1994, 2012; Bilsky, Janek, and Schwartz, 2011). Schwartz uses a technique called multidimensional scaling (MDS)[6] (he specifically warns against the use of exploratory factor analysis) to cull value structures from the questionnaire responses of large samples of students and teachers in over 70 countries. In earlier applications of his analysis, Schwartz uncovered seven value clusters: embeddedness (collectivism), intellectual autonomy, affective autonomy, hierarchy, mastery, egalitarian commitment, and harmony. Subsequent analyses have revealed as many as 10 dimensions. If we look just at rankings of our six countries on the dimension of intellectual autonomy (i.e., an aspect of individualism), where the mean value is 4.35, they are distributed in this way: Sweden, 5.09; Spain, 4.99; Italy, 4.91; Germany, 4.80; the United States, 4.19; and India, 4.02. If a pattern is emerging from these large-scale culture dimension research, it is one on instability leavened with more than a smidgen of fuzziness.

It is also possible to create cultural profiles for countries without the aid of thousands of survey responses and data reduction methods such as factor analysis, cluster analysis, or MDS. The method often used to do this is the constructed typology. As defined by McKinney (1966), a constructed type is "a purposive, planned selection, abstraction, combination, and (sometimes) accentuation of a set of criteria with empirical referents that serves as a basis for comparison of empirical cases" (p. 3). Put more simply, typologies are conceptual classifications resulting from the astute observation of historical and other empirical information that have a reasonable probability of being validated by other astute observers. Douglas and Wildavsky (1982) classify cultures on two criteria: first, high or low power hierarchy (grid) and, second, high or low group status emphasis (group). The resulting two by two table is then utilized to sort societies in this fashion:

High Grid—High Group = Hierarchy (Prewar Germany)
High Grid—Low Group = Fatalism (Sicily, southern Spain)

---

[6] MDS is a statistical technique which uses proximities among any kind of object to indicate how similar or different objects are on any measure(s) where a distance can be calculated. Rather than impose dimensions as in factor analysis, MDS attempts to uncover them in the data. See Kruskal and Wish (1978).

Low Grid—High Group = Egalitarianism (Sweden)
Low Grid—Low Group = Individualism (United States)

Fiske (1991) and Triandis (1971, 2002) cross-classify societies on the conceptual criterion of individualism–collectivism and horizontal–vertical power distance. In these schemas, the United States would be placed in the high individualism–vertical power distance cell, which Fiske called "market pricing" value orientation while Sweden, a high individualism–horizontal power distance country, would be classified as an "equality matching" nation.

The typology of national welfare states constructed by Gosta-Esping Andersen (1990, 2002) has proven to be very influential in the social science and public policy literature. As we stated in Chapter 1, the Esping-Andersen framework served as an important resource when we planned our strategy for selecting countries. This typology is more complex than those proposed by Douglas or Triandis; countries are ranked on criteria that include universality of income guarantee; commodification of welfare benefits, primacy of government in social and economic affairs, and extent of employment-protection measures. The last criterion, which deals with the labor market rigidity in a country is a factor closely linked to the demand for labor and ultimately to unemployment. Rigid markets manage flows of people in and out of employment through such mechanisms as minimum wages, unemployment insurance, severance pay, firing policies, etc.; flexible markets manage much less. On an index published by OECD entitled "Overall Strictness of Employment Protection," the United States has a rating of 0.2 while most EU countries are indexed at around 2.5 (see Blanchard, 2006). The OECD categorization and ranking process, however, might benefit from some of the nuance contained in the Esping-Andersen typology. For example, while Sweden and Italy have ratings that are very similar, Sweden conducts what Esping-Andersen calls an active labor market policy (i.e., full employment coupled with programs designed to move workers from one employment opportunity to another; Esping-Andersen, 1985, 1990). In Italy, worker protection policies have not been designed to adjust to changing economic conditions and have served simply to exacerbate long-term unemployment woes.

Cultural Components and Economic Performance

The identification of what Triandis (2002) has called "cultural syndromes," either through deep description, typology, or multivariate statistics, can tell us a good deal about the coherence of a nation's overall value orientation and can also point to incongruities among dimensions with the potential for generating dissonance and outright conflict (p. 19). These are compelling reasons enough for studying cultural values, but they are far from the most substantial if a better understanding of economic outcomes is the goal. Many of the typologies and dimensional analyses we have discussed, but not all, were undertaken with the clear intent of better understanding and improving economic performance. This is certainly the case in the Globe Study (House et al., 2004; Javidan et al., 2006) and in the work of Hofstede (2001; Hofstede et al., 2010) where business interests are clearly visible. While not as conspicuous, the economic implications of the typologies developed by Fiske (1991) and Triandis (2002) can be discerned swimming just below the surface. However, reading accounts of Esping-Andersen's classification in the social work or public policy literature could easily leave a reader with the impression that welfare policy has little to do with labor policy and nothing could be farther from this author's intentions.

Some efforts have been undertaken to test if the cultural components identified in factor analysis or typology construction can explain variation in economic outcomes like GDP growth, per capita income, or entrepreneurial activity. The results of these analyses remain mixed. Gorodnichenko and Roland (2013), for example, report that an increase in values favoring individualism over collectivism increase levels of income and the levels of innovation in a country. Mark Casson (2006), who has developed his own typology of cultures, finds that individualism plays an essential role in the creation of what he terms "enterprise culture" and "entrepreneurial associationism." Franke, Hofstede, and Bond (2002), on the other hand, report a negative impact of individualism and a positive effect of long-term orientation on GDP per capita growth in a study of 51 countries. In an analysis of entrepreneurial activity over a 20-year period, Hofstede et al. (2004) find that individualism surprisingly had a significantly negative effect on self-employment.

In Table 2.1, we collect the cultural classifications we have presented thus far along with an entry for Gannon and Pillai (2016), which we will consider at the chapter's end.

Table 2.1 Some Widely Used Cultural Classifications of Nation-States

Reference	Sweden	Germany	United States	Italy	Spain	India
Esping-Andersen (2002)	• Social Democratic • Full Redistribution • Decommodified welfare • Government pillar needs full employment	• Conservative/ corporatist • Negligible redistribution • Welfare depends on work • Rigid labor market	• Liberalism model with market pillar • No Redistribution of income	• Southern European family pillar • Negligible redistribution • Very rigid labor market	• Southern European family • Negligible redistribution • Very rigid labor market	
Gannon and Pillar (2016)	• Extreme egalitarianism • Horizontal individualism • Low power distance/legal penalties related to individual's assets	• Egalitarianism tempered by higher vertical Individualism • Inequality of outcomes is tolerated	• Egalitarianism with unbridled power distance tolerance • Market pricing culture • Inequality of outcomes is accepted	• Cleft culture • Difficulty integrating into a national culture because of geographic differences	• Torn culture (i.e, culture being amplified Differences) • Difficulty integrating into because of geographic differences	• Diverse, harmonious culture
Hofstede, Hofstede, and Minkov (2010)	• Low power distance • Relatively high individualism • Feminine • Very low uncertainty avoidance • Short-term orientation • Very high indulgence/ optimism	• Relatively high individualism • Masculine orientation • Relatively high uncertainty avoidance • Very high long-term orientation • Moderately low indulgence/ optimism	• Low power distance • Very high individualism • Masculine orientation • Relatively Low uncertainty avoidance • Very limited long-term orientation • High indulgence/ optimism	• High power distance • High individualism • Masculine orientation • Very high uncertainty avoidance • Relatively high long-term orientation • Very low indulgence/ optimism	• High power distance • Relatively low individualism • Relatively high masculine orientation • Very high uncertainty avoidance • Short-term orientation • Low indulgence/ optimism	• Very high power distance • Relatively low individualism • Masculine orientation • Relatively low uncertainty avoidance • Short-term orientation • Very low indulgence/ optimism

House, Hanges, Javidan, Dorfman, and Gupta (2004)						
House, Hanges, Javidan, Dorfman, and Gupta (2004)	• Future orientation, delayed gratification—well above mean • Gender equalitarianism—well above mean • Assertiveness, confrontational—below mean • Humane orientation altruism—well above mean • In-group collectivism loyalty—well below mean • Institutional collectivism redistribution—well above mean • Performance orientation reward excellence—below mean • Power distance stratification—below mean • Uncertainty avoidance—well above mean	• Future orientation, delayed gratification—Well above mean • Gender equalitarianism—below mean • Assertiveness, confrontational—above mean • Humane orientation altruism—At mean • In-group collectivism loyalty—below mean • Institutional collectivism redistribution—well below mean • Performance orientation reward excellence—above mean • Power distance stratification—above mean • Uncertainty avoidance—well above mean	• Future orientation, delayed gratification—Above mean • Gender equalitarianism—at mean • Assertiveness, confrontational—above mean • Humane orientation altruism—well above mean • In-group collectivism loyalty—below mean • Institutional collectivism redistribution—at mean • Performance orientation reward excellence—above mean • Power distance stratification—above mean • Uncertainty avoidance—at mean	• Future orientation, delayed gratification—well below mean • Gender equalitarianism—below mean • Assertiveness, confrontational—at mean • Humane orientation altruism—above mean • In-group collectivism loyalty—at mean • Institutional collectivism redistribution—below mean • Performance orientation reward excellence—below mean • Power distance stratification—above mean • Uncertainty avoidance—below mean	• Future orientation, delayed gratification—below mean • Gender equalitarianism—below mean • Assertiveness, confrontational—above mean • Humane orientation altruism—at mean • In-group collectivism loyalty—above mean • Institutional collectivism redistribution—below mean • Performance orientation reward excellence—at mean • Power distance stratification—above mean • Uncertainty avoidance—below mean	• Future orientation, delayed mean—above mean • Gender equalitarianism—well below mean • Assertiveness, confrontational—below mean • Humane orientation altruism—well above mean • In-group collectivism loyalty—well above mean • Institutional collectivism redistribution—above mean • Performance orientation reward excellence—above mean • Power distance stratification—above mean • Uncertainty avoidance—at mean

Continued

Table 2.1 Continued

Reference	Sweden	Germany	United States	Italy	Spain	India
Douglas and Wildavsky (1982)	• Opportunity resides in group solidarity and removal of social differentiation • Blame the system	• Opportunity resides in rule constrained rational action • Blame deviants	• Risk = Opportunity • Blame incompetents	• Opportunity resides in luck • Risk averse • Blame fate	• Opportunity resides in luck • Risk averse • Blame fate	• Risk = Opportunity • Blame incompetents
Fiske (1991) Triandis (2002)	• Equality matching • High Individualism • Horizontal power distance	• Equality matching • Market pricing hybrid	• Market pricing • High individualism • Vertical power distance	• Authority-ranking/ equality-matching hybrid	• Authority-ranking/equality-matching hybrid	• Market pricing • High individualism vertical power distance
Casson (2006)	• Entrepreneurial associationism	• Administrative associationism	• Enterprise culture	• Play the system culture	• Play the system culture	• Enterprise culture
Hofstede (1977)	• "Fox culture" • Small power distance • Small uncertainty avoidance	• "Fox culture" • Small power distance • Large uncertainty avoidance	• Not classified	• "Lion culture" • Large power distance • Large uncertainty avoidance	• "Lion culture" • Large power distance • Large uncertainty avoidance	• "Lion culture" • Large power distance • Small uncertainty avoidance
Bilsky, Janik, and Schwartz (2007)	• High Universalism/ benevolence • Low hedonism/ stimulation	• High universalism/ benevolence • Low hedonism/ stimulation	• High universalism/ benevolence • Low hedonism/ stimulation	• High universalism/ benevolence • Low hedonism/ stimulation	• High universalism/ benevolence • Low hedonism/ stimulation	• High Universalism / Benevolence • Low Hedonism / Stimulation

In what could be termed a typology of typologies, we indicate where each of our six countries fit in these classifications. Even a cursory glance at the table reveals that there are, ostensibly, a multitude of features that offer clues to labor force attachment decisions. From the multitude, we have extracted eight cultural components that have been explicitly linked to measures of economic activity.

Social Capital and Cooperation

In 1964, Gary Becker (1964, 1993), a subsequent Nobel Prize winner in economics, introduced the idea of human capital into the social science literature. Becker argued that just like physical capital (i.e., bank accounts, stock shares, manufacturing plants that yield income), personal schooling, healthy eating, and the virtues of honesty and punctuality are capital too, in the sense they are investments in self that pay dividends in the marketplace and in the quality of living. It was two noneconomists, James Coleman (1990) and Pierre Bourdieu (1986), however, that came to the conclusion, quite early on, that Becker's definition really combined two distinctive forms of capital, one that resided in the individual (personal human capital) and another that inhabits the social relationship between individuals (social capital).

Lest one believe that having social capital and good relations with others were simply laudable qualities of social etiquette divorced from real world economic consequences, Robert Putnam sought to dispel that notion in a series of books and articles (Putnam 1995, 2000, 2007) that were written based on his work in Italy. Turning his attention now to social relationships in the United States, Putnam provides evidence that Americans are experiencing the steady erosion of social capital in both its healthy (bridging) and less healthy (bonding) forms. Putnam et al. (1993) saw bonding social capital residing in the family and extended family as the illness of southern Italy, "a cancer eating up" healthy stocks of the kind of social capital (bridging) that make cooperation, interaction, sharing and trade possible across group boundaries. In America, Putnam places the blame for the decline in social capital on the individualization of leisure; immersion in social media; declines in volunteerism, civic club membership, and church attendance; and increased diversity. Putnam (2007) avers that "diversity seems to bring out the turtle in all of us [Americans]" (p. 151). Eiser (2008) also makes a strong argument that bridging and bonding forms of capital not only define individual relations but that they become institutionalized in societal systems where they can systematically help or hinder economic growth, competitiveness, and innovation.

There is some strong empirical evidence linking bridging social capital to economic activity. Using Bank of Italy survey data, Guiso, Sapienza, and Zingales (2004) report that in areas with higher levels of social capital, individuals were more likely to invest in stock, use checking accounts, and use institutional credit sources instead of informal sources. David, Janiak, and Wasmer (2010), with eight years of information from the European Community Panel Study, found that areas with high levels of bonding capital (most regions in Spain and Greece) exhibited high probabilities of unemployment and low probabilities of residential mobility. Tabellini (2008b) in his historical examination of nation-states identifies a "norm of cooperation" (i.e., the relationship that exists between the pattern of moral ties between individuals and patterns of economic interactions in nation-states). Cultures that champion a "norm of limited morality" mitigate this norm of cooperation that would lead to material advantages for all parties because the betrayal or abrogation of agreements outside the community with which older generations identify have limited costs for the deal-breaker. Some of the results for countries where this abrogation is a widespread norm are inefficient legal systems, political abuse, and exploitation and a state of "low betrayal" economic equilibrium.

Trust

Freitag and Buhlmann (2009) maintain that trust is the core of social capital (p. 1537). It is useful here to make the distinction, as do Glaeser et al. (2000), between trust and trustworthiness. The former references trusting behavior (i.e., the one doing the trusting) and the latter the one who is entrusted, someone who is worthy of receiving trust. Glaeser and his colleagues in their research with data from the General Social Survey find that social relationships in the United States have a strong relationship to trustworthiness but not to trust.

As in the case of social capital, trust has been connected empirically to a variety of economic outcomes. Easterly (2006) observes that societies in which people typically follow rules without coercion are generally less poor than those with widespread cheating problems. Guiso, Sapienza, and Zingales

(2006) define trust as the "subjective probability with which an agent assesses another agent or group of agents with performing a particular action" (p. 29). Armed with this definition and data from the World Values Survey, Guiso et al., find that trust in a country is correlated positively with thrift, tolerance, honesty, and a belief in hard work. This cluster of values, in turn, is related to saving, entrepreneurship, and the redistribution of wealth. Freitag and Buhlmann (2009) also employ the World Values Survey and discover that countries whose authorities are seen as incorruptible, whose institutions of welfare state reduce income disparities, and whose political interests are proportional to the power their constituents possess are more successful economically. Within the United States, Glaeser et al. (2000) find that the level of trust among African Americans is much lower than it is for Whites, and this is seen as a contributing reason for the income disparities between the two groups.

In a series of intriguing experiments around trust preferences, Bigoni and her research team (Bigoni et al., 2016, 2018) explore differences between northern and southern Italy. Counter to the findings of Banfield and Putnam, these researchers assert that the differences between the two regions do not reside in narrow self-interest (Banfield) or amount of bridging capital (Putnam). Rather, what distinguishes the two sections of the country and the differences in economic efficiency they represent is a "deep trait," they label "the preference for betrayal aversion" (Bigoni et al., 2016, p. 1338). Put simply, southern Italians have a higher distaste for being cheated. Some theoretical justification for the Bigoni et al. observation can be found in Anderlini and Terlizzese's (2017) endeavors to describe trust equilibrium.

Redistributive Justice

As we have previously noted, beliefs, attitudes, and economic preferences for both cooperation and trust have an association with beliefs, attitudes, and preferences for income redistribution. In a widely cited report released by the International Monetary Fund, Ostry et al. (2014) claim that wealth redistribution is necessary to promote a pro-growth economy. As research by Guillaud (2013) and Schuck and Shore (2019) demonstrate, there is a wide variation across nations in the appetite for income redistribution. Expectations of downward mobility (Schuck and Shore, 2019) and low rank in the labor market Guillaud (2013) are both positively correlated with preferences for redistribution as one would suspect. Some countries with highly active redistribution policies like France and Belgium, however, have slow or no-growth economies while others like the United States, with widening income inequality, have experienced strong growth. A much-watched experiment in Finland (Hannon, 2019), moreover, aimed at guaranteeing an income minimum for individuals out of work found that such a guarantee did nothing to spur the search for employment or for labor force attachment.

With the evidence we have at hand, it would be safe to conjecture that the preference for redistribution has a complex relationship with economic growth, if it has one at all. A bit of insight into this complex relationship can be found in a *New York Times* essay written by the columnist David Brooks (2013). He observes that income distributions are a downstream effect of human capital difference. In the United States where great emphasis is placed on meritocracy and people-sorting based on "the quest for distinction," income transfer policies are losing policies—they never catch up to the sorting dynamic. Although Brooks does not consider France in his contention, we will do so here. France is also a country where meritocracy is very important and where, arguably, efforts toward redistribution have been more successful. This begs the question, Is slow growth economy, the legacy of meritocracy overtaken by efforts to reduce income disparity?

Work Centrality

It might be seen as stating the obvious that positive attitudes toward work or, even better, the preference for work are a *sine qua non* for gainful employment. While there is a relationship, it turns out that the relationship is not as muscular as one would like to think. Perhaps the reason for this attenuation between attitude and behavior can be teased out from a declaration made by Herman Melville, the great American novelist: "In order that people may be happy in their work . . . they must not do too much of it" (Leyda, 1951, p. 795).

An important assumption made in research on work values is that employment is critical for personal growth and social integration (Freud, 1930; Deci and Ryan, 2000; Hauff and Kirchner, 2015). In Max Weber's analysis, work opened the gate to eternal salvation; for contemporary social scientists studying the subject, work allows individuals to reap more modest rewards and avoid governmental damnation in the balance. In the tradition of Weber, a good deal of research has been conducted on work commitment or centrality. Gallie (2019) in his cross-national research maintains that social democratic countries like Sweden exhibit higher levels of work commitment than liberal countries like the United States. The Mediterranean countries of Italy, Spain, and Greece rank even lower in this commitment. The reasons given by Gallie for these differences (i.e., coordinated economies like Sweden and Denmark place emphasis on skill-oriented work while plausible) are far from convincing. In their cross-nation research, Kittel et al. (2019) locate higher levels of work centrality in "Italy, in particular, the southern part, in Hungary, south eastern England and the British midlands, in the southern part of Germany, lower Saxony and in large parts of Greece" (p. 109). If there is a pattern here, it is scarcely visible to the naked eye!

While Gallie (2019) concludes that work commitment in national populations has been "remarkably stable" over time, this claim is disputed by a number of country-specific investigations. Twenge and her associates (2010) in a large study of baby boomers, Generation Xers, and millennials (N = 16,507) used data from a survey of high school seniors in the United States to examine work values in 1976 through 2006. Twenge et al. (2010) conclude from a series of confirmatory factor analyses that while baby boomers in America "live to work," millennials and Generation Xers "work to live" (p. 1122). An Australian study (Baron, Cobb-Clark, and Erkal, 2008) finds that the cultural transmission of a work ethic is strong for indigenous youth but not for immigrants. Surprisingly, the centrality of work may be declining even in full employment nations like Sweden. Ljunge (2011) finds that the take up rate in Sweden for sick leave has risen from 45 percent for the generation born in 1920 to 80 percent for the generation born in 1960.

The centrality of work in an individual's life is a function of a number of factors with the quality of the available jobs being critical. The work-values literature has, in addition, isolated a second influence: whether the motivation for working is the consequence of intrinsic values (i.e., work is interesting, helps others or society, stimulates personal growth) or extrinsic values (pay, job security, opportunity for advancement, fringe benefits package). Self-determination theory (Deci and Ryan, 2000; Twenge et al., 2010; Van Den Broeck et al., 2019), a conceptual framework quite popular in the study of work values, posits that extrinsic values emerge when intrinsic rewards are blocked or undermined in the job market. It has been hypothesized that millennials and Generation Z workers are more likely to seek out jobs that meet intrinsic values rather than more tangible rewards. In their study of 19

OECD countries (N = 43,179), Esser and Lindh (2018) report a picture of relative stability in work values from 1969 to 2015 with some small increase in the importance of intrinsic values evident in a handful of countries. Hauff and Kirchner (2015) use latent class analysis to study the work values of five capitalist democracies (United States, Great Britain, Germany, Norway, and Hungary; N = 8,280) and find evidence for four work patterns. While both extrinsic and intrinsic values are important in four countries, intrinsic values (e.g., work independently, interesting work) were more important in Norway. Van Den Broeck et al. (2019), in their examination of World Values Study, note that younger workers in countries where the predominant focus of the labor force is on intrinsic values tend to be happier and more satisfied with life. Several large-scale studies, however, have found that extrinsic values have assumed more importance in the lives of younger workers, at least, as far as workers in the United States are concerned. Kalleberg and Marsden (2013) monitor work values from 1973 through 2006 with the General Social Survey and see a general trend in valuing income and security more than work that provides a feeling of accomplishment. The previously mentioned study by Twenge et al. (2010) concurs, describing baby boomers (and not millennials) as the generation with the highest values for intrinsic rewards.

Risk-Taking

Taking risks to create wealth is a basic tenet of capitalism; it is the pathway to self-employment, entrepreneurship, innovation, and renewal of economic growth (Schumpeter, 1966; Casson, 2003; Baumol, 2010). As one might suspect, the belief in and the preference for risk-taking and self-employment vary widely, and some of the variation has been traced to differences in cultural value orientations. The Global Entrepreneurship Monitor developed by Bosma and Kelly (2018) ranks the United States at the very top of 54 countries with respect to cultural norms and values that help foster self-employment. The ranking of other countries in our study are India, 5; Spain, 16; Sweden, 18; Germany, 19; and Italy, 41. One of the key cultural values here is high regard placed on calculating risk-taking. In an effort to link Hofstede's six cultural dimensions to entrepreneurship, Wildeman et al. (1999) use information from the Executive Interim Management firm on business practices in 23 OECD countries. No clear relationships between these dimensions and self-employment were detected; the most compelling cultural effect found was a dissatisfaction with democracy. A comparison of risk-taking in the United States, China, and Germany conducted by Weber, Hsee, and Sokolowska (1998) asserts that the differences across these countries can be found in values responsible for setting "the equilibrium between greed and fear" (p. 177).

Individual Achievement

As is indicated in Table 2.1, many of the typologies and dimensional analysis of culture have pointed up the significance of an individualist vis-à-vis collectivist value orientation in a group or society. Individualism has been found to be negatively correlated to fatalism (Douglas and Wildavsky, 1982; Slovic et al., 2000) and has been connected both conceptually (Kraaykamp, Cemalcilar, and Tosun, 2019) and empirically (McClelland, 1961, 1964; Mazur and Rosa, 1977; Collins, Hanges, and Locke, 2004) to economic growth and entrepreneurial activity.

Preferences and Attitudes for Personal Human Capital Investment—Education and Training and for Labor Force Attachment

These very important components of acquiring knowledge and skills that can give a competitive advantage to prospective and employed workers, and using these skills to engage in productive work will be the primary concern of Chapter 3.

Testing Cultural Metaphors

When discussing our conceptual model in Chapter 1, we alluded to a component of value orientations identified as metaphors. Occupying a conceptual middle ground between deep description and cultural dimension approaches, the cultural metaphor method attempts to encapsulate a national culture within a symbol that "captures" what it means to be a German, or an Italian, or American. The method was developed by Martin Gannon and his associates (Gannon, 2009; Gannon et al., 2006; Gannon and Pillai,

Table 2.2 Cultural Metaphors for the Nations Included in Our Analysis

Sweden	Germany	United States	Italy	Spain	India
• Scandinavian egalitarian culture	• Other egalitarian culture	• Market-pricing culture	• Cleft culture	• Torn culture	• Multiculture
• The Stuga	• The symphony	• The athletic contest	• The opera	• The bullfight	• The dance of Shiva
• The "stroll down life's middle path"	• The unending search for the authentic	• The pursuit of liberty and happiness	• The twisting path to betrayal	• The running (late) with the bulls and the bears	• The cyclical journey to salvation (Mukti)

2016) as a means of introducing cultural sensitivity into international business transactions. In this respect, the method is similar to the original motivations of the Globe Study and Hofstede analyses. As Gannon notes, it is also strongly influenced by the early work of Clifford Geertz.

The metaphorical definitions that Gannon (2009) uses to describe our six countries are shown in Table 2.2. The second and third lines in the table provide the categorization that Gannon utilizes to classify general culture of the nation and the metaphorical symbol. Italy, for example, is defined as a "cleft culture" primarily because of its North–South divide while Spain is labeled as a "torn culture," reflecting the ongoing pressures for regional independence. In limited testing of these cultural metaphors, Gannon et al. (2006) conclude that they can, indeed, be used as a frame of reference for understanding culture. We put them to further test in this book examining their efficacy for distinguishing the perceptions of ordinary citizens in our six democracies.

We have taken some dramatic license in Table 2.2, in adding our own metaphor of cultural difference on line 4. As the reader may see, we take our inspiration from the deep descriptions introduced earlier in the chapter.

3

Human Capital and Labor Supply

Our labor preserves us from three great evils—Weariness, Vice and Want.

—Voltaire, *Candide or Optimism* (1979, p. 126)

Among the eight beliefs, attitudes, and presumptive preferences we listed in Figure 1.1 as the observable cultural correlates of economic activity, the preference for and intention to seek education and training would appear to be the most obvious. As Becker (1993) remarks, just as physical capital is created by making changes in materials so as to form tools and facilitate production, human capital is created by changing persons so as to give them skills and capabilities that make them able to act in new ways. Becker goes on to identify schools as the principal institution where this type of socialization takes place with families serving as the principal transmitters of the values for education and training.

Labor economists (Killingsworth, 1994; Borjas, 2008; Freeman and Wise, 1982) and critics of current labor policy (Crisp and Powell, 2017; Caroleo and Pastore, 2016; Vogel, 2015) remind us that while human capital creation typically provides only a partial explanation for labor force attachment, it can tell us a great deal about labor supply decisions. To more fully understand the problems of unemployment and underemployment, however, we also need to consider local/regional labor market conditions and how these conditions influence the demand for labor. We will have a bit more to say about labor supply–demand matches and mismatches in the next chapter.

Before beginning our exploration into the role that human capital investment plays in economic activity, we make a brief excursion into the nature of labor markets, believing that the digression will assist in motivating the discussion that follows.

In Figure 3.1 we offer a stylized depiction of two labor markets, one for high skills (E_{HS}) and the other for low skills (E_{LS}). The labor market equilibrium

Caught in the Cultural Preference Net. Michael J. Camasso and Radha Jagannathan, Oxford University Press (2021).

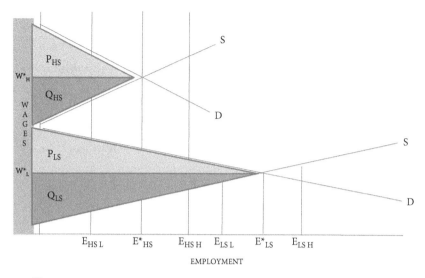

Figure 3.1 Equilibrium high and low skills labor markets.

in each market occurs when supply equals demand; E^*_{HS} high-skill workers are employed at W^*_H wages and E^*_{LS} low-skill workers are employed at W^*_L wages. The wages (W^*) are the market-clearing wages; other wages in both markets, either higher or lower, would precipitate pressures on those wages, leading to labor surpluses in the case of higher wages and labor deficits in the case of lower wages. The triangles (P) represent the producer (employer) surpluses, and triangles (Q) constitute employee surpluses. The quantity (P+Q) represents the maximum gain from these surpluses to the market (see Borjas, 2008).

When a labor market reaches equilibrium, unemployment is zero because the number of people who wish to work equals the number of available jobs. Individuals not willing to accept (W^*_H) or (W^*_L) will, of course, not participate in these markets and may enter if the wage rose or if circumstances force them to enter a market they do not prefer. In a recent report, the OECD (2016) classified countries and regions within countries into four principal groupings based on how well employee skill levels matched the available jobs requiring these skills. Most regions in Germany and Sweden were considered to be places in high-skills equilibrium, what we have defined as E^*_{HS}. Other areas, particularly in the southern Mediterranean (e.g., Italy, Spain, Greece, Portugal), were viewed as markets caught in a low-skills trap. Here, because of the weakness or nonexistence of high-skills opportunities, overeducated and/or overskilled individuals may out of necessity opt for work at E^*_{LS}. They can also choose to move geographically to a high-skills market in another region or country. Individuals might even decide to change careers and move from one high-skills economic sector to another. Countries like the United States have substantial skills surpluses in the low-skill labor market and substantial skills deficits in the high skills, especially STEM (science, technology, engineering, and mathematics) labor market (U.S. Bureau of Labor Statistics, 2018; Fayer, Lacey, and Watson, 2017). India, too, has large skills surpluses in the low-skill market but, unlike the United States, also has surpluses in the high-skills labor market.

The high-skill equilibrium of Sweden and Germany has consistently held unemployment rates both generally and for youth to modest levels. For the last 20 years these rates have averaged around 5.5 percent and 12 percent, respectively, in Sweden and 7 percent and 10.5 percent, respectively, in Germany. The overall and youth unemployment rates in Spain and Italy over this same time period averaged approximately 18 percent and 35 percent, respectively, and 9 percent and 30 percent, respectively, in Italy. Rates are much higher than these averages in southern Spain and southern Italy. In the United States unemployment rates have trended lower over the last 20 years, averaging about 7.5 percent overall and about 14 percent for youth. In India, overall rates have been very low with the mean of about 4.5 percent and the youth rate averaging about 10 percent.

The aforementioned 2016 OECD report pinpoints three remedies for unemployment, each calling for increasing the investment in personal human capital (supply-side solution) such as improvements in general education and vocational education and training, enhanced apprenticeship opportunities, and stronger efforts to bolster entrepreneurship and small-medium business enterprises (SMEs). The assumption here is that by increasing skills supply, labor force attachment will increase and unemployment will fall. If our stylized discussion of the competitive labor market has resonated, it should be evident now that these initiatives, at best, address only one very important segment of the youth unemployment problem.

Cultures of General and Vocational Education

In formulating his ideas about human capital development, Becker (1993, 1996) makes the distinction between two approaches or investment strategies, if you will. The first strategy is to provide broad general education, what in the United States is termed *liberal education*. The focus here, in essence, is its lack of focus; students are exposed to a broad spectrum of knowledge culled from the arts, sciences, and humanities. The goal is to create individuals capable of critical thinking with the capacity to learn how to learn, appreciate the arts and, perhaps most important, purvey the national culture to future generations. The second educational strategy is to stress specific knowledge and training, which, in principle, limits individuals who have been socialized in this fashion in the knowledge and skills necessary for negotiating an increasingly complex and diverse world of work.

The specific skill strategy does appear to have important advantages in capitalist labor markets since workers with specific and specialized skills are less likely to quit their jobs and their skills are more likely to compel company loyalty. And, as Becker (1996) points out, workers with specific skills are more likely to receive promotions and are among the last to be laid off during business downturns (p. 147). Bench or line workers can, with additional training, become managers, but the reverse is not feasible if the manager lacks specific technical skills when he or she entered the firm.

The selection of a general or specific educational path to human capital growth is a choice rooted in cultural values and preferences. In his study of democracy in America, De Tocqueville (1840/1945) observes that Americans show less aptitude and taste for general ideas than the French. He goes on to comment that the

> habit and taste for general ideas will always be greatest among a people of ancient culture and extensive knowledge. This is not to say the French approach to creating human capital is superior, on the contrary general ideas are no proof of the strength, but rather of the insufficiency of the human intellect; for there are in nature no beings exactly alike, no things precisely

identified, no rules indiscriminately and alike applicable to several objects at once. The chief merit of general ideas is that they enable the human mind to pass rapid judgment on a many great objects at once; but, on the other hand, the notions they convey are never other than incomplete, and they always cause the mind to lose as much in accuracy as it gains in comprehensiveness. (p. 14)

The French commitment to general ideas remains steadfast and is reflected in the French conceptions of *métier* (job; D'Iribarne, 2009) and *dirigisme* (managed capitalism; Bourdieu, 2005; Murphy, 2017; Peet, 2012), preference for income redistribution (Guillaud, 2013), weak support for entrepreneurship (Ulijn and Fayolle, 2004; Bosma and Kelly, 2018), and the centrality of *les gandes ecoles* (Bourdieu, 1996). It may also have contributed to the highly segmented labor market in the country and the neglect of specific knowledge initiatives like vocational education (OECD, 1984, 2016). Over the last few decades the United States has witnessed a steady growth in general education with either a two-year associates degree or a four-year college baccalaureate degree seen as the best tickets to insure economic success.

In the balance of this chapter, we will examine how the sensible remedies proposed by OECD (2016) to attack unemployment—vocational education, apprenticeship, and entrepreneurial opportunities—have been structured and are operating in our focal group of six nations. In undertaking this review we will attempt to show how the educational and training institutions and approaches in each country resonate significant underlying cultural beliefs, attitudes, and preferences.

The German Dual System

In what could be viewed as an earnest version of "a priest, minister, and rabbi walk into a bar," Ulijn and Fayolle (2004) examine work cultures in French, Dutch, and German engineering firms, and based on their observations, the authors delineate widely variant motivations for engaging in the work. The French engineers were drawn to the intellectual challenges that were immanent in product design; the Germans were motivated by the processes of competent fabrication and implementation, and the Dutch were stimulated by product sales and marketability. The study reveals what many others have described previously; that is, the French favor education that can be termed a "theory to practice model" while the Germans recognized the importance of "practice to theory" (OECD, 1984; McClelland, 1964; Murphy, 2017).

The Ulijn and Fayolle (2004) study is useful in highlighting one of the central features of human capital creation in Germany, which is that operational definitions necessitate both general (conceptual) and specific knowledge and skills. A second, and perhaps not so obvious, impetus comes from what McClelland (1964) has labeled the German value formula—"I must be able to believe and do what I should do for the good of the whole" (p. 80).

At a time in the United States and in a large part of Europe when human capital investments appear preoccupied with tertiary-level[1] university degrees, Germany and several of its geographic neighbors—Switzerland, Denmark, and Austria—have pursued a strategy that is designed around flexible meritocracy, innovative and high-quality production, and stakeholder collaboration. An integral component of this strategy is the dual education system or simply the dual system.

We present the basic architecture of the German education system in Figure 3.2. The rectangles are labeled with the credential or degree that signifies successful completion of a stage of schooling shown in parenthesis. The numbers within the rectangles reference the typical number of years required to complete each stage.

As is clear from the Figure 3.2, after finishing four years of elementary school (Grundschule), students are tracked into one of three programs of study: Gynasium, Realschule, and Hauptschule. Gymnasium comprises a demanding academic course of studies. Successful completion of Gymnasium curriculum in eight to nine years leads to a certificate of general college entrance and after three to six years of further study to a bachelor or bachelor/masters degree, analogues to BA and BS programs that epitomize so much of the college experience in the United States. Although this proportion has risen in recent years, about 50 percent of young Germans pursue upper secondary education (bachelor's level in the United States), and tertiary school graduate rates have remained stable in the low 20 percent range (Hoeckel and Schwartz, 2010; Fazekas and Field, 2013; Zimmermann et al., 2013).

In 2006, 47 percent of German students entered into vocational education either through the Realschule track, which can prepare the student

---

[1] A tertiary level of education is defined by the International Standard Classification of Education as education that occurs at a university, college, or trade school level typically after an upper secondary level diploma or certificate has been received. The International Standard Classification of Education descriptions of primary, secondary, and tertiary education are promulgated by UNESCO.

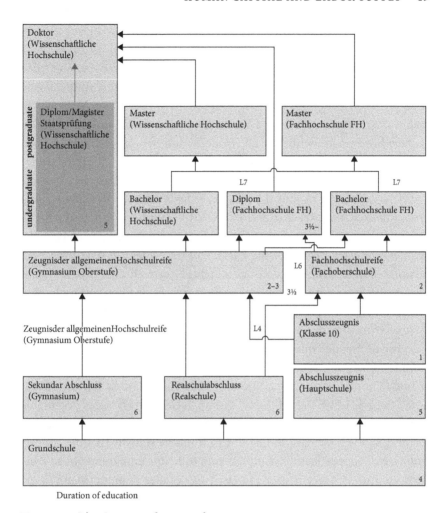

Figure 3.2 The German educational structure.

for either general or vocational educational opportunities, or Hauptschule, which is much more narrowly focused on preparation for manual skills work (Haeckel and Schwartz, 2010). By 2016 this proportion had dropped to about 43 percent (OECD, 2019c). Of students who continue on the vocational track beyond 10 years of schooling (upper secondary level), about 25 to 30 percent attend full-time vocational education training (VET) schools known variously as Fachschulen, Fachoberschule, or Berufsfachschulen, with the vast majority, mostly young men, enrolling in an apprenticeship (dual system) program. Figure 3.2 indicates that a student who initially follows a vocation studies path can switch over to a general education track if (a) he/she chooses to do so and (b) can pass the required examinations.

While entry into the secondary level vocational school like Fachoberschule requires a lower secondary school diploma, students who enter dual VET programs that feature apprenticeships do not. Many young men, in fact, enter with only a Hauptschule certificate, and a small percentage have no credential at all (Hoeckel and Schwartz, 2010; German Ministry of Education and Research, 2014). Questions have been raised regarding the amount of actual hands-off instruction that takes place in some Fachschulen programs, but this has never been an issue in German dual programs (see, e.g., Fazekas and Field, 2013; Zimmermann et al., 2013). Typical apprenticeships require that 80 percent of training take place in the business/industry firm with the balance of time spent in part-time VET schools—here conceptual skills are taught. Nearly all dual programs last for 3 to 3½ years with apprentices spending three or four days each week on the job at a business site. He or she is paid a salary that is, on average, a third of a full-time skilled worker and upon completion of training receives a license to practice one of over 350 skilled crafts or trades ranging from chimney sweep and diamond cutter or welder to millwright or auto mechanic (Zimmermann et al., 2013; CEDEFOP, 2018a). As Pastore (2018) notes, the goal of VET and the dual system in Germany is to develop highly qualified workers with exceptional specific knowledge. The evidence that the program is successful can be drawn from the statistic that the conversion rate of apprenticeship contracts into full-time employment has averaged around 55 percent over the last two decades (Zimmermann et al., 2013; German Ministry of Education and Research, 2014).

The success of the German manufacturing sector powered by highly skilled technicians with high school or two-year associates degrees has caused many economists, politicians, and government officials from around the globe to recommend the adoption of a German-style education system in their countries. Efforts to copy the German model have encountered a number of obstacles, however. The implementation of a functioning dual system or even a full-time vocational school program with application-oriented curriculum mandates a level of coordination among business, labor unions, and the government that has proven to be illusive in most capitalist democracies. German Chambers of Crafts and Commerce monitor whether working and training standards are met by participating firms; they also work with unions and government offices like the Federal Institute for Vocational Education and Training to reform or replace existing regulations, certifications, or training modules. They also work with VET schools and employers to ensure that students receive sufficient general education, allowing them to move and take advantage of different or emerging trades, crafts, or professions (Vogel, 2015; OECD, 2016; CEDEFOP, 2018b). If mistrust and hostility defines the relationships among these entities, as it does in many nation-states, the barriers to replication of the German approach might prove too high.

If we are correct in our conceptualization of human capital creation as a consequence of culture as well as economic conditions, merely requiring organizations to work together, while necessary, will probably not result in a successful outcome. In many OECD countries, apprenticeships are characterized as pathways to "dirty jobs" (OECD, 2016, p. 74; Eichhorst et al., 2015; Eichhorst and Rinne, 2016). As Werner Eichhorst and his associates maintain, the youth and parents in Germany accept VET as a solid alternative to general academic training. Through their conscious or unwitting application of the German value formula, these families have largely avoided many of the problems that have plagued other capitalist democracies—overeducation, underskilling, skill obsolescence, mismatches between employment occupation and field of training/education, and unemployment (McGuinness, Pouliakas, and Redmond, 2017; Valiente and Scandurra, 2017; CEDEFOP, 2018a,b).

Social scientists have labeled German society and economy as a "well-oiled machine" (Adher and Gunderson, 2007) and a "well-ordered machine" (Reiff, 2015); both of these metaphors convey an impression of the involuntary, habitual, and even inattentive. Based on the German approach to developing its human capital, a metaphor that stresses precision and synchronicity would appear more representative. As Gannon and Pillai (2016) assert, a fitting metaphor for German organization and culture is one of a symphony orchestra where even if everyone would like to play in the string section, it is understood that someone must play the tuba if the orchestra is to function properly. It is a very old metaphor in Germany as this observation from Karl Marx (1894/1967) will reveal:

In all kinds of work where there is cooperation of many individuals, the connection and unity of the process are necessarily represented in a will which commands and in functions which, as for the leader of an orchestra, are not concerned with partial efforts, but with the collective activity. (p. 76)

Democratic Education in Sweden

Human capital development in Sweden is both the antecedent and consequence of a value orientation that stresses equality of opportunity but not
equality of outcome. Esping-Andersen (1985, 2002) acknowledges this distinction, noting that while income inequality and redistribution pose severe
dilemmas for the Swedish social democracy a continued socialist commitment to effective redistribution would "alienate white collar strata and block
any chance of a broad wage-earner alliance" (Esping-Andersen, 1985, p. 323).
Sweden is often characterized as a culture that epitomizes the definition of
social justice attributed to John Rawls.[2] However, as Esping-Andersen (2002)
cautions, Sweden's adoption of a Rawlsian yardstick resonates well with its
broader ethos, which is built around the centrality of work. The Swedes appear to take Rawls (1999) quite literally when the philosopher asserts that the
most important primary good an individual can possess is self-respect and
that meaningful work and occupation is a primary pathway to its achievement (pp. 286–388).

Like Germany, the unemployed in Sweden face considerable shame and
stigmatization (Lahusen and Giuigni, 2016; Bergquist, 2016; Grimmer,
2016). Bergquist (2016) notes that the Swedish social structure presumes
a collective solidarity where citizenship is indistinguishable from duties
such as working and paying taxes. Inasmuch as the generous social security system is financed by full-time employment, "a proper job is a full-time
job" (p. 113). An exhaustive report commissioned by the Nordic Council of
Ministers (Albaek et al., 2015) is a splendid example of the seriousness with
which the unemployment issue is taken in Sweden.

Against this backdrop of moral economy one would expect to find an
educational system that facilitates school-to-work transitions. We provide
the general structure of this system in Figure 3.3. Compulsory schooling
(Grundskola) begins at age 7 and lasts for nine years; it typically follows a
preschool exposure (ages 1 to 6) that has been integrated into the school
system since 2011 (Carcillo et al., 2016; Kuczera et al., 2008). Since the

---

[2] John Rawls (1999) bases his theory of justice on the thought experiment of people behind a veil
of ignorance. In this experiment, people would not know what position they will have in society until
after they make up the social and moral rules. One person divides the known resources/rights, and
then the others get to choose first. This motivates the person making the division to make the worst
share as good as the rest of the shares, to make all the shares equal. Motivated by the expectation of
reciprocity, all primary goods including income and wealth, rights, and duties will, in principle, be
equally shared (p. 55).

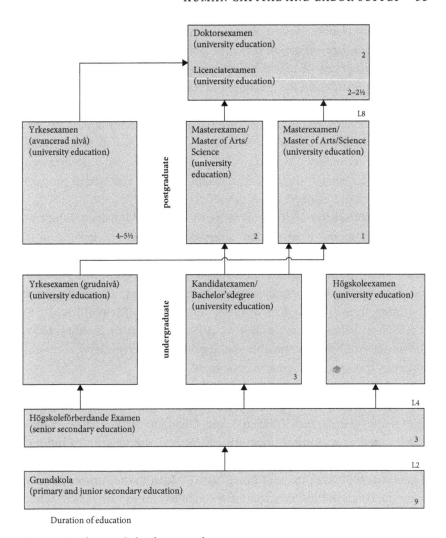

Figure 3.3 The Swedish educational structure.

early 1990s, when a series of large-scale school reforms took place, parents have the right to exercise school choice and enroll their child(ren) in a compulsory school other than the one to which the child(ren) were assigned as long as spaces are available. They can also send their children to privately run schools at costs paid by municipalities (Kuczera and Jeon, 2019). It is important to note that this compulsory education is delivered, publicly or privately, without tracking according to examinations or other measures of ability.

Upon completion of Grundskola, virtually all students enter senior (upper) secondary education for three years. Here they can choose from among 18 programs—6 of which are oriented toward general education and college preparation and the remaining 12 lead to vocational careers. Careers include building construction, business administration, property management, handicrafts, and tourism. Since the early 1990s enrollment on VET programs has dropped steadily from about 50 percent of all students enrolled in a senior secondary program to about 33 percent in 2018 (Kuczera and Jeon, 2019; Kuczera et al., 2008). This decline has been reflected in considerably higher youth unemployment rates.

In an effort to boost VET enrollments, the Swedish Ministry of Education initiated additional reforms that targeted vocational curriculum at the upper secondary levels, attempting to change from a predominantly school-based focus to more hands-on, on-jobsite apprenticeships. The transition has proven difficult in large measure because of a long tradition of isolating education from the world of work—a concomitant of school-based VET (CEDEFOP, 2018a; Kuczera and Jeon, 2019; OECD, 2016). Needless to say, the number of Swedish students that go on to university-level vocational training (Yrkesexamen) remains quite small.

Sweden's education reforms occurred at around the same time that a market-oriented government regained political power after nearly a 20-year hiatus (Fernandez-Villaverde and Ohanian, 2019). These changes can be seen as a cultural imperative to restore the balance of interests that make a social democratic society like Sweden possible (Esping-Andersen, 2002; Gannon and Pillai, 2016). Much to the consternation of many socialists in the United States, Sweden has now promulgated school choice, substantial cuts in its corporate tax rate, funded for-profit schools, and deregulated many business and industry sectors including the post office. These measures are without doubt confusing to many purists and ideologues but should not be surprising to individuals acquainted with a Swedish culture that avoids the rigidities and class resentments associated with ideologues. Schumpeter (1962) describes the country's great fortune in this way:

> the antagonism between intellectuals and labor men only shows under the microscope precisely because, owing to the level of both, there is no great cultural gulf between them and because, the Swedish social organism producing a relatively smaller supply of unemployable intellectuals than do

other social organisms, exasperated and exasperating intellectuals are not as numerous as they are elsewhere. (p. 325)

Capital Formation in the Southern Mediterranean

At first glance, it would appear that Italy and Spain are two interchangeable examples of the same southern European human capital formation problem—too much overeducation, not enough technical skills education, skill obsolescence, etc. To be sure, these countries, along with Portugal, Mediterranean France, and Greece, share many labor market characteristics that have hampered growth and prosperity in substantial sections of those countries. Italy and Spain, especially southern Italy and southern Spain, are simpatico in two respects—high unemployment and high upper secondary school dropout rates—which auger ill for many current job holders and prospective job seekers. The adult and youth unemployment rates in Italy, while declining since 2008, continue to be high (11 percent and 30 percent, respectively), but in regions like Calabria and Sicily, they remain close to 20 percent and 50 percent, respectively (OECD and Eurostat databases, 2019). In Spain, conditions are somewhat worse than in Italy with overall unemployment at 16 percent and a youth rate at 35 percent; Andalusia, however, continues to experience rates of 25 percent and 45 percent, respectively (OECD and Eurostat databases, 2019).

Italy and Spain continue to have extremely high secondary school dropout rates, despite large declines over the past two decades. The rate in Spain is now just under 20 percent (and the highest in Europe), and in Italy, it hovers around 14 percent. Once again, these rates are much higher in the south of these countries (Manca, Quintini, and Keese, 2017; Mullock, Quintini, and Keese, 2017).

The similarities between Italy and Spain begin to disappear however when we look more closely at the structures of secondary education in the two countries. In each case, the value orientations buried deep in culture reveal themselves with stunning clarity. In Figure 3.4 we introduce the reader to the educational system in Italy. Instruction is compulsory for all children aged 6 through 16 beginning in *scuola primaria* through lower secondary school (*scuola secondaria di primo grado*). Figure 3.4 shows that after five years of compulsory education, a student qualifies for diploma that allows him or her to continue on to a general education at a university or college

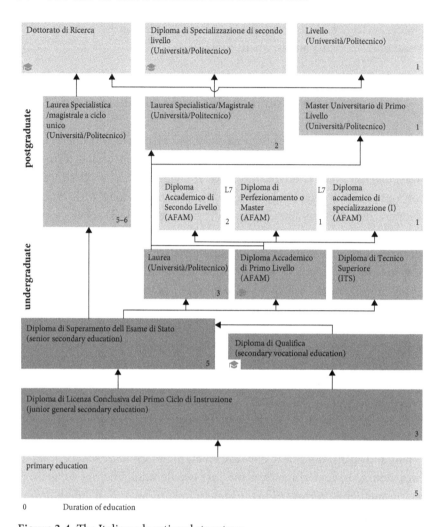

Figure 3.4 The Italian educational structure.

of arts and music or college of technology, Instituto Technico Superiore (ITS). Successful completion of a vocation track after three or four years of postcompulsory education leads to a Diploma di Qualifica. Underlying what seems to be a simple structure on the surface is a quite complex tangle of qualifications, auspices, and management. The first clue to this complexity derives from the fact that nearly 60 percent of all Italian students choose a technical or vocational educational pathway at the upper secondary level— a level much higher than even Germany. The second clue stems from the country's preference to operationally define technical and vocational as two different types of education (INAPP, 2016; Manca, Quintini, and Keese, 2017; CEDEFOP, 2018b).

Students who pursue the Diploma di Superamento Dell'Esame di Stato can do so in three ways: by attending academic high schools, upper secondary level technical schools, or upper secondary level professional schools. Hence, the qualifications for this diploma can be met with interests that range from Latin literature, business administration, and tourism to audio/visual/multimedia, stage/fashion design, and construction management. Many of these technical routes have a three- to six-month internship requirement. A recent study published by OECD shows that, unlike Germany, where there are clear differences in academic skills between students in general and technical education tracks, this is not the case in Italy where the socioeconomic background of families play a much more prominent role in enrollment decisions (Manca, Quintini, and Keese, 2017).

While technical education comes under the centralized control of the Ministry of Education, University, and Research, the majority of vocational training does not; instead, it is administered in the three- to four-year regional educational and vocational training programs. Here, training in such diverse areas as food processing/catering, automotive repair, artistic works operator, or electrician can vary considerably, almost never have a work-based component (OECD, 2019), and suffer from high rates of incompletion (Mullock, Quintini, and Keese, 2017). Since 2015, Italian students can also opt to gain vocational or technical skills through an apprenticeship program lasting three to four years. This option remains remote for most students since the collaborative relations between government, business, and labor unions remain contentious and are a work in progress (INAPP, 2016).

A complex vocational and technical education system such as the one constructed in Italy requires substantial investments in coordination for success. Instead, Italy appears to have constructed this edifice on the shifting sands of mistrust. In their opening chapter to an OECD report entitled "Getting Skills Right—Italy," Manca, Quintine, and Keese (2017) observe:

Italy suffers a profound lack of dialogue and trust between schools and firms and very much needed links between these stakeholders have not emerged spontaneously in the past. The status of Technical Vocational Education Training (TVET) is affected by a severe negative social stigma and the educational tracks that build links with the world of work have been traditionally perceived as leading to low-quality education. (p. 15)

And with the mistrust, according to these authors, comes the deception:

Qualifications in Italy do not provide robust signals of workers "true skills." This makes skill matching more difficult as employers have only partial and poor information to sort candidates into job and skills requirements. (p. 17)

The lack of coordination and distrust among institutions is not lost on students at the upper secondary and lower tertiary levels. Monticelli et al. (2016) and Lahusen (2016) cite case study and survey data demonstrating that young underemployed and unemployed blame the government (not themselves) for their circumstances. In her work on the diaspora of youth leaving southern European countries to find work, Ricucci (2017) observes that school is at the center of criticism from young people debating their future course of action. Quoting one of her field informants, an upper secondary school manager, "schools are still in the dock [in Italy]. I am not surprised that families and students do not trust them. Often teachers are too far removed from the world of work, sometimes even from reality itself" (p. 57).

In a recent *Economist* article entitled Metabolically Different (*The Economist*, 2019), the writer makes the point that Spain is not Italy, claiming the country lacks the decades-old fractiousness and stagnation of Italy. Our contention that the differences pointed out in this essay between "Spaniards' openness to change" and adoption of EU policies vis a vis Italian resistance is more a manifestation of "the resignation to follow" and the comfort of firm structure, both legacies of the Franco regime. Recall from the previous Chapter (Table 2.1) that Spanish respondents to both the Globe (House et al., 2004) and Hofstede (Hofstede et al., 2010) surveys scored more like Indian respondents than respondents from Germany, Sweden, Italy, and the United States on individualism–collectivism dimension. Spain and India are not individualistically oriented cultures if these large surveys are to be believed. And while the *Economist* article paints a fairly optimistic picture of Spain's economic activity—Spain's per capita gross domestic product overtook that of Italy in 2017—rigid educational curriculum and equally rigid labor markets forewarn of obstacles that need to be overcome.

The educational structure of Spain is given in Figure 3.5; it indicates a much simpler architecture than the Italian system. Ostensive simplicity should not

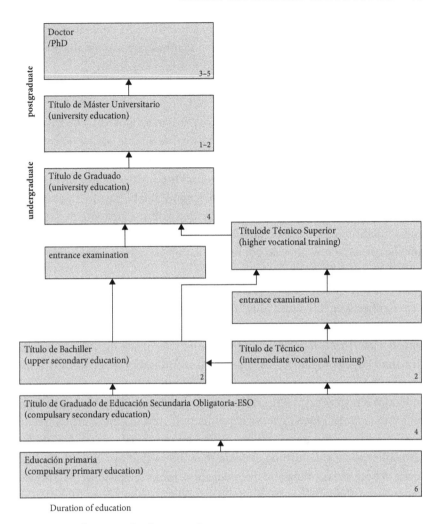

Figure 3.5 The Spanish educational structure.

be confounded with popularity, however. As Ricucci (2017) reports from Eurobarometer data, with the exception of Greek students, Spaniards are more likely than students in the other 28 EU countries to judge training/education in their country to "not be well adapted" to the current world of work.

Figure 3.5 shows that compulsory education ends at age 16 with a Titulo de Graduado de Educacion Secundaria Obligatoria. Upon graduation students have three choices: general education for two years (bachillerato); undertake vocational training, also for two years (*titulo de technico*); or drop out of school, which about 20 percent do. Only about 30 to 35 percent of students select vocational education, a proportion that has remained stable over the past decade (OECD, 2019; Mullock, Quintini, and Keese, 2017).

Vocational training in Spain continues to face formidable challenges of quality, reputation, and effectiveness (Lopez-Fogues, 2017; Prieto, 2014). The vast majority of vocational training takes place in school (OECD, 2019) despite governmental efforts to implement a dual education model (Formacion Professional Dual) in 2012. Zimmermann et al. (2013) contend that the vocational training endeavors have largely backfired with attendance in upper secondary level vocational education dropping due in part to an employer subsidy program that has actually increased youth employment turnover and shifted the occupational distribution toward less qualifications for jobs and, because the subsidies do not require lower job entry wages, encouraged school dropouts (p. 61).

Attempts to encourage apprenticeship programs have not fared much better either. Lopez-Fogues (2017) points to three barriers in Spain: strong opposition from trade unions and some parental organizations, a widespread view that proper learning can only take place in school, and the dearth of large companies—Spain's business and industry sectors are dominated by SMEs. The problem is exacerbated by the relatively large number of individuals with general skills and tertiary educations who are willing to take low-skill technical jobs in service, production, and manufacturing, freeing employers from the responsibility of developing social capital. CEDEFOP (2018b) reports a disturbing statistic that shows that Spain, with its high levels of both overskilling and overeducation, ranks lowest among European countries in the willingness of employees who have gravitated into lower-skill jobs to seek subsequent skill development and thus escape them (p. 88).

Career and Technical Education in the United States

In a 2014 press conference, then-President Barack Obama told reporters "We got to move away from what our Labor Secretary, Tom Perez calls our 'train and pray' approach. We train them and we pray that they can get a job" (White House Office of the Press Secretary, 2014). While Obama was speaking specifically to the problem of failed government efforts to stimulate labor demand through direct training programs, his aphorism could have just as easily been used to convey the nation's overall failures in vocational education.

Vocational education had, in fact, become so unpopular that during the 2006 reauthorization of the Perkins Act—the act that mandated an alternative to general education—the term *vocational* was replaced with the expression *career and technical education* (CTE). Notwithstanding the name change, vocational education continues to suffer from issues of quality, financial support, business commitment, and public acceptance (Kincheloe, 2018; Kuczera and Field, 2013; Zimmermann et al., 2013).

We depict the structure of the educational system in the United States in Figure 3.6. After completing eight years of compulsory education in elementary and lower secondary school (middle or junior high schools),

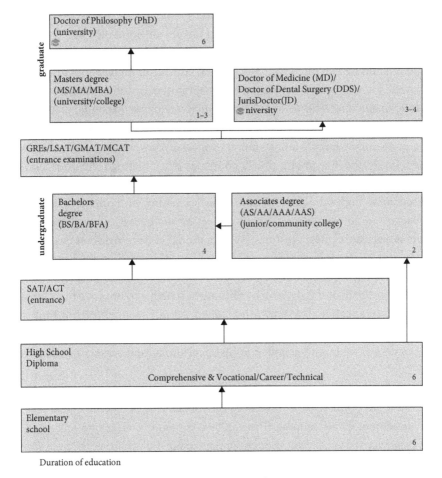

Figure 3.6 The educational system in the United States.

students enter four-year comprehensive high schools and can choose a general pathway leading to a four-year college or CTE track hopefully leading to training and a job. Most of this technical training takes place in comprehensive high schools rather than in separate vocational career centers in response to concerns that physical separation of students will set up segregation along racial grouping in violation of the Equal Education Opportunity Act of 1974 (Kuczera and Field, 2013, p. 21). Successful completion of high school/upper secondary school results in a general education diploma or a diploma and certificate in the case of vocational students. In principle, the American vocational student has both a general education and basic skills in a subject area that includes agriculture, business office operations, marketing, home health and economics, computer maintenance and operation, trade, or financial literacy. Critics however maintain that the typical U.S. vocational student has neither the general literacy or numeracy nor the basic technical skills to get a job that pays more than minimum wage. This indictment could be extended to many general education high school graduates as well. For example, results from the Programme for International Student Assessment continue to show that American upper secondary students lag well behind students from most European and many Asian countries in math and science. Math scores are especially low with the United States ranking in the 40s among the 70 countries participating (DeSilver, 2017). The math and science performance of Black and Hispanic students at comprehensive high schools is extremely disheartening with only 13 percent of Blacks and 26 percent of Hispanics meeting mathematics benchmarks on the American College Testing (ACT) national college readiness examination and 11 percent of Blacks and 22 percent of Hispanics reaching readiness in science (ACT, 2017).

Unlike Spain and Italy, which continue to struggle to improve their upper secondary vocational systems, the United States has attempted to find redemption at the lower tertiary level in the form of community college. President Obama said as much in his speech to a joint session of Congress in 2009:

I ask every American to commit to at least one year or more of higher education or career training. This can be community college or a four-year school, vocational training or an apprenticeship. But whatever the training may be, every American will need to get more than a high school diploma. (cited in Kuczera and Field, 2013, p. 17)

Two major weaknesses of vocational and technical education at the upper secondary level in the United States are low-quality training curricula and instruction delivered (a) without programmatic and financial oversight and (b) without the input and/or active involvement of actual/prospective employers (Zimmermann et al., 2013; Zirkle, 2017; Eichhorst et al., 2015). In their review of CTE obtained through community college, Kuczera and Field (2013) warn that dysfunction at the high school level could be repeated at the lower tertiary level with substantial financial cost to students if accountability is not improved.

It might appear puzzling to some as to why Americans, and particularly American businessmen, do not see value in an alternative school–work schema or long-term apprenticeships when other countries like Germany and Switzerland with strong economies apparently do. The rationale apparently stems from a literal and cultural application of Becker's (1993) human capital theory. As Lerman (2017) observes, in a perfectly competitive labor market, firms will provide specific training that enhances the productivity but not general training, which will not be cost-effective since the benefits will not offset training costs before other firms hire away the trained workers. Hence, the only way to finance general training is to lower wages of full-time workers (p. 306) or, possibly, as Ryan (2016) remarks, to allow the work-based learning to be financed entirely by the student-trainee, primarily through foregone earnings. Trainees will be paid the value of their marginal product, net of the direct cost to the employer training them (p. 15). When viewed through the prism of "self-interest rightly understood" and the American value formula, however, this strategy makes perfect economic sense in America's "free-wheeling" arena of largely unregulated capitalism—at least in the short run. If, on the other hand, one assumes a labor market for skilled employers with imperfect competition among employers, where the contest for employees is less intense and where wage differences do not cause large-scale quitting, then worker training would not affect the firm's profit margin. Such a market is consistent with what McClelland (1964) has called the "German value formula—I must believe and do what I should for the good of the whole" (p. 80). The preferred method of vocational education in the United States, in contrast, continues to be on-the-job training (Zimmermann et al., 2013; Eichhorst et al., 2015), an approach that does not require the close collaboration of government, employers, and unions and clearly signals low confidence in school-based CTE.

In 2017 the Trump administration issued an executive order expanding apprenticeships noting that "many colleges and universities fail to help students graduate with the skills necessary to secure high paying jobs in today's workforce" (White House Office of the Press Secretary, 2017). A key component of this order is the establishment of Industry-Recognized Apprenticeships, where third parties (i.e., business and industry trade groups, unions, and joint labor–management organizations) receive expedited review and registration in the U.S. Department of Labor. Working on the model of apprenticeship widely employed in the building/construction trades, the Trump measure promises to extend the model to retail, hospitality, and manufacturing (Scheiber, 2017). If the program is to be successful, it will require several fundamental changes in the way America conducts its school-to-work transition. First, students would need to be convinced that VET does not preclude further generic/cognitive development and career mobility (Valiente and Scandurra, 2017). Second, employers need to be convinced that the investment in dual programs and apprenticeships will lead to the creation of loyal future employees (Ryan, 2016). And, third, full-time employees and unions must be convinced that participation in these programs will not yield lower wages for full-time workers. In short, nothing less than a broad cultural change would seem to be in order, a change all the more difficult considering that real-wage increases of American workers has been substantially higher than most Scandinavian and all southern Mediterranean countries over the past decade (The Economist Intelligence Unit, 2014).

General and Vocational Education in India

In a 1997 article, Bhabani Gupta describes the Indian psyche as a mix of individualism and collectivism where the former plays an important role in social and economic activity so long as it does not violate social norms. The origins of individualism and pragmatism in Indian business and industry, moreover, can be traced to values learned from international interactions, particularly those during the long British occupation (Kumar, 2004; Singh, 2011). This value mixture has, of course, filtered through India's public education system where it has stimulated some sensational successes (e.g., widespread literacy in English in some regions of the country) and numerous failures, school-to-work transitions among them.

The structure of the Indian educational system is shown in Figure 3.7. Primary education typically begins at age 6 and ends at age 14; compulsory education also concludes at age 14. Secondary school is organized as two 2-year cycles called general/lower secondary school (Standard X) and upper secondary (Standard XII). Based upon student performance in lower secondary school and on his or her state examination results, students can enter one of four pathways, three of which offer vocational/technical training opportunities. Students may pursue a Standard XII diploma by entering an academic

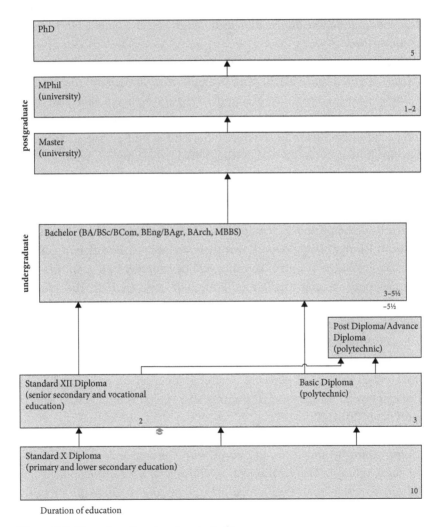

Figure 3.7 The educational system in India.

stream or a vocational one. The former is designed to prepare students for future study at a college or university science, commerce, and the arts and humanities while the latter can serve as a springboard for tertiary vocational education or to enter the labor force. Students seeking vocational and technical training can also choose to bypass the Standard XII curriculum and enter two-year Industrial Training Institutes and study subjects such as secretarial practices, computer operations, draftsmanship, electrical and plumbing trades, and food services (Zimmermann et al., 2013; Tara and Kumar, 2017). A third vocational route can be pursued through three-year polytechnical school; here, the training focuses on developing engineering skills in the construction, production, information technology, and civil/public services economic sectors.

There is widespread consensus among experts and governmental officials in India that VET has not been effective in meeting the needs of a rapidly growing economy. Majumdar (2016) points out that, like many European countries and the United States, India is churning out graduates and postgraduates from universities (about three million a year) who lack specific skills necessary for acquiring jobs in the growing sectors of the economy. He, along with other critics (Schmid, 2015; Tara and Kumar, 2017; Zimmermann et al., 2013), describes a formal and informal VET that impacts only about 4 percent of the half billion persons workforce and that is largely unsupported by company-based or workplace-based training. Tara and Kumar (2017) remark that there are at least 20 different government bodies in the country "running skill development programmes with little synergies and considerable duplication of work" (p. 152). The results of this largely uncoordinated effort to produce students with job-ready human capital has been relative declines, since the early 1990s, in the supply and wages of skilled workers (Zimmermann et al., 2103) and the high number of youth who do not attend even elementary school (14 percent), drop out of secondary school (11 percent), or after graduation are considered NEET (not employed, in education, or training; 28 percent; Schmid, 2015; Sateesh and Sekhar, 2014).

Efforts to reform secondary education in India have been influenced to a large extent by endeavors in Europe with German initiatives garnering the most interest. The creation of a Ministry of Skill Development and Entrepreneurship holds the promise of bringing some order to the VET process. But even while the National Skill Development Corporation was setting up skills councils under its auspices to deal with qualifications, educational quality, and transparency, both the Ministry of Labor and Employment and the Ministry of Human Resource Development were busily setting up their own sector skills councils (Tara and Kumar, 2017).

The capacity of India to set up dual-education and training systems or reframe vocational degrees as credentials equal or better than general education qualifications would appear to depend on how successful this multicultural society is able to balance its individualist and collectivist needs. It has been pointed out that the Hindu religion promulgates a cyclical view of time and a form of predestination that is largely outside the control of human exertions (Singh, 2011; Gannon and Pillai, 2016). Of course, there is a strain of predestination in Puritan teachings that states that even though God's plan is preordained, individuals may, in essence, "sneak a peek" at the plan through their achievements and failures here on earth. The correct application of self-interest (i.e., self-interest rightly understood) is the methodology that helps the observant distinguish the elect from the reprobate. There is some evidence to indicate the puritanization of Hindu predestination, at least among immigrants to the United States. Hindus comprise one of the most successful groups on measures of per capita family income, net family wealth, and similar measures of economic achievement (Pew Research, 2017; Sowell, 1996). The extent to which such a process unfolds in India remains an open question; how it is answered will have ramifications for the type(s) of education and training that is adopted—dual, general, school-based, pure on-the-job, or some amalgam.

Entrepreneurship Skills and Job Creation

Entrepreneurship, the dynamic process of creating incremental wealth, is at the very soul of the capitalist economic system (Schumpeter, 1939, 1964; Casson, 2003; Baumol, 2010). Increasing entrepreneurship is seen as a means for bringing disadvantaged and unemployed youth into the labor market (OECD, 2016; Vogel, 2015; Stam and Van Stel, 2011).

While entrepreneurial skills like creative thinking, calculated risk-taking, irreverence for consensual views, rule-challenging behavior, etc. are not necessarily popular qualities for new employees in established businesses, they are extremely important for the creation of small businesses build around breakthrough ideas and innovations. Innovative technologies created by small United States firms in the 20th century include air conditioning, the assembly line, fracking, the electronic spreadsheet, computerized axial tomography scanner, microprocessor, human growth hormone, and hundreds of others (Baumol, 2010; Vogel, 2015).

The obstacles to the development of entrepreneurial activity and small business formation are formidable and include attracting sufficient financing, obtaining necessary mentoring and consultation, and building a technical skill set containing human capital tools like negotiating ability, financial literacy, and presentation competence, among others. It is also paramount that the prospective entrepreneur be permitted to function within a social context that fosters bridging capital and network building. Svendsen and Svendsen (2004), for example, discuss how social capital in the form of network associations help break down market barriers by reducing the skepticism of customers around the quality and reliability of new product. Supportive networks are also viewed by OECD (2016) as a major barrier to entrepreneurship for disadvantaged youth.

All six countries on which we focus in this book have engaged in significant governmental initiatives to increase the self-employment of unemployed or underemployed youth. In Spain, the Ministry for Labor and Social Affairs launched the Strategy for Entrepreneurship and Youth Employment in 2013 with a goal of facilitating youth self-employment (OECD, 2016). Of the 100 measures identified in the strategy are reduced rates of social security contribution and the extension of unemployment benefits for six months during the business startup period. Sweden has undertaken a number of measures that have proven to be quite successful in promoting the formation of high value-added businesses (Semuels, 2017; Calvino, Criscuolo, and Menon, 2016). Changes in tax laws in 1990 have made it much easier for new companies to compete with large, established firms; Sweden has also deregulated many industries and has privatized many public services, which has had the joint impacts of forcing inefficient legacy business out of the market and helping new innovative firms to enter. In the summer of 2015, the Indian prime minister, Narendra Modi, announced Start-Up India, an ambitious collaboration of government, businesses, and education institutions to make entrepreneurship possible for individuals to become gainfully self-employed. The National Institute for Transforming India was given the responsibility for setting up business incubators across the country in addition to facilitating training and financial support for promising inchoate entrepreneurs (Thakur, 2016). The United States, of course, has a long history of supporting innovative SMEs. Through its Small Business Administration, Offices of Entrepreneurial Development, Women's Business Ownership, Entrepreneurial Education, HUB Zone Program, and the Department of Commerce, the government has sought to encourage business creation and innovation through financing, training, regulation, tax waivers, and management services (Reamer, 2017). These efforts have helped the United States retain its title as the country with the highest early-stage entrepreneurial activity rates among developed countries (Stam and Val Stel, 2011; Bosma and Kelley, 2018).

Each year Babson College (Wellesley, MA, USA) and several collaborating institutions publish a report entitled the *Global Entrepreneurship Monitor*. An important component of this report is a ranking of national environments conducive to entrepreneurial activity—the National Entrepreneurial Context Index (NECI). The ranking is based on 12 indicators of external context ranging from availability of financing and governmental support policies to availability of education/skills training and labor market structures. Out of the 54 developed and developing countries listed, our focal countries rank as follows: India (5), United States (6), Spain (16), Sweden (18), Germany (19), and Italy (41).

One important dimension of NECI is the level of complementarity between societal values and preferences and the norms of entrepreneurship. On this measure our focal countries rank in this order: United States (1), India (14), Spain (22), Sweden (26), Germany (38), and Italy (48; Bosma and Kelley, 2018). The relatively low rankings of Germany and Italy are consistent with value orientations that reflect comfort with employment in one of Germany's many large corporations and, in the case of Italy, an environment of low cooperation and trust. The relatively high rankings of the United States and India are also to be expected—both provide cultural backdrops that encourage risk-taking and individual achievement. The rankings for Sweden and Spain are puzzling both on overall NECI and on cultural favorability dimension. Swedes have created a business culture that encourages innovation and, along with it, widespread optimism (OECD, 2016; Calvino, Criscuolo, and Menon, 2016), while Spaniards, notwithstanding some recent improvement in their economic conditions, express more pessimism and much lower levels of entrepreneurship (Lopez-Fogues, 2017; Ricucci, 2017). A deeper dive into the NECI data shows that a good portion of Sweden's rather low ranking is due to absence of (largely irrelevant) post–high school entrepreneurial training and governmental support policies with Spain's rather high ranking the result of governmental support policies for entrepreneurial programs and school-based entrepreneurial education and training, which have, in reality, proven to be largely ineffective.

4

Skill Shortages, Skill Gaps, and Labor Demand

> *Laying stress upon the importance of work has a greater effect than any other technique of living in the direction of binding the individual more closely to reality; in his work he is at least securely attached to a part of reality, the human community.*
>
> —Sigmund Freud, *Civilization and its Discontents* (1930/1962, p. 9)

In the previous chapter we examined the educational structure that each of our six democracies have created to prepare (young) individuals for labor market participation. We attempted to link these nation-specific, human capital formation processes to underlying value orientations that have been in some instances successful and in others, less so in achieving the goal of employment. The human capital model is clearly a supply-side theory of underemployment and unemployment (i.e., the onus for overeducation, underskilling, skill obsolescence, etc.) is placed squarely on the shoulders of the prospective or out-of-work job applicant (Becker, 1964, 1993). As Caroleo and Pastore (2016) and Pastore (2018) counter, however, these problems of overeducation and underskilling can also be seen as the consequences of employers' labor demand decisions and labor market institutions (worker security programs, minimum wage requirements, trade union, firing restrictions) that create inflexible or rigid labor markets. Excessive schooling from this "job competition" perspective, in one scenario, leads highly educated graduates to accumulate credentials, which can more than qualify them to get the job, simply as a strategy to move up in the job queue.

Indeed, whether a Keynesian, Marxian, or classical school economist, the willingness of prospective workers to ply their education and skills in the labor market must necessarily be complemented by employers who are willing to hire these workers with the education and skills they present to produce goods and services that consumers want to purchase. As Borjas

Caught in the Cultural Preference Net. Michael J. Camasso and Radha Jagannathan, Oxford University Press (2021).
© Oxford University Press. DOI: 10.1093/oso/9780190672782.003.0004

(2008) explains, employers serve as agents for the consumer and in that role are responsible for the fashion in which the business's production function is shaped. In their role as job creators, then, employers typically have the upper hand over workers, adjusting their demand for labor as the consumer adjusts his or her demand for product or service.

When (youth) underemployment or unemployment is viewed as a labor demand problem, blame for these problems necessarily moves from the failings of individual workers to shortcomings emanating from the very nature of the capitalist labor market and its conditioning on short- and long-term business cycles (Schumpeter, 1939/1964; Dietrich and Moller, 2016; Vogel, 2015). The conceptual starting point for an employer's decision to hire proceeds logically from the business's production function, that is, $P = f(K, L)$, where P is the production output of the business; K the firm's capital in the form of land, equipment, physical plant, cash reserves, etc.; and L is the employees and the human capital they bring to the work place. Product output can be empirically estimated as a Cobb–Douglas[1] statistical model of the form:

$$P = aK^{b_1}L^{b_2} \tag{1}$$

where a, b_1, and b_2 are positive estimates, and K and L represent amounts of capital and labor inputs, respectively.

Over the long run, if businesses wish to remain profitable in a competitive market, they need to continuously examine their technical capital and labor costs and the relation these costs have to maximum profitability. Important for the firm's purposes is the marginal product of labor (MP_L) and the marginal product of capital (MP_K), that is, the stopping rules of rational capitalists that identify when the employer's labor (capital) cost(s) reach the point where the cost of producing an additional unit of a good or service (marginal cost) equals the revenue obtained from selling that good or service (marginal revenue). Even more important to our argument is how businesses determine when to begin substituting inputs either to maintain an existing level of production or to achieve a new and presumably more profitable level of production.

---

[1] Cobb–Douglas is often estimated using multiple log regression models that allow each partial slope coefficient to be interpreted as the partial elasticity of production with respect to the explanatory variable (labor or capital), holding all other variables constant (Gujarati and Porter, 2010).

In Figure 4.1, we introduce what in microeconomics is referred to as the marginal rate of technical substitution (MRTS; Perloff, 2001). The figure originates from the examination of Norwegian printing firm by Griliches and Ringstad (1971) and shows how this firm can produce the same amount of output (q = 10) with varying amounts of capital and labor. We see that by hiring one more worker ($\Delta L = 1$) production can be maintained with 18 fewer units of capital and the MRTS = $-\Delta K / \Delta L = 18$. Moving from point b to point c, the firm's MRTS is 7, indicating that each additional worker results in smaller amount of capital replacement. Inasmuch as the MRTS is a ratio of MP_L and MP_K, it can also be used to identify how many units of labor the business can replace with an extra unit of technical capital in the form of machinery, automation, outsourcing, etc. Even within a specific input (e.g., labor), the MRTS can be useful as in the situation where the firm weighs decisions to substitute overeducated workers for medium- or low-skilled workers.

If the Cobb–Douglas production function provides a useful representation of a rational, profit-maximizing employer's decisions around the use of labor and capital—and there is broad consensus it does even if the employer has never heard of the concept (i.e., another manifestation of the "invisible hand" at work; Borjas, 2008; Perloff, 2001; Samuelson and Nordhaus, 2010)—then it follows that businesses will find some MRTSs and resulting capital–labor configurations to be more optimal than others. In principle, substitution not

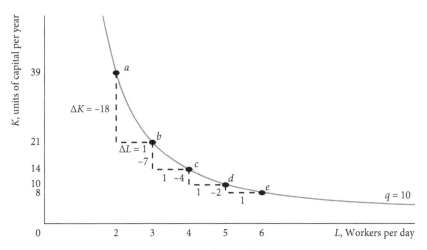

Figure 4.1 The variation of the marginal rate of technical substitution.
Adapted from Griliches and Ringstad (1971).

only provides the means for taking advantage of the best mix of available input resources; it also points the way to estimating how much input changes can increase or decrease output (i.e., returns to scale). If, for example, doubling labor (capital) inputs while holding capital (labor) constant results in output that also doubles, the firm will experience constant returns to scale.[2]

While providing a very useful conceptual framework for understanding labor demand in a competitive market, marginal product, MRTS, and Cobb–Douglas are not likely to be an entirely realistic description of hiring practices. This assertion is not merely an acknowledgement of the presence of labor market institutions and their role in modifying pure competition; its roots run much deeper and can be traced to what has been termed the Bourdieu paradox described in Chapter 1. Never a culturalist, Bourdieu nonetheless recognizes that participation and investment in the economic process is embedded in nationally and regionally defined value orientations. This is as true for the structure and functioning of labor markets as it is for the formation of human capital.

The Form of Youth Labor Markets

There are several factors that account for both the shape and the health of (youth) labor markets and, by extension, the creation of less than perfectly competitive markets in democratic, capitalist societies. Some of these factors are demographic (e.g., the age structure of the population, age-specific labor force participation rates, racial and gender composition; Freeman and Wise, 1982; Layard, 1982); others can be traced to slow or insufficient economic growth (Dietrich and Moller, 2016; Pastore, 2018; Vogel, 2015). There are also a host of labor institution influences like (a) minimum wage legislation, (b) active labor market policies (ALMPs) comprising government subsidized employment in the public and/or private sector, (c) employment protection legislation and regulations, and (d) wage subsidies in the forms of youth guarantees or earned income tax credits. Finally, labor market structures in Europe, the United States, and increasingly in India have been profoundly affected by the academization of potential workers, leading youth to stay in education for longer periods (Vogel, 2015; Coates and Morrison, 2016; Caroleo

---

[2] In a multiple log regression model, if we take the sum of the elasticity coefficients for labor and capital and the sum is equal to 1, we have constant returns to scale (i.e., doubling the inputs doubles the output). If the sum of the two coefficients is greater than 1, the result is increasing returns to scale; obversely, a sum of less than 1 indicates decreasing returns to scale (Borjas, 2008; Perloff, 2001).

and Pastore, 2016). These factors individually and in combination have been implicated in the formation of rigid labor markets,[3] the constriction of employer demand youth laborers, youth underemployment and unemployment, and persistent levels of skill shortages, skill gaps, and skill mismatches (Tasci and Zenker, 2011; McGuinness, Pouliakas, and Redmond, 2017; Zimmermann et al., 2013). We also believe these factors coalesce to form culturally distinctive production functions of the form:

$$P = aK^{b_1}L^{b_2}C^{b_3} \tag{2}$$

where C represents cultural value orientations that help sustain either economically or noneconomically efficient labor and wage levels even in the presence of economic recessions and expansions. Here we acknowledge the work on deeply rooted social customs in wage setting by Akerlof and Yellen (1990) and Agell (1999).

In the balance of this section of the chapter, we will profile the demographic and economic growth components of imperfect labor markets in our six capitalist countries and how they contribute to market rigidity, youth unemployment, and underemployment. In subsequent sections, we will then examine the roles played by government institutions and the interface between the educational and labor institutions. We will end the chapter with a brief discussion of how we believe cultural preferences influence the labor production elasticities in Sweden, Germany, India, Italy, Spain, and the United States—in essence, this is a discussion of the relative degrees of Bourdieuian paradox evident in each country's labor markets.

To help motivate our examination of important demographic and economic growth factors, we have constructed six country-specific tables (Tables 4.1–4.6) in time-series format. In each of these tables, we present 19 measures designed to give the reader a general overview of population

---

[3] The rigidity of labor markets refers to the level of protection workers receive when unexpected demand or supply shocks upset long-term contractual work attachments and employer–employee relationships. Protections associated with dismissals (firings) include severance pay, advance notice, and redundancy obligations of employers while protections around hiring include rules favoring disadvantaged groups, conditions for utilizing temporary or fixed-term contracts, probationary periods, and requisite training. Labor market theory suggests that rigid markets with high levels of protections will experience higher long-term unemployment rates (chronic unemployment) and less cyclical unemployment than markets with less employee protections (i.e., flexible markets; Borjas, 2008; Cahuc et al., 2013; Tasci and Zenker, 2011). OECD (2017) ranks countries using a Strictness of Employment Protection Legislation index with a zero indicating no protections and a six representing perfect protection. On the latest rankings available, our six focal countries score as follows: India, 3.29; Italy, 2.68; Germany, 2.68; Sweden, 2.61; Spain, 2.05; and the United States, 0.26.

Table 4.1 A Demographic, Economic Growth and Labor Force Profile of Germany

	2000	2001	2002	2003	2004	2005	2006	2007
GDP in U.S. constant $ (in billions)[1,2]	3,123.91	3,176.87	3,176.87	3,154.32	3,191.22	3,213.78	3,332.69	3,441.36
GDP per capita (computed)	37,998	38,578	38,513	38,218	38,674	38,969	40,457	41,832
GDP annual growth rate %[1]	2.82	1.52	−0.17	−0.76	1.19	0.76	3.82	3.40
GNI per capita [2]	36,529	37,019	36,821	36,649	37,694	38,051	39,828	41,080
Total population (in millions)[1]	82.21	82.35	82.49	82.53	82.52	82.47	82.38	82.27
Population, ages 15–24 years (in millions)[1]	9.04	9.16	9.30	9.41	9.49	9.50	9.48	9.42
% population, ages 15–24 (computed)	10.99	11.12	11.27	11.41	11.50	11.51	11.51	11.45
Unemployment rate (yearly)[1+]	7.9	7.8	8.5	9.8	10.7	11.2	10.3	8.7
Youth unemployment rate, ages 15–24[1+]	8.6	7.8	9.3	11	13	15.5	13.8	11.9
NEET (youth not in employment, education, or training)[3]	13.3	13.1	12.6	12.9	13.5	14.7	13.6	12.6
Labor force participation rate—ages 15+[1*]	57.55	57.54	57.22	56.92	57.13	58.48	59.02	59.2
Labor force participation rate—ages 15–24[1*]	51.5	51.3	49.7	47.4	48	50.2	50.9	52
Employment in general government as a % of total employment [4]								11.33
Exports in U.S. $ (in millions) [5]	549,607	571,427	615,997	748,531	911,742	977,132	1,121,963	1,328,841
Imports in U.S. $ (in millions) [5]	500,830	486,022	490,450	601,761	718,150	779,819	922,213	1,059,308
Per capita exports (exports/total population) (computed)	6,685	6,939	7,468	9,069	11,049	11,848	13,620	16,153
Per capita Imports (imports/total population) (computed)	6,092	5,902	5,946	7,291	8,703	9,456	11,195	12,877
Total early stage entrepreneurial activity[6]		6.28	5.16	5.22	4.4	5.09	4.21	
Established business ownership rate[6]		4.18	4.83	4.64	4.31	4.21	3.03	

[1]Source: https://stats.oecd.org/Index.aspx?DatasetCode=SNA_ (Appropriate Table) and World Bank Data Online https://databank.worldbank.org/home.aspx

[2]Source: https://data.worldbank.org/indicator/NY.GNP.PCAP.KD?_Locations=GNP. Gross national income (GNI) is equal to a country's gross domestic product (GDP) + the country's net property income from abroad. If a country has many multinational corporations that repatriate income from local country of production back to a home country, then GNI will be lower than GDP in the local country.

[1+]Unemployment Rate is the total number of unemployed individuals divided by the total number of individuals who are in the labor force (i.e., employed and unemployed seeking work). Youth unemployment rate is an age specific rate of the total number of 15- to 24-year-olds unemployed divided by the number of 15- to 24-year-olds in the labor force (i.e., employed and unemployed seeking work).

(2001—2017)

2008	2009	2010	2011	2012	2013	2014	2015	2016	2017
3,478.60	3,283.14	3,417.09	3,542.16	3,559.59	3,577.01	3,646.04	3,709.60	3,781.70	3,865.76
42,365	40,086	41,786	44,125	44,259	44,355	45,023	45,413	45,923	46,752
1.27	−5.38	4.24	5.60	0.30	0.22	1.51	0.87	1.12	1.79
41,393	39,673	41,236	43,770	43,827	43,888	44,429	44,766	45,203	
82.11	81.90	81.78	80.28	80.43	80.65	80.98	81.69	82.35	82.69
9.30	9.16	9.01	8.97	8.93	8.86	8.77	8.67	8.59	8.51
11.33	11.19	11.02	11.18	11.10	10.99	10.83	10.62	10.43	10.29
7.5	7.7	7	5.8	5.4	5.2	5	4.6	4.1	3.8
10.6	11.2	9.8	8.5	8	7.8	7.8	7.2	7.1	6.8
11.6	11.6	12.0	11.0	9.9	9.7	9.2	8.6	9.6	9.3
59.3	59.46	59.52	60.12	60.05	60.34	60.41	60.17	60.94	61.21
52.7	52.3	51.8	52.6	50.7	50.8	50	48.8	49.3	49.9
11.21	11.32	11.35	10.96	10.76	10.68	10.64	10.57		
1,466,137	1,127,840	1,271,096	1,482,202	1,410,130	1,450,951	1,498,158	1,328,549	1,340,752	1,450,215
1,204,209	938,363	1,066,817	1,260,298	1,161,213	1,187,315	1,214,956	1,057,616	1,060,672	1,173,628
17,856	13,771	15,543	18,464	17,533	17,992	18,500	16,264	16,281	17,539
14,666	11,457	13,045	15,700	14,438	14,723	15,003	12,947	12,880	14,194
3.77	4.1	4.17	5.62	5.34	4.98	5.27	4.7	4.56	5.28
4.03	5.15	5.69	5.64	4.95	5.07	5.15	4.82	7	6.05

[1]Labor force participation rate is the total number of individuals actively participating in the labor force (unemployed, employed, looking for work) divided by the number of individuals eligible to participate in the total working population group who are eligible to work but who do not participate are full time students, retirees, homemakers, prisoners, the disabled, and people who simply do not want to work.

[3]The NEET rate is more inclusive than the unemployment rate and is measured as the total number of youth aged 15 to 24 unemployed, economically inactive, not in education or training in the last 4 weeks divided by 15- to 24-year-olds in the population. https://data.oecd.org/youthinac/youth-not-in-employment-education-or- training-neet.htm

[4]Source: https://stats.oecd.org/Index.aspx?QueryId=78408#

[5]Source: https://wits.worldbank.org/CountryProfile/en/Country/SWE/Year/2015/TradeFlow/EXPIMP

[6]Source: https://www.gemconsortium.org/data/key-aps

Table 4.2 A Demographic, Economic Growth and Labor Force Profile of Sweden

	2000	2001	2002	2003	2004	2005	2006	2007
GDP in U.S. constant $ (in billions)[1,2]	396.53	402.73	411.08	420.89	439.07	451.44	472.61	488.70
GDP per capita (computed)	44,694	45,271	46,059	46,983	48,821	49,996	52,047	53,421
GDP annual growth rate %[1]	4.57	1.29	1.74	2.01	3.91	2.41	4.10	2.64
GNI per capita[2]	36,864	37,347	38,069	39,479	40,544	41,853	44,112	45,468
Total population (in millions)[1]	8.87	8.90	8.93	8.96	8.99	9.03	9.08	9.15
Population ages 15–24 years (in millions)[1]	1.03	1.04	1.05	1.07	1.09	1.11	1.15	1.19
% population ages 15–24 (computed)	11.56	11.63	11.75	11.90	12.09	12.32	12.62	12.96
Unemployment rate (yearly) [1+]	5.5	4.7	5	5.6	6.7	7.5	7.1	6.2
Youth unemployment rate age 15–24[1+]	9.5	11.7	12.9	14.3	18.5	21.9	21.5	19.3
NEET (youth not in employment, education, or training)[3]	7.9	7.3	7.9	8.4	9.5	9.2	10.5	10.1
Labor force participation rate—ages 15+[1*]	70.9	71.28	71.29	71.07	70.8	72.02	72.08	71.15
Labor force participation rate—ages 15-24[1*]	52.9	55.1	54.8	53.3	52.7	55.5	56.7	52.1
Employment in general government as a % of total employment[4]								30.26
Exports in U.S. $ (in millions) [5]	86,937	76,303	82,983	102,411	123,310	130,264	147,370	169,061
Imports in U.S. $ (in millions) [5]	72,767	63,536	67,121	84,199	100,833	111,351	127,101	152,823
Per capita exports (exports/total population) (computed)	9,799	8,577	9,298	11,432	13,711	14,426	16,229	18,480
Per capita Imports (Imports/total population) (Computed)	8,202	7,142	7,521	9,399	11,212	12,332	13,997	16,705
Total early stage entrepreneurial activity[6]		5.65	3.9	4.12	3.71	4.04	3.45	4.15
Established business ownership rate[6]		5.65	6.76	5.31	6.03	6.32	4.99	4.7

[1]Source: https://stats.oecd.org/Index.aspx?DatasetCode=SNA_ (Appropriate Table) and World Bank Data Online https://databank.worldbank.org/home.aspx

[2]Source: https://data.worldbank.org/indicator/NY.GNP.PCAP.KD?_Locations=GNP. Gross national income (GNI) is equal to a country's gross domestic product (GDP) + the country's net property income from abroad. If a country has many multinational corporations that repatriate income from local country production back to a home country, then GNI will be lower than GDP in the local country.

[1+]Unemployment Rate is the total number of unemployed individuals divided by the total number of individuals who are in the labor force (i.e., employed and unemployed seeking work). Youth unemployment rate is an age specific rate of the total number of 15- to 24-year-olds unemployed divided by the number of 15- to 24-year-olds in the labor force (i.e., employed and unemployed seeking work).

[1*]Labor force participation rate is the total number of individuals actively participating in the labor force (unemployed, employed, looking for work) divided by the number of individuals eligible to participate in the total working

2008	2009	2010	2011	2012	2013	2014	2015	2016	2017
485.98	460.78	488.38	501.39	499.95	506.16	519.34	542.83	560.39	573.21
52,711	49,554	52,076	53,062	52,520	52,723	53,562	55,395	56,473	56,992
−1.33	−5.99	5.09	1.89	−1.02	0.39	1.59	3.42	1.95	0.82
45,055	41,929	44,205	44,722	44,378	44,474	45,149	46,380	47,378	
9.22	9.30	9.38	9.45	9.52	9.60	9.70	9.80	9.92	10.06
1.23	1.26	1.27	1.28	1.27	1.26	1.23	1.20	1.18	1.15
13.29	13.50	13.54	13.52	13.37	13.08	12.70	12.29	11.85	11.38
6.2	8.4	8.6	7.8	8	8.1	8	7.4	7	6.7
20.2	25	24.8	22.8	23.6	23.5	22.9	20.4	18.9	17.9
8.7	11.0	10.3	9.1	9.7	9.4	9.4	9.1	8.2	8.0
71.23	70.58	70.48	70.92	71.12	71.48	71.94	71.97	72.06	72.67
52.7	50.8	51.4	52.8	52.5	54.3	55.3	54.9	54.7	54.4
29.37	29.43	28.97	28.5	28.48	28.51	28.45	28.59		
183,881	131,116	158,411	186,898	172,439	167,495	164,680	140,001	139,456	153,106
168,982	119,949	148,788	176,945	164,542	160,589	162,257	138,361	141,101	153,856
19,945	14,101	16,892	19,779	18,114	17,447	16,984	14,287	14,054	15,223
18,329	12,900	15,865	18,726	17,285	16,727	16,734	14,120	14,219	15,297
		4.88	5.8	6.44	8.25	6.71	7.16	7.58	7.29
		6.4	7	5.25	6.03	6.46	5.2	4.5	4.17

population group who are eligible to work but who do not participate are full time students, retirees, homemakers, prisoners, the disabled, and people who simply do not want to work.

[3]The NEET rate is more inclusive than the unemployment rate and is measured as the total number of youth aged 15 to 24 unemployed, economically inactive, not in education or training in the last 4 weeks divided by 15- to 24-year-olds in the population. https://data.oecd.org/youthinac/youth-not-in-employment-education-or- training-neet.htm

[4]Source: https://stats.oecd.org/Index.aspx?QueryId=78408#

[5]Source: https://wits.worldbank.org/CountryProfile/en/Country/SWE/Year/2015/TradeFlow/EXPIMP

[6]Source: https://www.gemconsortium.org/data/key-aps

Table 4.3 A Demographic, Economic Growth and Labor Force Profile of Italy

	2000	2001	2002	2003	2004	2005	2006	2007
GDP in U.S. constant $ (in billions)[1,2]	2,060.21	2,096.72	2,101.93	2,105.11	2,138.41	2,158.72	2,202.04	2,234.49
GDP per capita (computed)	36,181	36,801	36,838	36,730	37,070	37,239	37,872	38,237
GDP annual growth rate %[1]	3.66	1.72	0.10	−0.29	0.93	0.45	1.70	0.96
GNI per capita [2]	36,394	37,046	37,030	36,907	37,370	37,661	38,392	38,642
Total population (in millions)[1]	56.94	56.97	57.06	57.31	57.69	57.97	58.14	58.44
Population, ages 15–24 years (in millions)[1]	6.68	6.52	6.39	6.27	6.18	6.09	6.03	6.00
% population, ages 15–24 (computed)	11.73	11.44	11.19	10.95	10.70	10.50	10.38	10.26
Unemployment rate (yearly)[1+]	10.8	9.6	9.2	8.9	7.9	7.7	6.8	6.1
Youth unemployment rate, ages 15–24[1+]	31.5	27.8	27.1	26.8	24.4	24.1	21.8	20.4
NEET (youth not in employment, education, or training)[3]	23.3	22.2	20.7	20.5	21.1	20.1	20.0	19.2
Labor force participation rate—ages 15+[1*]	48.49	48.69	48.95	49.24	49.47	49.05	49.08	48.75
Labor force participation rate—ages 15–24[1*]	39.5	37.6	36.3	35.3	35.7	33.6	32.3	30.8
Employment in general government as a % of total employment [4]								14.34
Exports in U.S. $ (in millions) [5]	239,932	244,252	254,216	299,466	353,543	372,957	417,153	500,203
Imports in U.S. $ (in millions) [5]	238,069	236,127	246,609	297,403	355,267	384,836	442,565	511,823
Per capita exports (exports/total population) (computed)	4,214	4,287	4,455	5,225	6,129	6,434	7,174	8,560
Per capita Imports (imports/total population) (computed)	4,181	4,144	4,322	5,189	6,159	6,639	7,612	8,758
Total early stage entrepreneurial activity[6]		9.11	5.74	3.11	4.32	4.94	3.47	5.01
Established business ownership rate[6]		3.6	3.63	2.26	4.72	6.41	3.03	5.56

[1]Source: https://stats.oecd.org/Index.aspx?DatasetCode=SNA_ (Appropriate Table) and World Bank Data Online https://databank.worldbank.org/home.aspx

[2]Source: https://data.worldbank.org/indicator/NY.GNP.PCAP.KD?_Locations=GNP. Gross national income (GNI) is equal to a country's gross domestic product (GDP) + the country's net property income from abroad. If a country has many multinational corporations that repatriate income from local country production back to a home country, then GNI will be lower than GDP in the local country.

[1+]Unemployment Rate is the total number of unemployed individuals divided by the total number of individuals who are in the labor force (i.e., employed and unemployed seeking work). Youth unemployment rate is an age specific rate of the total number of 15- to 24-year-olds unemployed divided by the number of 15- to 24-year-olds in the labor force (i.e., employed and unemployed seeking work).

[1*]Labor force participation rate is the total number of individuals actively participating in the labor force (unemployed, employed, looking for work) divided by the number of individuals eligible to participate in

2008	2009	2010	2011	2012	2013	2014	2015	2016	2017
2,211.02	2,089.81	2,125.06	2,137.31	2,077.06	2,041.17	2,043.49	2,062.94	2,080.64	2,111.90
37,585	35,363	35,849	35,994	34,885	33,887	33,616	33,969	34,318	34,886
−1.70	−5.91	1.37	0.40	−3.08	−2.86	−0.80	1.05	1.03	1.63
37,608	35,688	36,128	36,251	35,178	34,161	33,946	34,115	34,733	
58.83	59.10	59.28	59.38	59.54	60.23	60.79	60.73	60.63	60.54
5.96	5.93	5.89	5.85	5.81	5.77	5.73	5.70	5.69	5.68
10.14	10.04	9.94	9.86	9.76	9.58	9.43	9.38	9.38	9.38
6.7	7.8	8.4	8.4	10.7	12.2	12.7	11.9	11.7	11.2
21.2	25.3	27.9	29.2	35.3	40	42.7	40.3	37.8	34.7
21.2	23.0	23.2	24.6	26.1	27.7	27.4	26.0	25.1	
49.1	48.48	48.21	48.14	49.08	48.79	49.06	48.97	49.5	49.81
30.7	28.8	28.1	27.1	28.6	27.1	27.1	26.2	26.6	26.2
14.19	14.28	14.17	13.93	13.69	13.79	13.75	13.62		
541,786	406,479	446,840	523,256	501,529	518,095	529,529	456,989	461,529	503,054
560,960	414,784	486,984	558,832	489,104	479,336	474,083	410,933	404,578	451,416
9,210	6,878	7,538	8,812	8,423	8,601	8,711	7,525	7,613	8,310
9,536	7,019	8,215	9,411	8,215	7,958	7,799	6,766	6,673	7,457
4.62	3.72	2.35		4.32	3.43	4.42	4.87	4.42	4.28
6.48	5.82	3.7		3.32	3.67	4.27	4.51	5.2	5.95

the total working population group who are eligible to work but who do not participate are full time students, retirees, homemakers, prisoners, the disabled, and people who simply do not want to work.

[3]The NEET rate is more inclusive than the unemployment rate and is measured as the total number of youth aged 15 to 24 unemployed, economically inactive, not in education or training in the last 4 weeks divided by 15- to 24-year-olds in the population. https://data.oecd.org/youthinac/youth-not-in-employment-education-or- training-neet.htm

[4]Source: https://stats.oecd.org/Index.aspx?QueryId=78408#

[5]Source: https://wits.worldbank.org/CountryProfile/en/Country/SWE/Year/2015/TradeFlow/EXPIMP

[6]Source: https://www.gemconsortium.org/data/key-aps

Table 4.4 A Demographic, Economic Growth and Labor Force Profile of Spain

	2000	2001	2002	2003	2004	2005	2006	2007
GDP in U.S. constant $ (in billions)[1,2]	1,149.49	1,195.48	1,229.91	1,269.12	1,309.30	1,358.05	1,414.74	1,468.06
GDP per capita (computed)	28,335	29,265	29,685	30,083	30,504	31,110	31,865	32,460
GDP annual growth rate %[1]	4.82	3.28	1.44	1.34	1.40	1.99	2.43	1.87
GNI per capita [2]	29,853	30,624	31,044	31,554	31,961	32,422	33,110	33,494
Total population (in millions)[1]	40.57	40.85	41.43	42.19	42.92	43.65	44.40	45.23
Population, ages 15–24 years (in millions)[1]	5.95	5.83	5.69	5.53	5.36	5.21	5.10	5.01
% population, ages 15–24 (computed)	14.66	14.28	13.73	13.10	12.50	11.93	11.50	11.08
Unemployment rate (yearly)[1+]	13.8	10.4	11.2	11.3	11.1	9.2	8.5	8.2
Youth unemployment rate, ages 15–24[1+]	25.3	20.7	21.5	22.3	22.5	19.6	17.9	18.1
NEET (youth not in employment, education, or training)[3]	15.6	14.7	15.0	15.0	14.7	17.1	15.9	15.6
Labor force participation rate—ages 15+[1*]	53.83	53	54.61	55.84	56.71	57.79	58.64	59.28
Labor force participation rate—ages 15–24[1*]	48.5	46.8	48.1	48.9	49.4	52.4	52.7	52.5
Employment in general government as a % of total employment [4]								13.36
Exports in U.S. $ (in millions) [5]	113,343	116,149	125,872	156,005	182,727	192,798	214,061	253,754
Imports in U.S. $ (in millions) [5]	152,898	154,993	165,920	208,549	259,265	289,611	329,976	391,237
Per capita exports (exports/total population) (computed)	2,794	2,843	3,038	3,698	4,257	4,417	4,821	5,611
Per capita Imports (imports/total population) (computed)	3,769	3,794	4,005	4,943	6,040	6,634	7,432	8,651
Total early stage entrepreneurial activity[6]		6.32	4.59	6.65	5.15	5.65	7.27	7.62
Established business ownership rate[6]		4.72	8.39	4.03	7.79	7.71	5.45	6.38

[1]Source: https://stats.oecd.org/Index.aspx?DatasetCode=SNA_ (Appropriate Table) and World Bank Data Online https://databank.worldbank.org/home.aspx

[2]Source: https://data.worldbank.org/indicator/NY.GNP.PCAP.KD?_Locations=GNP. Gross national income (GNI) is equal to a country's gross domestic product (GDP) + the country's net property income from abroad. If a country has many multinational corporations that repatriate income from local country production back to a home country, then GNI will be lower than GDP in the local country.

[1+]Unemployment Rate is the total number of unemployed individuals divided by the total number of individuals who are in the labor force (i.e., employed and unemployed seeking work). Youth unemployment rate is an age specific rate of the total number of 15- to 24-year-olds unemployed divided by the number of 15- to 24-year-olds in the labor force (i.e., employed and unemployed seeking work).

[1*]Labor force participation rate is the total number of individuals actively participating in the labor force (unemployed, employed, looking for work) divided by the number of individuals eligible to participate in the total working

2008	2009	2010	2011	2012	2013	2014	2015	2016	2017
1,484.47	1,431.42	1,431.62	1,417.32	1,375.82	1,352.36	1,371.02	1,418.07	1,464.51	1,509.20
32,303	30,874	30,737	30,322	29,415	29,008	29,496	30,532	31,506	32,391
−0.48	−4.42	−0.45	−1.35	−2.99	−1.38	1.68	3.51	3.19	2.86
33,248	32,044	32,045	31,512	30,888	30,516	31,088	32,217	33,307	
45.95	46.36	46.58	46.74	46.77	46.62	46.48	46.44	46.48	46.59
4.92	4.82	4.71	4.60	4.50	4.42	4.37	4.34	4.32	4.32
10.71	10.40	10.11	9.84	9.63	9.49	9.40	9.33	9.30	9.28
11.3	17.9	19.9	21.4	24.8	26.1	24.4	22.1	19.6	17.2
24.5	37.7	41.5	46.2	52.9	55.5	53.2	48.3	44.4	38.6
16.7	22.6	23.6	24.3	25.6	27.2	24.3	22.8	21.7	19.9
60.08	60.18	60.28	60.33	60.4	60.02	59.6	59.54	59.23	58.83
52.4	49.5	46.9	44.9	43	41.7	39.6	38.8	36.9	37.3
13.66	14.79	15.2	15.61	15.88	16.21	15.99	15.72		
279,231	223,132	246,265	298,171	285,936	310,964	318,649	278,122	281,777	319,622
418,728	287,502	315,547	362,835	325,835	332,267	350,978	305,266	302,539	350,922
6,076	4,813	5,287	6,379	6,113	6,670	6,855	5,988	6,062	6,860
9,112	6,201	6,775	7,762	6,966	7,127	7,551	6,573	6,509	7,532
7.03	5.1	4.31	5.81	5.7	5.21	5.47	5.7	5.23	6.19
9.05	6.4	7.72	8.85	8.74	8.39	7.03	7.7	6.2	7.05

population group who are eligible to work but who do not participate are full time students, retirees, homemakers, prisoners, the disabled, and people who simply do not want to work.

[3] The NEET rate is more inclusive than the unemployment rate and is measured as the total number of youth aged 15 to 24 unemployed, economically inactive, not in education or training in the last 4 weeks divided by 15- to 24-year-olds in the population. https://data.oecd.org/youthinac/youth-not-in-employment-education-or- training-neet.htm

[4] Source: https://stats.oecd.org/Index.aspx?QueryId=78408#

[5] Source: https://wits.worldbank.org/CountryProfile/en/Country/SWE/Year/2015/TradeFlow/EXPIMP

[6] Source: https://www.gemconsortium.org/data/key-aps

Table 4.5 A Demographic, Economic Growth and Labor Force Profile of United States

	2000	2001	2002	2003	2004	2005	2006	2007
GDP in U.S. constant $ (in billions)[1,2]	12,713.06	12,837.14	13,066.42	13,433.17	13,941.71	14,408.09	14,792.30	15,055.40
GDP per capita (computed)	45,056	45,047	45,429	46,304	47,614	48,756	49,575	49,980
GDP annual growth rate %[1]	2.94	−0.02	0.85	1.93	2.83	2.40	1.68	0.82
GNI per capita [2]	46,267	46,318	46,690	47,656	49,074	50,240	50,973	51,582
Total population (in millions)[1]	282.16	284.97	287.63	290.11	292.81	295.52	298.38	301.23
Population, ages 15–24 years (in millions)[1]	39.01	39.61	40.22	40.84	41.49	42.16	42.55	42.96
% population, ages 15–24 (computed)	13.83	13.90	13.98	14.08	14.17	14.27	14.26	14.26
Unemployment rate (yearly)[1+]	4.0	4.7	5.8	6.0	5.5	5.1	4.6	4.6
Youth unemployment rate, ages 15–24[1+]	9.3	10.6	12.0	12.4	11.9	11.3	10.5	10.5
NEET (youth not in employment, education, or training)[3]	12.2	13.3	13.6	14.3	13.9	13.1	12.9	13.2
Labor force participation rate—ages 15+[1*]	67.07	66.82	66.58	66.24	65.99	66.04	66.18	66.04
Labor force participation rate—ages 15–24[1*]	65.8	64.5	63.3	61.6	61.1	60.8	60.6	59.4
Employment in general government as a % of total employment [4]								
Exports in U.S. $ (in millions) [5]	781,831	729,080	693,068	724,737	814,844	901,041	1,037,029	1,162,538
Imports in U.S. $ (in millions) [5]	1,217,933	1,140,900	1,200,096	1,302,834	1,525,304	1,734,849	1,918,997	2,017,121
Per capita exports (exports/total population) (computed)	2,771	2,558	2,410	2,498	2,783	3,049	3,476	3,859
Per capita Imports (imports/total population) (computed)	4,316	4,004	4,172	4,491	5,209	5,871	6,431	6,696
Total early stage entrepreneurial activity[6]		11.07	10.62	11.85	11.27	12.44	10.03	9.61
Established business ownership rate[6]		5.83	5.74	5.41	5.45	4.67	5.42	4.97

[1]Source: https://stats.oecd.org/Index.aspx?DatasetCode=SNA_ (Appropriate Table) and World Bank Data Online https://databank.worldbank.org/home.aspx

[2]Source: https://data.worldbank.org/indicator/NY.GNP.PCAP.KD?_Locations=GNP. Gross national income (GNI) is equal to a country's gross domestic product (GDP) + the country's net property income from abroad. If a country has many multinational corporations that repatriate income from local country production back to a home country, then GNI will be lower than GDP in the local country.

[1+]Unemployment Rate is the total number of unemployed individuals divided by the total number of individuals who are in the labor force (i.e., employed and unemployed seeking work). Youth unemployment rate is an age specific rate of the total number of 15- to 24-year-olds unemployed divided by the number of 15- to 24-year-olds in the labor force (i.e., employed and unemployed seeking work).

[1*]Labor force participation rate is the total number of individuals actively participating in the labor force (unemployed, employed, looking for work) divided by the number of individuals eligible to participate in

(2001—2017)

2008	2009	2010	2011	2012	2013	2014	2015	2016	2017
15,011.49	14,594.84	14,964.37	15,204.02	15,542.16	15,802.86	16,208.86	16,672.69	16,920.33	17,304.98
49,365	47,576	48,377	48,797	49,517	50,000	50,909	51,982	52,373	53,222
−1.23	−3.62	1.68	0.85	1.46	0.96	1.80	2.09	0.74	1.55
51,095	49,190	50,178	50,708	51,389	51,878	52,752	53,741	54,104	
304.09	306.77	309.33	311.58	313.87	316.06	318.39	320.74	323.07	325.15
43.33	43.64	43.86	44.17	44.37	44.44	44.39	44.25	44.15	43.95
14.25	14.23	14.18	14.18	14.14	14.06	13.94	13.80	13.67	13.52
5.8	9.3	9.6	9.0	7.9	7.4	6.2	5.3	4.9	4.4
12.9	17.6	18.4	17.3	16.2	15.6	13.4	11.6	10.4	9.2
14.7	16.9	16.1	15.9	15.2	16.0	15.0	14.4	14.1	13.3
65.99	65.37	64.7	64.11	63.7	63.25	62.89	62.65	62.79	62.85
58.8	56.9	55.2	55	54.9	55	55	55	55.2	55.5
15.89	16.71	16.91	16.45	16.05	15.79	15.49	15.26		
1,299,899	1,056,712	1,278,099	1,481,682	1,544,932	1,577,587	1,619,743	1,501,846	1,450,457	1,545,609
2,164,834	1,601,896	1,968,260	2,263,619	2,274,462	2,265,911	2,410,855	2,313,425	2,248,209	2,407,390
4,275	3,445	4,132	4,755	4,922	4,991	5,087	4,682	4,490	4,754
7,119	5,222	6,363	7,265	7,246	7,169	7,572	7,213	6,959	7,404
10.76	7.96	7.59	12.34	12.84	12.73	13.81	11.88	12.63	13.64
8.34	5.87	7.68	9.05	8.56	7.49	6.95	7.33	9.2	7.75

the total working population group who are eligible to work but who do not participate are full time students, retirees, homemakers, prisoners, the disabled, and people who simply do not want to work.

[3]The NEET rate is more inclusive than the unemployment rate and is measured as the total number of youth aged 15 to 24 unemployed, economically inactive, not in education or training in the last 4 weeks divided by 15- to 24-year-olds in the population. https://data.oecd.org/youthinac/youth-not-in-employment-education-or- training-neet.htm

[4]Source: https://stats.oecd.org/Index.aspx?QueryId=78408#

[5]Source: https://wits.worldbank.org/CountryProfile/en/Country/SWE/Year/2015/TradeFlow/EXPIMP

[6]Source: https://www.gemconsortium.org/data/key-aps

Table 4.6 A Demographic, Economic Growth and Labor Force Profile of India

	2000	2001	2002	2003	2004	2005	2006	2007
GDP in U.S. constant $ (in billions)[1,2]	802.75	841.48	873.49	942.15	1,016.79	1,111.20	1,214.14	1,333.15
GDP per capita (computed)	762	785	802	850	903	971	1,045	1,130
GDP annual growth rate %[1]	2.02	3.02	2.06	6.09	6.19	7.57	7.58	8.15
GNI per capita [2]	2,470	2,549	2,607	2,763	2,935	3,157	3,394	3,684
Total population (in millions)[1]	1,053.05	1,071.48	1,089.81	1,108.03	1,126.14	1,144.12	1,161.98	1,179.68
Population, ages 15–24 years (in millions)[1]	204.44	208.44	212.44	216.31	219.89	223.09	225.76	228.05
% population, ages 15–24 (computed)	19.41	19.45	19.49	19.52	19.53	19.50	19.43	19.33
Unemployment rate (yearly)[1+]	2.7	2.9	3.1	3.2	3.1	3.1	2.7	2.4
Youth unemployment rate, ages 15–24[1+]	7.9	8.1	8.6	8.9	8.8	8.9	8.3	7.8
NEET (youth not in employment, education, or training)[3]	32.2				26.1	30.4		
Labor force participation rate—ages 15+[1*]	57.5	57.7	57.9	58.1	58.3	58.5	57.6	56.7
Labor force participation rate—ages 15–24[1*]	44.7	44.7	44.7	44.8	44.9	44.9	43.2	41.5
Employment in general government as a % of total employment [4]								
Exports in U.S. $ (in millions) [5]	42,358	43,878	50,098	59,361	75,904	100,353	121,201	145,898
Imports in U.S. $ (in millions) [5]	52,940	50,671	57,453	72,431	98,981	140,862	178,212	218,645
Per capita exports (exports/total population) (computed)	40	41	46	54	67	88	104	124
Per capita Imports (imports/total population) (computed)	50	47	53	65	88	123	153	185
Total early stage entrepreneurial activity[6]		10.81	16.04				10.09	8.53
Established business ownership rate[6]		8.76	12.15				5.6	5.53

[1]Source: https://stats.oecd.org/Index.aspx?DatasetCode=SNA_ (Appropriate Table) and World Bank Data Online https://databank.worldbank.org/home.aspx

[2]Source: https://data.worldbank.org/indicator/NY.GNP.PCAP.KD?_Locations=GNP. Gross national income (GNI) is equal to a country's gross domestic product (GDP) + the country's net property income from abroad. If a country has many multinational corporations that repatriate income from local country production back to a home country, then GNI will be lower than GDP in the local country.

[1+]Unemployment Rate is the total number of unemployed individuals divided by the total number of individuals who are in the labor force (i.e., employed and unemployed seeking work). Youth unemployment rate is an age specific rate of the total number of 15- to 24-year-olds unemployed divided by the number of 15- to 24-year-olds in the labor force (i.e., employed and unemployed seeking work).

2008	2009	2010	2011	2012	2013	2014	2015	2016	2017
1,385.02	1,502.46	1,656.62	1,766.59	1,862.98	1,981.95	2,128.82	2,302.41	2,466.18	2,630.95
1,157	1,237	1,346	1,416	1,475	1,550	1,645	1,759	1,862	1,965
2.38	6.95	8.76	5.25	4.13	5.10	6.14	6.90	5.89	5.49
3,764	4,026	4,357	4,595	4,771	5,010	5,322	5,691	6,026	6,359
1,197.15	1,214.27	1,230.98	1,247.24	1,263.07	1,278.56	1,293.86	1,309.05	1,324.17	1,339.18
230.03	231.86	233.65	235.28	236.89	238.48	240.03	241.51	243.09	244.49
19.21	19.09	18.98	18.86	18.76	18.65	18.55	18.45	18.36	18.26
2.3	2.5	2.4	2.5	2.7	2.8	2.8	2.8	2.7	2.6
7.8	8.6	8.9	9.3	10.0	10.4	10.4	10.6	10.7	10.3
		27.9		27.5					
55.8	54.9	54.1	53.2	52.3	52.3	52.2	52.2	52.1	52.0
39.8	38.2	36.5	35.0	33.5	33.1	32.7	32.2	31.4	30.6
181,861	176,765	220,408	301,483	289,565	336,611	317,545	264,381	260,327	294,364
315,712	266,402	350,029	462,403	488,976	466,046	459,369	390,745	356,705	444,052
152	146	179	242	229	263	245	202	197	220
264	219	284	371	387	365	355	298	269	332
11.49					9.88	6.6	10.83	10.59	9.28
16.5					10.66	3.73	5.5	4.6	6.22

[1]Labor force participation rate is the total number of individuals actively participating in the labor force (unemployed, employed, looking for work) divided by the number of individuals eligible to participate in the total working population group who are eligible to work but who do not participate are full time students, retirees, homemakers, prisoners, the disabled, and people who simply do not want to work.

[3]The NEET rate is more inclusive than the unemployment rate and is measured as the total number of youth aged 15 to 24 unemployed, economically inactive, not in education or training in the last 4 weeks divided by 15- to 24-year-olds in the population. https://data.oecd.org/youthinac/youth-not-in-employment-education-or- training-neet.htm

[4]Source: https://stats.oecd.org/Index.aspx?QueryId=78408#

[5]Source: https://wits.worldbank.org/CountryProfile/en/Country/SWE/Year/2015/TradeFlow/EXPIMP

[6]Source: https://www.gemconsortium.org/data/key-aps

structure and economic performance from 2000 to 2017. The endpoints for these time series reflect the availability of comparative data for all six countries.

In Table 4.1, we profile Germany, Europe's largest economy. In addition to the 19 indicators shown in the table, we provide detailed notes on sources of the data, methods of calculation, and definitions where necessary. In Germany, we observe a relatively stable population size with a declining proportion of youth aged 15 to 24. And while these demographic components tend to reinforce rather rigid German labor markets (Rinne and Schneider, 2017; Cahuc et al., 2013; Zimmermann et al., 2013), the country's strong economic growth measured by gross domestic product (GDP), gross national income (GNI), and export/import ratios, which are among the highest in Europe, tend to support the need for a good deal of business–government coordination to insure strategic flexibility in the country's labor market.

The data in Table 4.1 also describe a country with relatively low and stable overall unemployment and youth unemployment rates and steadily rising labor force participation rates among of workers regardless of age. Youth unemployment and youth not in employment, education, or training (NEET) rates have remained substantially below European averages of 15 and 20 percent, respectively, for the 17 years depicted. It is also noteworthy that unemployment and labor force participation rates in Germany were largely unaffected by the 2008 fiscal crises. As is expected from our discussion in Chapter 3, rates of total early-stage entrepreneurial activity (TEA) and the businesses of these entrepreneurs that have survived for 42 months or more (established business rate) are quite low in the country; German workers tend to seek out established firms rather than begin their own businesses (Bosma and Kelley, 2018). Over the 17-year period, German TEA rates (per 100 businesses) are typically less than half of the activity witnessed in the United States.

Germany's dynamic economy with its emphasis on complex, value-added products and services requires a labor force with requisite skills and qualifications that is responsive to changing consumer market demands. As Rinne and Schneider (2017) assert, "the role of the dual apprenticeship system cannot be overrated in achieving this outcome" (p. 4). The dual system, notwithstanding its costs, acts as a reliable counterbalance to hiring barriers by offering employers very reliable signals about a prospective worker's productivity, worker receipt of standardized certificates, and overall qualifications (Rinne and Schneider, 2017). It would be incorrect, however, to attribute employer dedication to the dual system to simply a pecuniary interest in creating firm-specific capital. One incentive that has received substantial attention by labor economists, at least in Germany, is the importance of demonstrating social commitment (Cahuc et al., 2013; Eichhorst and Rinne, 201; Dietrich and Moller, 2016), a commitment that has helped insure that dual-system graduates have sufficient skills to move across different professions (Zimmermann et al., 2013; Vogel, 2015) and that employers avoid poaching and monopsony[4] because norms of fairness are routinized within and across firms competing in the same business/industry sectors (Council of Economic Advisors, 2016; Ryan, 2016; Hirsch, Jahn, and Schnabel, 2018).

The recent trend of young people in Germany seeking general academic education over vocational training and apprenticeships, however, could undermine Germany's dual system and the prosperity it has brought to the nation (Rinne and Schneider, 2017; Eichhorst and Rinne, 2016). In a recent piece in the *Wall Street Journal*, the Association of German Chambers of Commerce and Industry reported that 32 percent of companies were unable to fill at least some of their apprenticeship slots in 2018, well up from the 12 percent with vacancies in 2006 (Morath, 2019). This trend promises to exacerbate the increasing difficulty that employers report in finding skilled and talented workers in manufacturing, information and communication technology, engineers and technicians, and skilled trades and machine operators (CEDEFOP, 2018b).

Sweden, like Germany, has been able to negotiate rigid labor markets to help insure the relatively smooth school-to-work transitions for a large majority of young people but has done so without the help of a dual vocational/educational system. Instead, the country has relied on a rather unique application of ALMPs, often referred to as the Nordic model (Carcillo, Hyee, and Keane, 2016; Richardson and Van den Berg, 2006; Pastore, 2018). Unlike ALMPs in Italy, Spain, Greece, and elsewhere in Europe, which tend to be uncoordinated,

[4] Monopsony or employer wage-setting power refers to any labor market where firms have labor markets that allow them to determine wages either because there is a single buyer of labor in the market or because firms collude to set (lower) wages in what would otherwise appear to be competitive markets. Rather than base wages at the equilibrium point where the marginal revenue product of labor is equal to the marginal cost of labor, the employers set pay at the equilibrium point where marginal revenue product is equal to the average cost of labor, thus sacrificing efficiency for profit-taking through lower wage payments to workers. Markets comprising firms exercising monopsony power have an incentive to employ fewer workers at lower wages and limit output and revenue more than they would in a competitive market (Hirsch, Jahn, and Schnabel, 2018, Council of Economic Advisors, 2016; Ryan, 2016).

following a "one and done" intervention strategy (see, e.g., Lopez-Fogues, 2017; Pastore, 2018; Carcillo, Hyee, and Keane, 2016), Sweden, through its Public Employment Service and its over 300 municipal governments, offers a veritable smorgasbord of vocational and nonvocational training and continuing education programs designed to keep youth, as well as older Swedes, in close contact with the nation's capitalist enterprise. Youth employment endeavors include the Municipal Youth Programme, the Youth Guaranteee (YG; Ungdomsgarante), the Youth Practice Programme, and labor market training, most notably, the AMU employment training program (Byambadorj, 2007; Richardson and Van den Berg, 2006). The YG, with its 90-day waiting period designed specifically to avoid the risk of program participants reducing their job search intensity, is credited along with AMU for the country's low long-term unemployment rate (Carcillo, Hyee, and Keane, 2016). This intensity and often overlapping nature of these programs also signal the Swedes' aversion to youth idleness and inactivity (Bergquist, 2016; Albaek et al., 2015).

As Table 4.2 indicates, Sweden exhibits GDP and GNP per capita levels that are among the highest in the world. The close tracking of these two indicators suggests that repatriated money from foreign multinationals does not comprise a significant portion of the country's GDP. This is also the case in Germany. Exported goods and services, per capita, for this relatively small population nation shows steady growth, as do rates of TEA. Notwithstanding Sweden's aging population, the country boasts some of the highest overall employment and labor force participation rates in Europe. The wide differentials in the high youth unemployment and NEET rates are indicative of the very high number of Swedish youth in school or participating in one or more of the country's ALMPs but who are not included in the labor force denominator.

The measures that the Swedish government has taken to insure that a social balance is maintained between robust economic production and full employment, on the one hand, and the decommodification of welfare benefits, on the other, should give socialists, whether in America or elsewhere, reason to pause before proclaiming Sweden as a socialist nirvana. After the severe economic downturn in 1991, which was caused to a large extent by social program spending that had risen to 70 percent of GDP, Sweden began taking extraordinary steps to rein in large parts of its public healthcare, education, and welfare systems (Gottfries, 2018; Fernandez-Villaverde and Ohanian, 2019). The electricity and transportation industries were deregulated and parts of the national health insurance program were privatized.

To further increase the incentives to work, a number of reforms were introduced in 2006 including an earned income tax credit, an increase in mandatory age for retirement from 65 to 67, reductions in welfare benefit levels, and limitations on pension access for early retirement (Gottfries, 2018; Carcillo, Hyee, and Keane, 2016). In a series of measures beginning in the late 1990s, the corporate tax rate was cut from confiscatorially high levels to 22 percent, with more decreases scheduled (Fernandez-Villaverde and Ohanian, 2019).

As Gannon and Pillai (2016) point out with a more than a bit of irony, it has been Sweden's social welfare programs—their success as well as their costs—that have led to a revitalization of "individualism through self-development" (p. 109). Self-development, moreover, appears to be closely aligned with productive, full-time work. Sweden's exceedingly high labor participation rates (in the upper 70 percent range for both men and women), an operational definition of this individualism, are also essential if its safety net is to continue functioning at a high level.

In Sweden's version of the cultural production function, corporate income and investment are taxed at low levels, labor is engaged to the fullest extent possible, and the culture continues to resist socialist pressures for complete egalitarianism and income redistribution.[5] The country's highly coordinated approach to the problems of unemployment and inactivity have proven to be successful in avoiding the segmentation of the labor market into high- and low-skill niches and the wage inequality that such segmentation all but guarantees. Education and employment legislation have been designed and/or negotiated to obviate the necessity for short-term contracts and their negative impact on employer and employee investment in firm-specific skills (Pastore, 2018).

The costs of Sweden's full employment economy remain steep, financially and perhaps psychologically. The proportion of individuals employed in government (Table 4.2) is nearly twice that of Germany, Italy, or Spain. The nation's personal income tax rate of nearly 62 percent is the highest in the world and helps pay for an extensive system of prenatal care, paid family leave, and institutionalized daycare. The latter service, which facilitates women's rapid return to the labor force, may not be as beneficial to young

---

[5] Esping-Andersen (1985) notes that egalitarianism is not the very essence of socialism. "From all available evidence it seems exceedingly clear that a continued socialist commitment to effective income redistribution will alienate white-collar strata and thus block any chance of a broad wage earner alliance. . . . The problem of income inequality and redistribution poses a severe dilemma for social democracy . . . because powerful labor organizations (unskilled unions especially) insist on equalization" (p. 323).

children in care, however. Komisar (2018), for example, reports that teen suicides reached a 25-year high in 2013 and instances of self-harming behavior were reported by 20 percent of adolescents.

Italy, like Germany and Sweden, also has extremely rigid labor markets, possessing all of the necessary components described earlier (see especially footnote 3) and introducing a few additional wrinkles as well. There is broad consensus, however, among economists and labor policy experts that the nation's responses to this rigidity and the problems of long-term unemployment, bifurcated labor markets, overeducation, and overskilling this rigidity produces have been unenthusiastic and disorganized (Pastore, 2018; Monticelli et al. 2016; Manca, Quintini, and Keese, 2017; Nuti, 2018).

An examination of the time-series data we have compiled in Table 4.3 shows that Italy's large economy has experienced slow growth that has taken considerable time to recover from the 2008 recession. Overall, GDP and GNI have remained largely unchanged over the series as has per capita GDP. Italy continues to experience high unemployment and very low labor force participation rates, and these rates among youth are indicative of major labor demand problems. The increasing ratios of youth unemployment rates to NEET rates after 2011, moreover, indicate a decrease in job-seeking activity, an inference readily verified by the examination of the declining labor force participation rates of Italian youth aged 15 to 24 years. No doubt adding to this distressing employment environment are the low TEA levels and established business ownership rate. Italy ranks near the bottom on both measures (Bosma and Kelley, 2018) with the share of "necessity entrepreneurship" very low due to Italy's generous welfare system.

Unlike Germany or Sweden where governmental data provide a reliable description of economic activity, a sizable share of production in Italy is concentrated in the shadow economy (Marino and Nunziata, 2017; OECD, 2016). In addition to the negative consequences for efficiency and labor standards of this shadow economy, this "off the book" activity contributes to the skill gaps and mismatches that plague significant sectors of the economy. Manca, Quintini, and Keese (2017) point out that skill matching in Italy, and especially in southern Italy, suffers from a "severe lack of transparency" (p. 148). In a study by Mandrone (2016), the author contends that as many as two thirds of available vacancies are not publicly advertised and are only visible through informal and personal networks. Hence, qualifications in Italy possess rather poor skill-signaling qualities, when compared to Germany or Sweden.

Lest one come away from the discussion with the impression that the Italian labor market is bereft of rational calculation, at least as it is practiced widely in America, we again invoke the Bourdieu paradox and the mistaken belief that economic efficiency and rational calculation are synonymous. As rigid labor markets go, Italy has one of the most inflexible, especially when it comes to unfair dismissals. The monetary compensation, according to Manca, Quintini, and Keese (2017), is in the form of two monthly salaries per year of tenure (a minimum of four months and a maximum of 24 monthly wages), an amount that is considerably higher than the OECD average. And, while France introduces flexibility into its highly rigid labor market through the use of more and shorter short-term contracts (Askenazy, 2018), Italy augments short-term contracts by keeping some labor activity in the shadows, employing workers without either formal contracts or legal protections. It is a strategy imminently practical given a value orientation where trust is not readily conveyed and where the penalties for making employee mistakes are severe.

An additional disturbing feature of the Italian economy can be discerned by examining the real GDP per hours worked. Marino and Nunziata (2017) note that while this indicator has been flat from 2000 through 2016, the trend has been increasing in the Euro zone as a whole with Germany and France distancing themselves from Italy, and countries like Spain catching up to Italy. Marino and Nunziata trace this stagnation to factors including low investments in human and physical capital, insufficient research and development, a post-2008 crisis credit crunch, and the slow pace of labor reforms. However, there may be another determinant at work here that stems from employer wage-setting power due to practices that limit workers' job information and choices and cultural preferences that limit workers' mobility, leading to the exercise of monopsony power (Ryan, 2016; Council of Economic Advisors, 2016).

The rigid and weakly competitive labor markets in many regions of Italy appear to be fertile breeding grounds for the confluence of workers reluctant to quit their jobs when confronted with wage stagnation and employers willing to take advantage of this reluctance by limiting their firms' output (and revenue) and substituting profits made from lower wages. Evidence has accumulated that employees are much less responsive to wage changes than would be expected if labor markets were very competitive (see, e.g., Ransom and Sims, 2010; Mas and Pallais, 2016). Monopsony, because of its capacity to prosper in the shadows of inefficient and inflexible labor markets, appears to us to have found a very desirable home in large parts of Italy.

We now turn our attention to the youth labor market in Spain. As can be observed from the data we present in Table 4.4, the country has experienced a dramatic turn-around in economic growth from the years of negative GDP that immediately followed the 2008 financial crisis. Data from 2018 (not shown in the table) indicates that GDP per capita has overtaken that of Italy (Charlesmagne, 2019). Notwithstanding this slow but steady economic growth, Spain faces a host of social and economic problems that continue to plague businesses and workers. Youth unemployment rates, in the 35 percent range, and labor force participation rates, also in the low 40 percent range, are symptoms of the dual nature of the Spanish market, characterized by a large share of short duration temporary contracts with limited transition probabilities (Zimmermann et al. 2013; Sanz-de-Galdeano and Terskaya, 2017; Mullock, Quintini, and Keese, 2017). Spain's above-average NEET rates, moreover, do not readily translate into jobs at either the low-skill or high-skill levels because of the rigid labor market with its barriers to entry. The problem here may actually be more significant than in Italy due to a less developed shadow economy.

Spain's utilization of short duration, temporary contracts are distinctive from other European countries in a rather unique fashion (i.e., they are of longer length than in other OECD countries; OECD, 2016; Mullock, Quintini, and Keese, 2017). This use of longer term yet temporary employment contracts has resulted in more frequent unemployment spells and the lowest transition rates from temporary employment to permanent employment in the OECD (Sanz-de-Galdeano and Terskaya, 2017).

Bolstering the contention that Spain has begun to turn the corner on economic growth and prosperity is the upward trend in TEA since 2008. An upward trend in established business ownership is also evident form Table 4.4. Given employers' limited interest in formal vocational training and in hiring individuals with such skills, self-employment could become an increasingly important factor in promoting Spanish youth's economic and social mobility.

Spain's dual (i.e., segmented into permanent and temporary workforces) labor market has helped the country garner a number of distinctions, many of them rather dubious. For example, Lopez-Forgues (2017) points out the country has the most pronounced educational bifurcation in Europe, with nearly 40 percent of 25- to 34-year-olds in university and nearly 40 percent of the same age group terminating their education in primary or lower secondary school. According to OECD (Mullock, Quintini, and Keese, 2017), Spain has the highest primary and lower secondary school dropout rate in Europe, nearly 20 percent in 2016. Although Spain does not have the highest incidence of overskilling at the start of a job in the EU (30 percent)—a distinction earned by Greece (35 percent)—it boasts the lowest level of overskilled employees (7.2 percent) who seek to develop additional skills that could improve both their extrinsic and intrinsic work rewards (CEDEFOP, 2018b). Spain shares with Greece the further distinction of having a higher proportion of overeducated workers (32 percent) in Europe (McGuinness, Pouliakas, and Redmond, 2017). Not surprisingly, in a recent comparative study of 10 European countries, the researchers report that Greek and Spanish youth (aged 18–34) expressed the lowest levels of satisfaction with their current financial circumstances, the former at 25 percent and the latter at 35 percent (Tosun et al., 2019).

Employers in Spain have appeared to adapt quite well to the labor market they helped create with the sometimes intentional and sometimes inadvertent help of the Spanish government and educational establishment. Lopez-Forgues (2017), for example, observes that the rigidity of demand results in excessive education with employers favoring higher level degrees regardless of job specifications (p. 358). This mismatch, in turn, creates disequilibrium between qualifications and salaries (wage penalties) that has encouraged the outmigration of the skilled workforce. The additional consequences of this mismatch and skills gap include lower productivity, increases in on-the-job searches, turnover, slower economic growth and, as previously noted, low levels of job satisfaction (CEDEFOP, 2018b; Mullock, Quintini, and Keese, 2017).

To date, no employment protection legislation has successfully addressed the problems of duality in Spain where the firing-cost gap between temporary and permanent contracts remains large (Sanz-de-Galdeano and Terskaya, 2017). The country's long-term unemployment levels exhibit a recalcitrance that disregards both recent economic growth and the latest ALMPs instituted by government. Molina and Rhodes (2007) observe that since the government helped create its dual labor market in 1984, little has been done to remove worker exit barriers that have characterized permanent employment since the time of Franco (p. 237). This point has been made more recently by Sanz-de-Galdeano and Terskaya (2017) and can be observed in the paternalism of many small and mid-size entreprises (SMEs) where the ghost of the Generalissimo manifests itself in weak or nonexistent worker unions.

As we noted earlier in this chapter (see especially the discussion leading to footnote 3), the United States represents the nation in our six country analysis with the most flexible labor market. On the OECD Strictness of Employment Protection Legislation index, the United States scores consistently in the 0.20 to 0.28 range and with zero signifying "no protection at all," America has garnered the image of "free-wheeling capitalism" at its worst, if its many European critics are to be believed. Workers especially are viewed by many policy experts—both in America and in Europe—as particularly vulnerable (OECD, 2017; Tasci and Zenker, 2011).

Yet, as Table 4.5 shows, there are considerable strengths in the U.S. economy that, in many ways, offset some persistent structural weaknesses. Since the 2008 financial crisis, the country's GDP and GNI per capita have increased steadily. In recent data published by OECD for 2018, the United States' per capita GDP of $62,480 far surpasses that of Germany ($53,752) or Sweden ($52,767). The U.S. Bureau of Labor Statistics also reports that real weekly earnings have increased to record highs when deflated for inflation (Hammermesh, 2017). Overall unemployment in America before COVID-19 was at record lows (in the 3.7–3.9 range) and youth unemployment rates, while not as low as Germany, were substantially lower than Sweden and other Nordic countries. Labor force participation rates have continued to track lower since 2000 (with recent upsurges in 2018 and 2019), but long-term unemployment rates have not diminished appreciably since 2008 (Hammermesh, 2017; Kosanovich and Theodossiou Sherman, 2019). The NEET rate and the youth unemployment rate have been declining indicating that both employment-related and educational activities are increasing as the economy expands.

Table 4.5 also exhibits the high and growing level of TEA in the country. The trend for established business ownership is not as strong, however, possibly reflecting the increased competition faced by entrepreneurs in an era of rapid growth.

As we have seen, Germany introduced flexibility into its rigid labor markets by equipping workers with a panoply of technical and cognitive skills, and Sweden does the same through labor market coordination. America, in contrast, introduces flexibility through economic growth, worker mobility, and on-the-job training (Pastore, 2018; Cappelli, 2015; Tasci and Zenker, 2011) to reduce the experience gap of young people. Pastore (2018) provides this example:

> In the U.S. the annual job finding rate is above 60 percent, which means that 60 out of every 100 unemployed people find a job within a year. Hence, if

chances are equally distributed among unemployed individuals, every un-employed person has, on average, a chance to find a job in less than two years, which is a relatively short period of time. (p. 3)

Cappelli (2015) argues that the mobility of American workers has greatly reduced the problems of skill shortages and skill gaps. He cites research showing that job requirements are not exogenous from the supply of applicants, which is another way of saying that a shortage of job seekers that leads to higher wages causes employers to substitute capital for labor to create new jobs with lower skill requirements. In addition, employers tend to lower the skill requirements for given jobs when labor is scarce and raise them when more qualified workers are plentiful (p. 253).

One issue that the United States shares with Europe is the skills mismatches resulting from the oversupply of college-educated youth (OECD, 2016; McGuinness, Pouliakas, and Redmond, 2017) and the undersupply of STEM-trained applicants (U.S. Bureau of Labor Statistics, 2018; DeSilver, 2017). Coates and Morrison (2016) lament the push under the Obama administration urging more and more young people to go to college. The administration's focus on community college attendance was especially pronounced with an associate degree touted as opening pathways to technical careers and to four-year degrees as well. This gesture to the German model has provided underwhelming results in both respects to date (Coates and Morrison, 2016; Levin et al. 2017), further clouding the community college educational mission.

The academization of America's labor force has not yet led to the skill mismatch problems witnessed in Italy, Spain, Greece, and many eastern European countries. One indicator is the current job vacancy rate, which can suggest something about the difficulty in hiring and therefore information about the supply and demand for qualified applicants (Cappelli, 2015). Since 2000, when the United States began reporting data on job openings (vacancies), the rate is at its highest levels (Hammermesh, 2017). When you combine this statistic on vacancies with the low overall and youth unemployment rates, you have evidence of an economy with full employment and more job openings than applicants in both skilled and unskilled segments of the labor market.

India, too, has flexible labor markets but differs dramatically from the United States in the degree of flexibility: it is estimated that about 90 percent of India's labor force is employed in the informal sector, which is largely outside the scope of the country's labor regulations governing working conditions, wages, benefits, and other protections (Dasgupta and Kar, 2018). This informal sector spans not only the estimated 400 million workers in agriculture and self-employment but also includes an estimated 50 million individuals in the organized manufacturing and service sectors where employment generally follows government mandates including written employer–worker contracts.

As we show in Table 4.6, India's economy has expanded appreciably over the time series presented. However, as a number of observers have maintained, the growth in the formal sector, especially in manufacturing, remains too low to absorb the large number of youth entering the labor market (Zimmermann et al. 2013; Schmid, 2015). With nearly 30 percent of prospective and actual workers in the 15- to 29-year-old age group, this take-up problem is likely to become more urgent in the next several years.

Compared to many European countries, India's unemployment and youth unemployment rates are quite low. The latter has averaged around 10 percent from 1991 through 2017 (Dasgupta and Kar, 2018). But, as Table 4.6 also shows, the labor force participation rates of young people has declined from 2005 to 2017. The share of youth categorized as NEET has continued to hover around 26 percent, consisting primarily of girls and young women involved in domestic duties (Zimmerman et al., 2013). When these unemployment, NEET, and labor force participation rates are examined collectively, they point to a dynamic where an increasing proportion of India's youth are attending postsecondary education—with some estimating the increase from about 28 percent in 2005 to over 40 percent in recent years (Zimmermann, et al. 2013).

The academization movement in India promises to have more serious repercussions for economic growth for that country than the movement has thus far had in the United States. Schmid (2015) calls our attention to the situation in the country where the unemployment rate among higher educated youth (about 20 percent) is substantially higher than it is for low-educated youth (about 3–4 percent). This is a reversal of the pattern found in Mediterranean and eastern European countries where the unemployment rate for educated youth is about three fifths (60 percent) of that of the low educated. In fact, the only European country that shares India's education-adjusted profile is Greece (Schmid, 2015).

As we have seen in our discussion of labor markets in Italy and Spain, overeducation in India has resulted in serious skills mismatches, which have, in turn, led to production inefficiencies, unemployment and underemployment, monopsony conditions, and worker discouragement and disaffection. One outlet available to workers is self-employment, and, indeed, this pathway has been taken by many Indians. Table 4.6 indicates that TEA has stabilized at about 10 percent. Established business ownership rates, on the other hand, have dropped significantly since 2013, signaling that governmental policies and initiatives require further evolution (Majumdar, 2016; Thakur, 2106).

Influencing Labor Demand Through Active Labor Market Policies

As we have attempted to make clear in our country-specific descriptions of labor market demand, market corrections for skill and/or education mismatches, skill gaps, underemployment, and unemployment have not proven sufficient in some instances. Growth, for example, has not been strong enough (Dietrich and Moller, 2016; Bruno et al., 2017; Pastore, 2018) or mobility has not been frequent enough (David, Janiak, and Wasmer, 2010; Cappelli, 2015; Tasci and Zenker, 2011) in some countries and over some market cycles to impact youth unemployment and labor force participation rates. Hence, governments, in Keynesian-compliant fashion, have sought to assist the market through these rough patches by means of various legislations and administrative practices, which we referred to earlier as ALMPs.

It is possible to classify ALMPs into one of four categories with some of these categories more pertinent to the youth unemployment problem than others. First, there are efforts designed primarily in educational institutions—sometimes in consultation with employers, sometimes not—to increase school-to-work transitions through vocational education and training, apprenticeship training, creation of dual systems, and on-the-job training (Eichhorst and Rinne, 2016; Vogel, 2015; Zimmermann et al. 2013). We have covered this type of ALMP initiative in some detail in Chapter 3.

A second ALMP effort has manifest itself through minimum wage legislation (Jardim et al. 2017; Zimmermann et al. 2013; Layard, 1982) or in the form of wage subsidies (Caliendo and Schmidt, 2016; Pastore, 2018), the most widely known in the form of YGs. The conventional wisdom, supported by many labor economists and businessmen, is that the former reduces the demand for workers by disincentivizing employers to pay lower entry wages for new workers with skills and experience deficits. The latter, on the other hand, have been viewed favorably as a means of bridging the gap between often-times low entry-level wages and wages that incentivize work over inactivity.

A third form of ALMP manifests itself as measures to protect employees from the unfair labor practices of employers; capricious reductions in wages, hours, benefits, or working conditions; summarial firings; and business closings without notice and/or severance. Worker protection legislation and collective bargaining agreements, while increasing worker security in some sectors of the market, have had any number of pernicious impacts in some nations including the responses of more rigid labor markets, dual labor markets, a rise in short-term work contracts, lower levels of economic growth, and higher unemployment rates (Zimmermann et al. 2013; Schmid, 2015; Bruno et al. 2017). This is not to say that all worker legislation has produced significant unintended consequences; for example, the moral hazards of unemployment insurance when coupled with active job search have proven to be very low (O'Leary, 2017; Eberts, 2017; Michau, 2009). However, since legislation like this (workman's compensation for injury is another) typically targets the permanent, adult workforce, and not entry-level youth, we will conclude our discussion of this form of ALMP at this point by offering this single note. The effects of protection legislation have not benefited youth; on the contrary, they have resulted in a seemingly endless variety of fractional and disadvantageous work contracts, culminating in the zero-hour employee called to work on a moment's notice and terminated in much the same way (Rainsford, Maloney, and Popa, 2019; Askenazy, 2018).

We will term the fourth and final class of ALMPs, labor market training and employment strategies (LMTES). Within this particular category are programs and policies that provide job search assistance, subsidized hiring incentives, paid directly to employers, and public sector work programs. We distinguish LMTES from human capital creation programs like the dual system, work-based vocational education and training, apprenticeship systems, and entrepreneurial training and support covered in Chapter 3, arguing that LMTES are government-directed efforts to influence the demand side of the employment market.

How successful have ALMPs been in combating youth unemployment? While there is some empirical evidence to suggest that wage supplementation may expedite youth transition from inactivity or temporary employment to full-time work, the effect of a minimum wage has proven less encouraging. Likewise, evidence for the effectiveness of public sector labor force training and employment strategies remains a topic of controversy with subsidized private sector employment apparently achieving more impact than public sector jobs programs. A short synopsis of the representative research findings with respect to employee wage supplements and employer subsidies (categories 2 and 4) is presented.

Subsidies Paid to Employees

Perhaps the most widely known example of wage subsidies is the YG (Ungdomsgaranti) provided in Sweden to youth aged 20 to 24 (Byambadorj, 2007; Pastore, 2018). The municipal and state governments work cooperatively to provide a training allowance that is coordinated with other ALMPs like labor market training in either the private or public sector. The success of this approach, at least in Sweden, can be culled from the country's consistently low youth unemployment rates. In 2013, buoyed, no doubt, by the success of YGs in Sweden, Finland, and Denmark, the European Commission launched its own YG targeting high youth unemployment countries like Spain, Italy, and Greece (O'Reilly et al., 2015). If youth labor force participation and unemployment rates in these countries are any indication of YGs success, then a great deal more work needs to be done. It appears the Nordic success arises from its embeddedness in a value orientation of broad institutional cooperation, a condition lacking in these Mediterranean countries (Pastore, 2018; Eichhorst et al., 2015; Dietrich and Moller, 2016). The same can be said of the more limited use of ALMPs in Germany where wage subsidies are carefully integrated into the dual system (Schmid, 2015).

So as not to leave the reader with the impression that wage subsidies, properly utilized, are a panacea for the unemployment problem, we offer a recent example from Finland. In a first of its kind experiment in Europe, a random sample of 2,000 individuals were paid a tax-exempt income of approximately $650 a month, regardless of other sources of income (including wages from work) or whether they were looking for a job. After two years, those individuals did not have significantly higher employment levels or wages from employment than individuals in a control group who did not receive this guaranteed income (Hannon, 2019). Even in the Nordic countries, apparently a guarantee cannot be guaranteed to produce a positive impact!

The payment of a minimum wage is another way of providing a wage subsidy to employees, except in this instance, the subsidy originates directly from the employer, potentially reducing the firm's profits and/or investment/expansion capital. The principal arguments for enacting a minimum wage are rarely based on criteria such as economic efficiency, labor market flexibility, and business growth; rather, they proceed from the tenets of social justice. The Economic Policy Institute (2019), an American think tank based in Washington, DC, for example, argues that a $15 per hour federal minimum wage is necessary to lift pay for nearly 40 million workers, reverse decades of growing pay inequality between the lowest paid workers and the middle class, and help significantly level the wages of White Americans and American workers of color. The Economic Policy Institute also cites the importance of this minimum wage for spurring business activity and job growth; however, this contention has been challenged by a broad spectrum of business and economic organizations including the U.S. Chamber of Commerce, the National Federation of Independent Businesses, and the National Association of Manufacturers. If economic theory is correct and if the empirical record is to be taken seriously, proscriptions against using a minimum wage as an economic growth tool would appear to have a great deal of merit.

One economic study touting the economic benefits of a minimum wage is the widely cited work of Card and Krueger (1995) entitled *Myth and Measurement: The New Economics of the Minimum Wage*. In their book, these researchers find that, contrary to what many businessmen conjecture and economists predict, a dramatic increase in the minimum wage of fast-food workers in New Jersey actually increased employment level by 2.7 full-time equivalents per restaurant when compared to a state, Pennsylvania, that did not raise its minimum wage. This translated into employment elasticities ranging from 0.5 to 0.9 whereas the elasticities usually observed in such studies ranged from −0.1 to −0.3 (Borjas, 2008). These findings soon captured the imagination of a host of minimum wage increase proponents, including the then U.S. Secretary of Labor (Dilworth, 1996). As the study came under increased scrutiny, however, it became increasingly evident that the data collection methods (telephone interviews with managers) generated substantial amounts of measurement error, which, in turn, produced positive labor demand elasticities (Borjas, 2008; Dilworth, 1996). A reexamination of this same set of New Jersey and Pennsylvania restaurants by Neumark and Wascher (2000) utilizing payroll data concluded that the raise in the New Jersey minimum wage actually had resulted in a decrease of 4 percent in employment in New Jersey relative to Pennsylvania with an employment demand elasticity of −0.22 (i.e., in the direction expected by neoclassical economics).

In the United States and in Europe, the controversy over the minimum wage rages on in a more nuanced form with advocates opining that economic consequences are conditioned upon the size of the increase as well as the base wage from which the increase has been calculated (Card and Krueger, 1995; Borjas, 2008). It would be expected, for example, that raising the minimum wage in a state or city that has a high wage already in place would see very little employment impact compared to a low-wage state or city. A recent high-profile experiment in Seattle, Washington—an American city with one of the nation's highest minimum wages at $9.47—calls even these assumptions into question. The city increased its minimum wage to $11 in 2015 and $13 in 2016. Using administrative data spanning all industries in the city, Jardim et al. (2017) report that the 2015 increase produced disemployment effects that offset the wage increases (an elasticity of −1). The subsequent 2016 increase to $13 yielded much more pronounced reductions in employer payroll expenses and by extension employee earnings, with a net elasticity of −3. Thus, it would appear that even in circumstances where increases proceed from a high wage base, the net results are reductions in employee hours and fewer employees.

Subsidies Paid to Prospective or Actual Employers

An important ALMP designed to help workers gain the general and specific skills they need to be successful in the job market is the individually targeted employer subsidy program. In their meta-analysis of 207 evaluations of ALMP impact, Card, Kluve and Weber (2017) classify nearly 25 percent of the interventions as subsidies to private sector employers (15 percent) or to public sector employment programs (9 percent). As we have attempted to do, Card, Kluve, and Weber (2017) are careful to distinguish employer subsidized initiatives from ALMPs that support on-the-job or classroom training, on the one hand, and employee wage subsidies, on the other.

Government subsidies to private sector employers have been utilized in both Germany and Sweden to ease worker transitions or dislocations due to technological or market shocks, providing employers with the resources to retrain, recapitalize, or both (Eichhorst et al. 2015; Schmid, 2015; Pastore, 2018). They have also been used in the United States to fund transitional jobs to increase short-term employment but have proven less successful over the long term (Dutta-Gupta et al. 2016). In their meta-analysis, Card, Kluve, and Weber (2017), however, find that private sector ALMPs have their most positive average impacts in the medium and longer term, increasing employment by 21 percent (p. 14). The size of this effect, however, appears to be a function of the disproportionately large number of programs of this type in the sample emanating from Germanic or Nordic countries.

Returns to subsidies in the public sector have not been nearly as noteworthy; in point of fact, they have often been negative. Caliendo and Schmidt (2016) in their analysis of 37 evaluations of ALMPs directed at youth unemployment in Europe find that public sector work programs had zero effect on subsequent job quality or stability. These researchers assert that "instead of providing a bridge to regular employment they [public job subsidies] seem to entail locking-in or even stigmatization effects." (p. 16). Card, Kluve, and Weber (2017) come to much the same conclusion in their meta-analysis, reporting medium-term impacts of −1.1 percent and long-term impacts of zero.

The United States, more than any other nation, has sought to increase youth and adult employment and labor force participation through the use of subsidized public sector jobs and training programs. In each of the several iterations of the country's principal (federal) employment/jobs training legislation—for example, the Comprehensive Employment and Training Act (1973), the Job Training Partnership Act (1982), the Workforce Investment Act (1998), and the Workforce Innovation and Opportunity Act (2013), sizeable proportions of funds have been earmarked or have found their way to public sector employment. The results have been underwhelming and, in many cases, quite costly as well.

Numerous evaluations of the Comprehensive Employment and Training Act programs indicated that many of the funds were used by governments to supplant local efforts. When new public sector jobs were created (and this apparently did not happen often), the employment benefits were more often than not quite modest and benefited women and not men (Maynard, 1995;

Lalonde, 1995). Assessments of the Job Training Partnership Act show that while discounted benefits for adults over seven years averaged about $3,000, the returns to public sector employment for youth amounted to a net *cost* for males of $6,000 and $1,200 for females (Carneiro and Heckman, 2003). An evaluation of the residential Job Corps program, directed at unemployed youth also demonstrated very little employment impact (Burghardt and Schochet, 2001). Finally, evaluations of the Workforce Investment Act (WIA) and the Workforce Innovation and Opportunity Act (WIOA) have produced mixed and, at times, confusing estimates of program benefit. Both WIA and WIOA have announced concerted efforts to insure that more subsidies target employers in the private sector. If this is true, then findings by Hollenbeck (2009) indicating a negative benefit of $8,000 for dislocated workers is especially disheartening.

Stimulated perhaps by the Trump administration's renewed efforts to revitalize worker training and apprenticeship in a rapidly expanding economy, the popular press in the United States has once again brought the failures of worker training in America (Fadulu, 2018; Thrush, 2018; Scheiber, 2017) to the public's attention. Fadulu (2018), for example, rails against "Reagan's JTPA" but neglects to recount the shortcoming of Clinton's WIA or Obama's WIOA. Job Corps, a political staple since 1964, continues to underperform badly, as Thrush (2018) points out, with participants' average yearly earnings at $12,486, barely above the poverty level for a single individual. Notwithstanding these public sector employment failures, this form of ALMP in America continues to be promulgated by sizeable numbers of academics, public policymakers, politicians, and members of the press. Cynically, opponents in the business community and in government appear to acquiesce treating such advocacy as a cost of doing business.

In this chapter, we have set out to show that even on the demand side of the labor market equation the value orientations of nations (i.e., cultural beliefs, attitudes, and preferences) exert a pervasive influence in how capitalism is practiced. Just as the structure of human capital formation is formulated (Chapter 3) on qualities that are valued by a nation, so too are the ingredients for labor demand, including the commitment to economic growth, the level of government and private sector cooperation, the choice of market rigidity antidotes, the feasibility of geographic and/or labor sector mobility, and the appetite for ALMPs and the particular form they take. Nationalism or regionalism provide texture—that is, *symbolic interests* if one prefers the language of Bourdieu (1986)—that may conflict with pure economic interests like productivity or efficiency. This texture can even have the effect of circumscribing the amount of time and other resources individuals are willing to invest in playing the economic game as it has been envisioned by its neoclassical authors.

5

Investigating the Cultural Transmission of Economic Values

Survey and Sampling Methods

But throughout all this history of survey research one fact remained, a very disturbing one to the student of social organization. The individual remained the unit of analysis, no matter how complex the analysis, how numerous the correlations, the studies focused on individuals as separate and independent units. . . . As a result, the kind of substantive problems on which such research focused tended to be problems of "aggregate psychology," that is within individual problems, and never problems concerned with relations between people.
—James S Coleman, *Relational Analysis* (1958)

In the opening chapter we presented a conceptual model that is used to address the three research questions around which the book is organized. There, in addition to our queries around the differential impacts of national cultures in fostering economic opportunity and the extent to which the effects of these national cultures are independent of pre-existing economic conditions, we introduced intergenerational cultural transmission as the socializing mechanism that can help us answer both the differential impacts and culture exogeneity (independent contribution) questions. We described our intention to focus on the cultural value orientations of three generations—baby boomers, Generation Xers and millennials—hypothesizing that the relative stability of beliefs, attitudes, and preferences spanning the 1940s through 2017 could facilitate disentangling more or less persistent constellations of beliefs, attitudes, and preferences from the changes in economic conditions that have characterized each of the six countries we compare over this same timeframe.

The independent impact of enduring cultural values on a nation's economic activity has never achieved widespread acceptance in the field of economics.

Caught in the Cultural Preference Net. Michael J. Camasso and Radha Jagannathan, Oxford University Press (2021).
© Oxford University Press. DOI: 10.1093/oso/9780190672782.003.0005

Yes, there is that seminal work by the economist-turned-sociologist, Max Weber, and more recent examples of culture's impact on economic structure and functioning—for example, McCloskey's (2006) examination of the 17th-century bourgeois culture of England and Netherlands; Mokyr's (2019) investigation of technological and economic consequences of disinterested and open scientific inquiry by Frances Bacon and his contemporaries; and Mark Casson's (2006) typology of pro-innovation and entrepreneurial cultures. Each of these economists makes the case that it is cultural values and ideas, not capital or economic opportunity per se, that is responsible for economic growth and prosperity.

Even the notion of enduring cultural values has been de-emphasized in much of the economic literature. A recent essay in *The Economist* entitled "The Uncultured Science" (2019) boasts that "culture factors are but temporary barriers to diffusion of development and economic growth." This article and much of the literature that can be termed *cultural economics* (Spolaore and Wacziarg, 2018, 2009; Fernandez, 2008) or *behavioral economics* (Becker, 1996), while acknowledging the importance of cultural norms, emphasize their fragility in the face of changing economic conditions such as prices or wages. Becker (1996), for example, agrees that economic interests more than traditions and customs can permanently account for both the internalization and stability of cultural norms (in the form of preferences) that remain useful for maximizing individual utility (p. 350). Becker also maintains that "personal interest theories" are more parsimonious in explaining changes in norms and preferences than theories proposed by sociologists and anthropologists where individuals are typically viewed as having few or no choices (pp. 17–19). He does, however, acknowledge that stable behavior in an economic environment of changing opportunities, incomes, prices, etc. might contradict the primacy of self-interest in the utility maximization argument (p. 35).

Indeed, over the past 20 years or so, there has been renewed interest in the field of economics to more closely examine the "nearly always endogenous" presumption underpinning the role of cultural norms, beliefs, attitudes, and preferences in economic analysis. One approach, which for want of a better term we will refer to as the *majority of agents* perspective, focuses on how the prevalence of a cultural norm or preference in a population can independently influence and even shape subsequent economic activity. In his work on European unemployment and the provision of unemployment insurance,

Michau (2013), for example, posits the idea that cultural evaluation in a society can be traced to changes in cultural heterogeneity, specifically in the proportions of civic and economic agents present at any given point in time. With respect to the configuration of a welfare state, Michau maintains that if a majority of agents (citizens) have a preference for working hard and also show a high degree of "civicness," policies supporting generous unemployment benefits receive broad support. Guilt for unduly relying on such welfare benefits would be so widespread that the proportion of the population that abuses society's largess would be small. Should the degree of civicness evolve, however, to the point where the preference for hard work as the principal means of achieving self-sufficiency declines in favor of a preference for broader economic redistribution, irrespective of work ethic, then one should expect this "new civicness," divorced of commitment to work to have serious ramifications for economic growth and productivity. We are reminded here of the economic restructuring that Sweden embarked upon in the 1970s and again in the 1990s and the current challenges facing the country (see Ljunge, 2011).

Michau's (2013) argument is reminiscent of the multiple trust equilibria model promulgated by Anderlini and Terlizzese (2017). These economists focus on the dramatic impacts that the addition of a sizable proportion of "cheaters" or "noncheaters" can have on civic culture. Adding a fraction of the former will tend to increase the overall frequency of societal dishonesty while adding, instead, a fraction of noncheaters will raise the social sensitivity to the cost of cheating but would not affect its frequency. In other words, the larger the number of people adhering to a preference, whether social justice, trust, hard work, or a myriad of other qualities, the stronger it is felt by individuals.

Cultural Transmission

The "majority of agents" perspective, as we have identified it here, anticipates that the level of preference heterogeneity (or homogeneity) in a society will remain stable so long as this equilibrium does not exceed a society's resource or budget constraints. If these are broached and the current preference level is too costly financially and/or emotionally, then one could expect that a change in value orientation would occur if the nation-state is to remain viable politically and economically. Hence, the exogeneity of values and preferences here are established through the lag[1] in impact that new institutional policies (incentives and/or disincentives) have on subsequent economic behavior. The problem we see with this identification of exogeneity as a process established through changes in a population's preference heterogeneity and concomitant incorporation into political and economic institutions is the seemingly ahistorical nature of the process. Preference exogeneity from this viewpoint is manifest as population thresholds or tipping points in a kind of demographic, dialectic of inevitability, the essence of which has been captured in Samuel Johnson's maxim:

> It is thus that mutual cowardice keeps us in peace. Were one half of mankind brave and one-half cowards the brave would be always beating the cowards. Were all brave, they would lead to a very uneasy life; all would be continually fighting; but being all cowards we go on very well. (cited in Boswell, 1934/1971, p. 326)

That is, until the next time the preference for bravery achieves broad favorability.

A second approach used to establish the exogeneity of cultural preferences and values, and the one we employ in the analysis we undertake in this book, is the explicit modeling of cultural transmission from parents to children. Intergenerational analyses of the impact of culture on economic activity attempts to establish the presence of a lag between an economic activity such as employment seeking at time (T) and a prior set of values and preferences held by individuals at time (T−1) or earlier (T−N). Thus, intergenerational models provide two ways of falsifying the hypothesis of cultural exogeneity: (a) value orientations across generations do not persist in the face of changes in the economic environment (prices, wages, etc.) in a country, and (b) there are changes in intergenerational value orientations but the economic environment remains unaffected by these changes. In either instance, evidence of a lag between cultural values influencing economic behavior is not apparent.

The use of the parent (or grandparent) as an instrumental variable in the study of cultural transmission can be traced to the work of Bisin and Verdier

---

[1] It is common practice in economics and in demography to incorporate past values of explanatory variables in regression models if it is believed that the relationship between X and Y is not contemporaneous. As Gujarati and Porter (2010) note, the reasons for lags include inertia, force of habit, resistance to change, and institutional arrangements like long-term contracts. We would add culturally established preferences, beliefs, and attitudes.

(2011). These researchers began from the premise that the resilience of ethnic/religious/cultural traits across generations plays an important role in determining a wide range of economic outcomes, specifically the traits, social norms, and ideological tenets that determine discounting, risk aversion, altruism, attitudes toward family and job market, and the interpretation of and reaction to choice environments (p. 340). Bisin and Verdier identify two forms of cultural transmission: the first, inside the family, which they refer to as "direct vertical socialization," and the second, "oblique and horizontal socialization," which emanates from other socialization sources like educational, political, or economic institutions. Vertical socialization proceeds through a transmission mechanism that Bisin and Verdier (2011) identify as "imperfect empathy":

> There is a fundamental friction in potential altruism which sustains cultural transmission by biasing parents toward their own cultural traits. While parents want the best for their children (altruism) they evaluate their choices for their children using their own and not their children's preferences. (p. 341)

Cultural heterogeneity in the Bisin and Verdier (2011) model derives not from some impersonal, demographic process but instead obtains from the utility-maximizing choices of parents who take into account past performance of social and economic institutions and prospects of their future performances. Moreover, when vertical and horizontal socialization fail to exhibit complementarity in a society, it can be expected that the homogeneity required for widespread civicness, cooperation, and honesty will also be in short supply.

In their examinations of social capital and its effect on economic efficiency in Italy, Guiso, Sapienza, and Zingales (2008) also utilize intergenerational culture transmission as an instrument to study the circumstances responsible for the formation of exogenous cultural beliefs, attitudes, and preferences. They begin their analysis by making this observation: "economic models are generally silent on how people acquire priors, e.g., probability distributions over events with which they have no firsthand experience" (p. 292). Their tentative hypothesis is that parents pass on these prior beliefs, attitudes and preferences after weighing future and current events (choices) by the costs of their children's mistakes when the children are still at home. If parent trust decisions have yielded negative economic returns, parents tend to adopt pessimistic attitudes toward trade, investment, and other economic activities, setting up a "no trust–no trade" equilibrium. If, in turn, there is no countervailing evidence available to a child through oblique socialization avenues, to borrow from Bisin and Verdier (2011), then there is little incentive for the child to invest and learn, and there is no updating of the received prior. If the norm in the region or country becomes one of the transmissions of pessimistic priors that go unchallenged (perhaps because the pathways of horizontal socialization are unreliable or corrupt), then it is easy to see how environments of betrayal (Bigoni et al., 2016, 2018), excessive bonding capital (Putnam et al., 1993), amoral familism (Banfield and Fasano, 1958), or limited morality (Tabellini, 2008a, 2008b) are created and maintained.

Fernandez and Fogli (2006) and Fernandez (2008) approach the issue of intergenerational transmission by studying second-generation Americans, specifically women who were born in the United States but whose parents were born elsewhere and their labor force participation and fertility behavior. Fernandez makes the argument that past values of labor force participation and fertility in the country of origin reflect three types of influences: (a) institutions like markets, minimum wages, and worker protections; (b) the economic environment—supply and demand for labor, access to child care, transportation costs; and (c) cultural preferences and beliefs. If past (country of origin) labor force participation and fertility rates (T−1) can explain how much second generation American women work notwithstanding their residence in the United States in a different time period (T) and facing a different set of institutions and economic variables, then these old-country labor force participation and fertility rates are deemed by Fernandez and Fogli (2006) to serve as cultural proxies capable of predicting economic behavior. And, indeed, in a series of regression analyses, these economists find that cultural proxies exert a significant, independent impact on labor force participation in the United States after controlling for family factors like income, education, and unobserved human capital.

A number of researchers have examined the intergenerational transmission of values that would indicate the continuing support for capitalism. Some of this work finds that the preferences for the centrality of work, the rewards possible from free-market capitalism, entrepreneurial activity, etc. remain stable while other research appears to demonstrate erosion or even rejection of these values and preferences. Kalleberg and Marsden (2013, 2019) employ the General Social Survey (GSS) from 1973 through 2006 to explore whether millennials in the United States are more or less likely

than earlier generations to value wage-producing work, high income, potential for advancement, and a number of intrinsic job rewards (altruism,
interesting work, etc.). Controlling for potentially confounding effects like
historical time-trend and life course (aging) with hierarchical logit regression, Kalleberg and Marsden (2013) report no birth cohort diminution of
the value of work and small differences across generations in the importance
of job, income, and security with millennials valuing these more (p. 264).[2]
Twenge et al. (2010) in their study of high school seniors in the United States
(1976–2006) begin from the premise that different generations face different
experiences and events producing differing preferences and expectations
about work and market capitalism (p. 1120). Among their conclusions, motivated by a confirmatory factor analysis, Twenge et al. find that millennials
have the highest value for leisure and, perhaps not so ironically, the lowest
value for intrinsic job rewards like self-realization. They conclude that while
baby boomers "live to work," millennials and Generation Xers "work to live"
(p. 1122). More recent indications that the American commitment to capitalism might be in transition can be found in recent polls conducted by Pew,
the Cato Institute, and Gallup. According to recent Gallup polls (Saad, 2019),
only about 50 percent of millennials view capitalism favorably, down from
66 percent in 2010.

While the apparent softening of support for capitalism in the United
States remains a topic of considerable debate (the same previously mentioned Gallup poll shows overwhelming intergenerational support for entrepreneurship and small- and medium-sized enterprises), there are signs in
Europe and elsewhere of a diminution in the values central to its maintenance. Cross-national research by Michau (2008), Hauff and Kircher (2015),
Guillaud (2013), and Esser and Lindh (2018) suggests that countries with
more income inequality are subject to the transmission of higher levels of
anticapitalism expressed primarily through concerns for income and job
security. Even in capitalist countries known for their egalitarianism like
Australia (Baron, Cobb-Clark, and Erkal, 2008), Canada (Lemieux and
Macleod, 2000), and Sweden (Bergquist, 2016; Ljunge, 2011), there are

---

[2] Establishing generational (cohort) effects in longitudinal data can be statistically challenging if
there are confounding effects with age (developmental) and/or historical factors (time-trend). In a
stylized cohort table, age and period effects occur jointly in each cohort diagonal; age and cohort,
in the cross-sectional data in each column; and cohort and period effects, in each row. Hence, in a
typical regression analysis, only two of these three effects can be identified simultaneously (Glenn,
1977). See Yang and Land (2013) for the simultaneous test of these factors using generalized linear
mixed models.

signs that the "spirit of capitalism" may be on the wane. While modernization theory (Hauff and Kircher, 2015; Hancke, Rhodes, and Thatcher, 2007) predicts some convergence of values due to global economic forces affecting nations, it would seem prudent to us, however, not to overstate the importance of oblique forms of value transmission, especially when these values conflict with the more traditional values of parents. We have presented a great deal of research (see especially Chapter 2) that points to strong stability in work related values and preferences over time, notwithstanding changing economic and social contexts. We agree with Gallie (2019), Cook and Furstenberg (2002), and others that while it would be incorrect to ignore intergenerational value variation (or stability) within country, it would be equally problematic to disregard the cross-national accounting of approaches and commitment to free market capitalism. Both components are necessary if we are to gain a clear understanding of the conditions responsible for the permanence and change in value orientations either because of or in spite of economic factors.

Transition to Adulthood

Understudied in the economic literature but a staple in sociology, is the critical role that the achievement of adulthood exerts on youth values and preferences. The timing and conditions under which the transition occurs could influence the degree to which parental priors are adopted, the new adult's receptivity to extrafamilial sources of values and preferences, and his or her capacity to effectively prioritize competing and/or conflicting expectations.

There are a set of conventional markers that have been used to describe youth transition to adulthood (e.g., finishing secondary school, finding that first permanent job, leaving home, getting married, having children; Furstenberg et al., 2002; Settersten, Furstenberg, and Rumbaut, 2008). Studies in the United States over the last four generations (baby boomers, Generation Xers, millennials, and Generation Zers, the last born 2001–2020) indicate that adulthood no longer begins when adolescence ends. Settersten, Furstenberg, and Rumbaut (2008) make the point that beginning with Generation X, a lengthy period developed, often spanning into individuals' 20s and extending into their 30s, that is devoted to further education, job exploration, and experimentation with relationships. These more complex transitions, perhaps due to their sheer length, have, in turn, resulted in social and economic consequences for both the parental family and the adult children.

There appears to be some consensus in the sociology and demography literatures that the cost–benefit ratio of prolonged transition to adulthood are more a consequence of cultural values and expectations than economic conditions (see, e.g., Musick and Bumpass, 1999; Furstenberg et al., 2002; Settersten, Furstenberg, and Rumbaut, 2008). Danziger and Rouse (2007) find that student debt, housing costs, and job instability are not defining factors, at least in the United States. They note that children, perhaps with the tacit approval of parents, delay leaving home, entry into the workforce, and marriage and children in anticipation of attaining high-status jobs. The assumption here is that the delays are critical to the formation of higher levels of human capital. We should note that these economic factors do play a role in Europe (Iacovou, 2002; Aassve et al., 2002; Newman and Aptekar, 2007).

Cross-national analysis of youth transitions reveals that the reasons for both staying at home and leaving can vary widely. Breen and Buchmann (2002) identify at least four key elements influencing transition decisions. The first element they list is the structure of tertiary education in the country. If it is provided locally, it can be expected that youth will not find it necessary to relocate before finishing this stage of their education. A second factor, also linked to the education system, is the degree to which secondary-level instruction is connected to the labor market. Breen and Buchmann (2002) maintain that education–labor links defined by "qualification space" (i.e., Germany, Switzerland) provide a much clearer signal to employers of potential productivity than do links characterized by "organizational spaces" (i.e., France, Italy). A third element is the degree of labor market regulation, a topic we have covered under labor market rigidities in Chapter 4. Finally, Breen and Buchmann (2002) call attention to the overall welfare regime operating in a country; here, they cite the importance of Esping-Andersen's (1990, 2002) model.

Breen and Buchmann (2002) see these four factors as sociocultural filters shaping the transition to adulthood through the impact they exert on family dynamics. In corporate-conservative Germany, the family exercises high levels of control over children but tolerates high dissociation between youth and adult cultures. While one would expect substantial differences between youth and adult value orientations, Breen and Buchmann aver that these differences are attenuated by an orderly pathway to adulthood.

Mediterranean countries like Spain and Italy also have a conservative welfare regime and a dissociative relationship between youth and parental elements; however, they differ from Germany by their construction of a precarious path to employment where dissociation is attenuated by family intervention.

Breen and Buchmann (2002) also contrast the family dynamics of these corporate welfare states with social democratic Sweden and laissez-faire United States, following the Esping-Andersen typology. In Sweden, dissociation between generations is replaced by egalitarianism and close intergenerational value orientations, resulting in orderly, managed transition to the workforce and adulthood. In the United States, too, family relations are egalitarian, bolstered by strong beliefs in self-reliance and the necessity of taking advantage of opportunities. Any dissociation between youth and adults is constrained by beliefs and norms in America as a "land of opportunity."

Cook and Furstenberg (2002) view transition to adulthood as culturally conceived and approved pathways to economic self-sufficiency. Like Breen and Buchmann, they examine the transitions to adulthood in Italy, Germany, Sweden, and the United States but do not focus on family dynamics. Instead, they chart the transitional trajectories of youth in each country, focusing primarily upon their distinctive educational institutions. They observe that in Italy the path to adulthood has been shaped to a large extent by the geographic diffusion of mass education at the upper secondary and tertiary levels in the 1980s. One consequence of this diffusion is that fewer students found it necessary to travel away from home to pursue their field of choice. This ability to commute to school from their parents' home dovetailed with a penchant for prolonged matriculations (driven by rigid labor markets and falling wages), compelling Italians to slow down the process of transitions. Cook and Furstenberg (2002) remark that while the retardation is not without costs to both parent and child, the latter is often able to enjoy a consumption lifestyle equal to that of more independent young people residing in northern and western Europe (p. 263).[3]

---

[3] In their essay "Failure to Launch," a title reprised from the 2006 motion picture, Lisa Bell and her colleagues (Bell, Burtless, Gornick, and Smeeding, 2007) contrast the psychological and financial costs of young adults living at home in Italy and the United States. Bell et al. (2007) point up the dramatic differences in parental response to this phenomenon in the two nations. In Italy, parents have been found to draw utility from young men living at home; that is, parents buffer against the young adults' economic problems, and in exchange, they stand to benefit from the child's emotional support and, in many cases, their increasing stocks of human capital. "It can be useful to have an unemployed or underemployed lawyer in the house" (p. 17). In the United States, this utility is more tenuous with "living at home" viewed as personal failure or as a harbinger of difficult family dynamics. See Manacorda and Moretti (2006) and Giuliano (2007) for interesting discussions of this issue.

Whereas over 60 percent of 18- to 34-year-old Italians live with their parents, Cook and Furstenberg (2002) declare that most Swedes are out of their parental home by 25 years of age. With a national focus on preparing a productive and self-reliant citizenry and a tertiary education dominated by the principle of numerous clauses (i.e., limited seats in a specialty or subject at a university or upper level technical school), most Swedes live away from home in dormitories or lodgings. Given the penchant of young Swedes to find permanent work and eschew extended upper secondary or tertiary education, it is not surprising that Cook and Furstenberg find far fewer quasi-professional students here than in countries like Italy, France, or Greece (p. 269), perhaps limiting the number of future disgruntled, unemployed intellectuals as well (Schumpeter, 1962). Bottom line, the key family transitions here are compressed and autonomy is achieved at an early age in Sweden.

The educational system in Germany, like Sweden, also compresses that transition-to-adulthood process. Full-time wage-earning youth are prepared efficiently through the VET and apprenticeship pathways we discussed in Chapter 3. Labor market realities are the centerpiece of German education and training; and occupational pride is the foundation of adult identity. Lastly, Cook and Furstenberg (2002) contrast the compressed but guided transitions of Germany and Sweden with the "sink or swim" transitions they say are emblematic of the United States. Lacking the duel system of Germany or the comprehensive active labor market policies of Sweden, America relies on a poorly coordinated amalgam of vocational schools, community colleges, universities, and on-the-job training to help prepare young people for economic self-sufficiency. Notwithstanding this seemingly disordered state of education in the United States, successful transitions to adulthood are viewed as uncomplicated as they are inevitable. This is best conveyed in the often-repeated quote of William Galston (n.d.) of the Brookings Institution.

> You need only do three things in this country to avoid poverty—finish high school, marry before having a child and marry after the age of 20. Only 8 percent of families who do this are poor; 79 percent of those who fail to do this are poor.

To Galston's three admonitions, we would add two additional rules for the "pursuit of happiness": do not acquire a felony record and attain literacy in English if this is not the language of the country of origin.

Observing Cultural Exogeneity Through
Naturalistic Sampling

A principal source of data used to study cultural beliefs, preferences, and attitudes and their transmission in Europe and America has been the social survey. Large numbers of potential respondents are selected from a target population, usually on the basis of the variable of principal concern (ordinarily the dependent variable), by probabilistic or judgmental techniques. Individual respondents are then contacted by one or more survey approaches: face-to-face interviews, mailed questionnaires, telephone interviews, and/or internet-available (online) questionnaires. In recent years, self-administered online modes of contact and computer-assisted face-to-face and telephone interviews have become increasingly popular (Dillman, 2000). We ourselves have referenced a number of the most widely administered surveys like the European Social Survey, the European Value Survey/World Value Survey (WVS), European Community Household Panel, the Luxembourg Income Study, and the GSS in our review of research on cultural and economic activity.

The use of large-scale social surveys to examine the family transmission of cultural values and preferences and to establish an exogenous relationship of this transmission to economic outcomes like labor force attachment has proven exceedingly challenging. These difficulties can usually be traced back to one or more of these features of research design, e.g., the sampling unit, the unit of observation, and/or the unit of analysis. In the typical social survey, all three of these units are the individual, and this can pose a problem if the nature of the research question requires an inference to be made about a unit that is different from the individual.

First, there is a problem of establishing the individual's association to other influential actors in a geographically identifiable social space (community). Individuals randomly sampled or selected through some type of cluster method are highly unlikely to be related by meaningful social interactions; they are merely co-located in physical proximity. To make ecological inferences plausible, social survey researchers have used a variety of statistical techniques, including fixed effects (country or regional dummy variable) or more sophisticated hierarchical linear modeling. While both approaches sidestep the issues of aggregation bias, they leave the cultural acquisition process in a "black box" (Fernandez, 2008). The country or regional dummy or level is used as an instrument to account for the unmeasured features of community, and this often yields theoretically unsatisfactory explanations for why geographic locations matter. Recall in Chapter 2 the counterintuitive congeries of regions reported by Kittel, Kalleitner, and Tsakloglou (2019) in the examination of work centrality in Europe.

Survey samples of individuals also face a second issue in explaining the process of culture transmission, and this stems from their capacity to establish parent–child transmission only indirectly. The principal vehicle used by researchers who utilize sample surveys to study value conveyance is the intercohort analysis. We have reviewed quite a few of these studies earlier (see, e.g., Kalleberg and Marsden, 2013; Fernandez and Fogle, 2006; Twenge et al., 2010; Michau, 2008; Bell et al., 2007). Inasmuch as both cohorts are juxtapositions of a set of periodically drawn cross sections that share a common birth date, any intercohort analysis (Generation Xers vs. millennials) necessarily must infer family socialization, the acquisition of priors, etc. from "cohort effects," purged for age and time trend. We see this as another manifestation of a black-box explanation based on temporal coincidence. To directly study intergenerational cultural transmission through the family, social surveys would need to incorporate multiple panels that link actual families across generations and countries.

A third limitation of survey samples is that the sampling unit and unit of observation often restrict the unit of analysis to individual-level problems. Coleman (1967) provides an excellent example from his early work with public schools in the United States. When investigating the reasons underpinning variation in student academic achievement, he concluded that it was not individual attitude and belief responses to a survey that proved to be important; rather, it was student roles and statuses in school that shed more light on the problem. Coleman's argument has relevance for the unit of analysis that best captures the transmission of economic preferences. Unlike attitudes and beliefs, which are affective and cognitive states that reside in the individual and therefore can legitimately be analyzed at the individual level, preferences are manifestations of choices that are best analyzed at the decision level (Phillips et al., 2002; Ben-Akiva and Lerman, 1994). Hoffman and Duncan (1988) have labeled this distinction as the modeling of attributes of the decision maker versus modeling the attributes of the decision.

We would like to offer one final observation about the use of large social surveys and their capacity to provide strong evidence of culture's impact on economic outcomes. We believe we can make this point with a few examples that are representative of a general pattern. Using the WVS in his intracohort analysis of the acceptability of recurring governmental benefits, Michau (2008) reports a series of regression models that explain around 7 percent of the variance in this dependent variable. Schuck and Shore (2019) investigation of attitudes around the meaning of work and the receipt of government assistance using Cultural Pathways to Economic Self-Sufficiency and Entrepreneurship survey data yields a series of R^2s (i.e., proportion of variation explained in the dependent variables) that range from 5 to 10 percent. Tabellini's (2008a) use of the GSS to determine if the value of trust is transmitted across generations yields R^2s in the 8 to 10 percent range. When Guiso, Sapienza, and Zingales employ multiple waves of the WVS to study the intergenerational transmission of trust and cooperation, their explanatory statistical models account for between 4 and 9 percent of the total variance in these dependent variables. We can provide additional examples, but we hope these are sufficient to convince the reader that social surveys of unconnected individuals do not adequately illuminate either the transmission process or any influence it may have on beliefs, attitudes, or preferences.

In this book we have taken a different approach to units of sampling, observation, and analysis, one that allows us to preserve the spatial (community) and family associations between individual respondents and also facilitates the study of stability or change in actual economic decision processes. Referred to variously as naturalistic sampling and analysis (Denzin, 1978), theoretical grounded sampling (Glaser and Strauss, 1967), sampling for relational analysis (Coleman, 1967), and place-based investigation (Boruch, 2005), the rudimentary principle underlying this approach is to preserve as much as possible of the spatial connections and social relations of the individual respondent, recognizing that these connections and relationships are essential for any thorough understanding of personal behavior. As Glaser and Strauss (1967) suggest, naturalist inquiry can proceed down either a qualitative or quantitative pathway, with a mixture of these approaches a viable third option. The qualitative path takes us into the realm of the case study or multiple case study analysis (i.e., in-depth investigation into some phenomenon; Stake, 1995, 2006). When this phenomenon is culture and its consequences, the detailed study is termed *ethnography*.

Selltiz, Wrightsman, and Cook (1976) refer to case studies as "the analyses of insight stimulating" examples. Such insights are possible, according to these authors, because the researcher assumes a posture toward the phenomenon under study of "alert receptivity" and intensity and a reliance on integrative ability to draw together diverse pieces of information (p. 98). Implicit in this description is the supposition that the phenomenon, whatever it may be, is identified at the outset and that the case(s) is an opportunity to study it.

How the case or cases get selected in the qualitative case study literature is subject to some debate. Glaser and Strauss (1967) draw the distinction between theoretical and circumstantial sampling, stating that the former selects case(s) to the degree to which they provide simultaneous maximization of similarities or differences while the latter relies on the data collected to point out these similarities or differences. Stake (2006) contrasts case(s) science and professional services based sampling (p. 24), citing science-based sampling as an effort to obtain a representative case(s) of a broader population that facilitates generalizability while professional service sampling's purpose is to select cases that provide knowledge about system or organizational functioning. The business cases collected by Harvard Business School (https://hbsp.harvard.edu/cases/) or the International Institute for Management Development (https://www.imd.org/research-knowledge/) are good examples of professional services sampling. For Stake (2006), the best sampling approach is the one that binds the phenomenon of interest to the case or cases.

In contrast to qualitative, naturalistic inquiry, there is a quantitative path, which to paraphrase the poet, Robert Frost, is a road not taken very often. It is a road, however, that has been trail-blazed by the sociologist James Coleman with his work on relational analysis (Coleman, 1958) and the associational basis of social capital (Coleman, 1990). Coleman was a proponent of multiple case analysis, which he labeled *contextual analysis*, but he believed a quantitative approach to case analysis was preferable for a variety of methodological reasons. First, there was his belief that statistical methods allowed for strong tests of hypothesis without any sacrifice of rich data description and inference. Second, there was the added advantage of estimating the amount of error that accompanied inference. All research designs are subject to bias, some of which is due to measurement (observation) issues, and some, an effect of the quality of the inference itself. To gain a more through appreciation for Coleman's quantitative approach to naturalistic inquiry, we strongly recommend *Medical Innovation*, a study of the adoption and diffusion of medical technology by Coleman, Katz, and Menzel (1966). It is an example of relational analysis at its finest.

Quantitative case study analysts like Coleman have little quarrel with their qualitative counterparts when it comes to the selection of sample cases. As before, cases need to be exemplars, that is, insight-stimulating examples that maximize similarities and differences in the phenomenon under investigation, which is ordinarily defined as the dependent variable of interest.

In our investigation of the national and multigenerational influence of cultural beliefs, attitudes, and preferences on economic behavior, we have chosen to chart the middle path of naturalistic inquiry—a quantitative journey guided by some useful historic and qualitative signposts. This qualitative influence shows up first in our selection of countries and regions within the countries; it manifests itself again in our choice of multigenerational families and reveals itself a third time in our statistical modeling. We begin with the selection of nations.

If the goal of sampling is to maximize differences and similarities between cultures with respect to the phenomenon of youth unemployment then the Esping-Andersen (1990, 2002) typology is a very good sampling frame from which to draw cases that exhibit maximum variability on economic performance. The typology also takes into account a rich collection of contextual factors (independent variables) that differ quite dramatically in some instances across welfare capitalist types. Recall our discussion in Chapter 4 of the coordinated active labor market policies of social-democratic Sweden and the ad-hoc, uncoordinated youth employment initiatives promulgated in Spain. Our selection of Sweden (social-democratic), Germany (conservative/corporatist), Italy and Spain (southern European), and the United States and India (free market/liberal/Anglospheres[4]) comprises the first stage of our naturalistic sampling process.

The second stage in our selection of national cases required us to drill down to a spatial observational level that maximized the similarities and differences evident at the aggregate country level. Here the guiding principles can be stated as follows: find a region and city in that region of the country that provides a distillation of the qualities portrayed in the Esping-Andersen typology, perhaps exaggerates these qualities a bit, and facilitates the identification of actively interacting three-generation families. The last principle interjects an element of realism, perhaps stating the obvious—that regional and/or city access and compliance were necessary and sufficient conditions for sampling families there.

---

[4] *Anglosphere* is a term used by James Bennett (2004) and others to refer to English-speaking countries that are, or were at one time, members of the British Commonwealth or, as in the case of the United States, were a former colony. These countries (Great Britain, the United States, Australia, Canada, India, and others) tend to practice a style of capitalism characterized by reliance on free markets. See also Hall and Soskice (2001).

Cook and Furstenberg (2002) have made the point in their advocacy for a cross-disciplinary, case synthesis approach that by ignoring within-country variation we have distorted the cross-national account (p. 260). The bias from aggregation introduces measurement error into analysis that cannot be adequately addressed using fixed effects or other statistical techniques. As a 2016 OECD report on local economic development makes clear, country profiles are, in actuality, mosaics of local and regional areas that have distinctive intracountry employment growth (decline) patterns and different skill supply and demand profiles (OECD, 2016). We recognize that by selecting families from only one small area within a region, the generalizability of our findings may be more difficult to establish beyond the regional level of observation. Still, this level of generalizability can be quite significant if our sampling unit (case) resonates, to use a term promulgated by Paul Steinberg (2015), to other regions with similar economic conditions and institutions, which we will show our case selections clearly do.[5]

In Sweden, we selected a labor market within the Jönköping region located between the large cities of Stockholm and Malmo, which we will refer to under the pseudonym of Johnholm.[6] Over the last 10 to 15 years, the general employment and youth unemployment rates in Johnholm were within a half standard deviation of the country-as-a-whole rates. OECD (2016) has designated Jonkoping as a low-skill trap region that borders with regions with a skill surplus to the south and high-skills equilibrium to the north.

The labor market chosen in Germany was Baden-Wurttemberg, in the extreme south-western part of the country. Christineberg, as we shall call the area, has experienced relatively low unemployment rates even by German standards. Baden-Wurttemberg has experienced modest economic growth over the past decade and, according to the OECD (2016), is in a state of high-skills equilibrium.

Our Italian families reside in Sicily in the subregion of Catania. In a labor market, we will term Reggio Maurizio on Sicily's east coast, local economic growth has averaged about 0.5 percent over the last 15 years and the unemployment rate is characteristically high. The OECD (2016) characterizes

---

[5] Steinberg (2015) makes the point that like social surveys, quantitative and qualitative case studies have generalizability criterion (i.e., the justification of inference to a larger set of observations). In social surveys, the generalization flows from an observed sample to a population of individuals. In case studies, generalization flows from observed cases to spatial/community systems, economic systems, or political systems that resonate with those in the observed case.

[6] As part of our Institutional Review Board protocol we agreed to make every effort to protect the identity of the families in the study. Our use of pseudonym is one component of this overall effort.

Catania as a province with high-skill surplus bordering a low-skills trap subregion on the west (Enna) and high-skills equilibrium subregion on the south (Siracusa).

Andalusia served as our sampling frame in Spain. Our labor market, San Arco, lies at the center of the region along the coast, and it typifies the economic environment throughout much of southern Spain (e.g., high adult and youth unemployment and negative economic growth) until quite recently. The OECD (2016) has designated the entire Andalusia region as low-skills trap, in stark contrast with Catalonia and Basque country, which have consistently exhibited high-skills equilibrium.

The sampling of regional cases in the United States and in India was especially challenging given the vastness of these countries, large population sizes, and ethnic/racial diversity. In America, we selected the state of Delaware with its small land mass of less than 2,500 square miles and population of about 950,000. We focused on a labor market area that provided a mix of urban, suburban, and farming settings and that facilitated the identification of closely interacting three-generation families. This area, which we will identify under the pseudonym Sherianne, also provided us with the opportunity to locate White, Black, and Hispanic respondents. On several economic measures—namely, job creation, economic growth, and unemployment—Delaware is representative of the nation's overall economic expansion over the past 10 years. According to the OECD (2016), the Sherianne market has been in high-skills equilibrium with some pressure from skills deficits and surpluses in adjacent states' labor markets.

In India, we selected a labor market we call Raazpuram, located in the state of Tamil Nadu in south India, a state that is considered to be India's higher education hub, boasting the highest number of universities in the country. However, the closure of thousands of small- and medium-sized enterprises in 2016–2017 has cost nearly half a million jobs in the state, driving up the youth unemployment rates and resulting in high levels of mismatch between levels of education and job opportunities. All our study families reside in Chennai, the largest city in the state that also serves as the state capital and its primary center for commercial and industrial activities. With slightly over 10 million residents, Chennai is considered a melting pot of cultures exhibiting tremendous diversity that is representative of many major Indian cities. Chennai's economy is fueled by car manufacturing ("the Detroit of South Asia"), IT and financial services, and a healthy dose of medical tourism.

In the third and final stage of our naturalistic sampling process, we sought to interview millennials who lived in geographic proximity with both their Generation X parent(s) and their baby boomer grandparent(s). These youth could be permanently employed, temporarily employed, or unemployed. Inasmuch as our research objectives called for us to observe cultural transmission, it was essential that this spatial closeness was accompanied by social interaction—interviewing the estranged, we felt, could only alienate our prospects of observing transference.

Using contacts that we had developed in each local labor market— key informants from business, government, social organizations, and academia—we were able to create rosters of families who met these criteria. From these lists, we selected 10 families where all three generations agreed to participate in a lengthy face-to-face interview and to make themselves available if follow-up was necessary. It is important to note that this sample selection is not random inasmuch as it does not represent all three-generational families in the region or even the local labor market. Notwithstanding this limitation, we do believe these cases resonate (Steinberg, 2015) conditions for familial socialization that are most likely to signal value transmission.

Relatively small numbers of observations have been a hallmark of both qualitative and quantitative naturalist inquiry. Stake (2006) notes that "the benefits of multi-case study will be limited if fewer than say 4 cases are chosen or more than 10" (p. 22). In their classic study of value orientations, Kluckhohn and Strodtbeck (1961) selected 20 adults each from five communities in a western state in the United States. When examining long-term unemployment in Europe, Lahusen and Giugni (2016) chose a sample of 120 long-term unemployed youth, 20 each from a city located in one of six European countries: Lyon, France; Cologne, Germany; Karlstad, Sweden; Turin, Italy; Geneva, Switzerland; and Kielce, Poland. Their objective was to explore in-depth any cross-national differences in hardship, stigmatization, source of blame, and kinship support. The previously mentioned medical innovation study by Coleman (Coleman, Katz, and Menzel, 1966) provides still another example, and there are many more. What ties these studies together is their need to generate intensive, in-depth data, a condition that often places substantial resource constraints on the number of cases and respondents that can be entertained.

One component of our in-depth interviews with family members was to have the respondent participate in a very demanding experiment in which each family member was asked to make a series of decisions from a set of

16 choice scenarios. We will have a good deal more to say about the stated preference experiment in Chapter 7; suffice it to say here that this process generated 2,880 separate decisions (16 × 180) and could not be carried out over the internet, by mail, or telephone—it had to be conducted face to face. Hence, the intensity of the experiment placed resource constraints on the case sample size (i.e., selection of skilled interviewers, the cost of those interviewers, etc.).

It is a fair question to ask if the inclusion of a rather complex experiment was necessary to examine cultural transmission: Could the interview have provided adequate information without it? If one believes that individual beliefs and attitudes (characteristics of the decision maker) are sufficient, the answer is yes, and the correct unit of observation and analysis is the individual. If you believe as we do that economic preferences are best measured and analyzed at the decision level, then the answer is no. This opinion is shared by Glaeser and his colleagues (2000) when they write: "Using experiments and surveys together allow you to measure preferences, behavioral propensities and other individual attributes more convincingly than surveys, since experiments provide direct observation of behavior" (p. 841). It is also shared by Caprar et al. (2015) as critical for the advancement of cultural studies in international business and management. In our view the field of cultural economics could benefit from more studies like those undertaken by Bigoni et al. (2013, 2016). The trust "games" (experiments) these researchers ran in four Italian cities provided insights on risk preference that we believe are more compelling than responses to social survey questions.

Family Interview Process

The interview schedule we utilized to elicit family member responses was structured around the conceptual model we adumbrated in Chapter 1 (see Figure 1.1). It contains two sections: the first contains questions around a cluster of eight attitudes and beliefs (characteristics of the individual family member) that we believe coalesce to form a direct measure of value orientation around work and employment. To reiterate, this cluster comprises the elements of trust, redistributive justice, education, training, work centrality, labor force attachment, risk-taking, cooperation, and individual achievement. Items used to measure these beliefs and attitudes were drawn from European Social Survey, the World Value Survey, European Community

Household Panel–Community Version, the GSS, and the Jagannathan, Camasso, Walker Project Access Work History Study. The first section of the instrument also contains a series of questions about cultural metaphors and is a direct test of the relevance of the deep measure of value orientations proposed by Gannon and his colleagues (Gannon and Pillai, 2016; Gannon, 2009). Responses to questions in this section of the interview schedule generate observations at the individual respondent level, which are analyzed at the individual respondent level.

In Section 2 of the schedule, we present the respondent with 16 choices (decisions/scenarios) designed to elicit how individuals value a set of five job attributes believed to be important factors in the literature on job acquisition and retention: job type, salary, skill set, prestige level, and job setting. This set of scenarios form the core of our experiment to observe actual preferences leading to behavior. In our conceptual model, they are viewed as deep measures of value orientation, providing us with observations at the decision level, which are, in turn, analyzed at the decision level. A copy of the entire interview schedule in English is provided in Appendix A. Copies of the document in Swedish, German, Italian, and Spanish are available from the authors.

Paid interviewers were selected from each local labor market on the basis of their familiarity with the geographic area, their capacity to conduct confidential and professional interviews and their willingness to disburse remuneration to respondents who completed the entire interview. Interviewers also had to agree to complete a short interviewer reaction sheet that was used by the authors to gauge the overall quality of each individual-interviewer interaction and to provide additional insights on data quality.

Each respondent was introduced to the interview through the reading of an explanation of the study and an informed consent protocol. The protocol, which appears as the second page in the interview schedule (see Appendix A), provides an assurance of confidentiality and describes the voluntary nature of the interview and the remuneration amount for completing the interview (25 euros or equivalent in country currency, if desired). All components of the interviewing process were reviewed under and approved by the Institutional Review Board process at Rutgers University. All family interviews except half of those in the United States were conducted in 2018; the balance of the American interviews was completed in early 2019.

In Table 5.1 we provide a profile of our multigenerational sample. The annual income distributions in each country labor market mirror to a large extent national level data presented in Chapter 4. The United States

Table 5.1 Description of the Study Sample

Demographic Characteristics	Johnholm				Christineberg				Reggio Maurizio				San Arco				Sherianne				Raazpuram			
	BB	GenX	Mill	All	BB	GenX	Mill	All	BB	GenX	Mill	All	BB	GenX	Mill	All	BB	GenX	Mill	All	BB	GenX	Mill	All
Gender (percentage of males)	40	50	40	43.3	20	20	50	30	20	30	80	43.3	50	50	60	53.3	20	20	30	23	60	70	70	66.7
Marital status percentage																								
Married	x	x	x	x	50	50	10	51	40	60	0	33	40	70	10	40	50	50	10	33	70	100	10	60
Never Married	x	x	x	x	10	0	90	31	0	0	70	30	0	10	90	31	10	0	100	33	0	0	90	30
Divorced/ Separated	x	x	x	x	0	50	0	17	10	33	0	13	10	10	0	7	0	30	0	10	0	0	0	0
Widowed	x	x	x	x	40	0	0	13	50	10	0	20	50	10	0	20	40	20	0	20	30	0	0	10
Religion: Mean religiosity scale (0 = min 10 = max)	4.1	7.0	1.8	2.9	6.8	2.3	3.7	4.3	6.8	6.4	4.1	5.8	6.6	4.7	1.6	4.3	6.2	6.9	4.5	5.9	8.5	8.5	6.8	7.9
Annual Income: Mean in euros (thousands)	18.5	47	23	31	32	51	30	37	21	26	17.5	23	22	31	17.5	26	28	66	24	46	17	13	11	15
Education level percentage																								
Completed Primary	100	100	100	**100**	100	90	**100**	98	60	100	100	**87**	70	100	100	**90**	100	100	100	**100**	90	80	80	**87**
Completed Secondary	100	60	100	**86**	100	90	**90**	93	60	80	100	**80**	60	70	100	77	100	90	80	70	80	80	80	**80**
Completed Tertiary	30	40	50	**40**	20	40	**40**	33	40	50	60	**50**	40	50	70	**53**	60	50	70	**60**	30	30	60	**40**

Notes: BB = baby boomer. Gen X = Generation Xers. Mill = millennials.

and Germany demonstrate the highest levels (most evident in the prime working age respondents of Generation X), followed closely by Sweden. The income distributions of the families in Italy (Sicily) and Spain (Andalusia) are considerably lower than national average, and this would be expected given the poorer economic performance of these regions. The relatively low and uniform income levels of Indians also comport well with national published data and are no doubt the consequence of surfeit of both skilled and unskilled labor.

When we examine the education distribution of our family respondents, in light of discussions in Chapter 3, the expected pattern of tertiary education becomes evident. Our samples indicate that Italians and Spanish achievement of a tertiary-level education is consistently higher across generations than it is in Sweden and Germany. India, especially the millennials in the sample, demonstrates an increased orientation to postsecondary education. Our American sample, however, reveals the highest tendency toward tertiary education, a phenomenon we have also detailed in Chapter 3.

As we have shown in previous research on cultural economics, religion has often been used to gauge culture in countries. In a recent study by the Pew Research Center (2018), researchers find that Sweden ranks lowest on the importance of religion in daily life (17 percent) followed in order by Germany (46 percent), Spain (49 percent), Italy (70 percent), the United States (72 percent), and India, where 90 percent of survey takers report that religion is important in their lives. Note that this same order can be found in our intergenerational sample. What is also clear from both the Pew Center and our respondents is that millennials rank lowest in religiosity, dramatically so in Spain and much less so in India, the United States, and Italy.

With respect to marital status, our sample is an imperfect representation of the crude marriage rate rankings that distinguish the six countries. According to the most recent OECD and United Nations figures, these rates per thousand population are as follows: Italy, 3.4; Spain, 3.7; Germany, 5.0; Sweden, 5.4; the United States, 6.9; and India, 7.8. As Table 5.1 shows in the study sample, India exhibits the highest percentage of married respondents and Italy, the lowest. The United States sample, however, has a proportion of married respondents (33 percent) that is not different from that of Italy and is slightly less than proportions found in Germany and Spain. The marital status of respondents was not asked in Sweden so we do not know where our Swedish sample ranks on this variable.

In conclusion, Table 5.1 indicates that the overall sex ratios of our country sample (i.e., men to 100 women) range from a low of 23 per 100 in Sherianne to well over 60 men to 100 women in Raazpuram. The ratios in the other labor markets range from 30 per 100 in Christineberg to 53 per 100 women in San Arco. The relatively low sex ratios in some of our samples are driven in part by the higher age-specific death rates of men.

Our profile of individual characteristics show wide variation across labor markets on a number of demographic measures, which is to be expected given the cultural and economic variations that we have witnessed in our national comparisons of labor market supply and demand. Hence, it is important to take these characteristics into consideration when performing any statistical analyses to help obviate their potential confounding effects, which we do.

6

Attitudes, Beliefs, Intentions, and Metaphors Over Time and in Place

Description and Analysis

As time goes on the underlying realities of situations tend to disappear in a tissue of metaphor.

— Thorstein Veblen, *The Place of Science in Modern Civilization* (1919/1990)

In this chapter we contrast national and intergenerational responses of our study samples to a constellation of attitudes, beliefs, and the behavioral intentions they signal that have been linked to economic activity. In Chapter 1 (Figure 1.1), eight components of this constellation were identified as the measurable manifestations of value orientations with the potential to serve as the stimuli for updated value orientations in the subsequent generations.

We examine these data in three ways: (a) we first provide descriptive information on country similarities and differences along with intergenerational stability and/or changes; (b) second, we conduct more direct comparisons of country and generation effects using a variety of multivariate statistical techniques; and (c) third, we discuss how our findings correspond or diverge from existing literature. Keeping in mind Becker's (1996) admonition that preferences for individual consumption should be assumed endogenous unless empirically shown to be otherwise, we extend this same caveat to a set of beliefs, attitudes, and intentions that can be interpreted as indirect measures of utility seeking behavior. As we articulated in Chapter 5, our approach to establishing the independent impact of cultural values is to utilize multigenerations as a proxy measure of changing economic conditions including wage and price fluctuations and economic growth and decline within a country. If country differences in beliefs, attitudes, and intentions persist while controlling statistically for the within-country economic changes

Caught in the Cultural Preference Net. Michael J. Camasso and Radha Jagannathan, Oxford University Press (2021).
© Oxford University Press. DOI: 10.1093/oso/9780190672782.003.0006

signaled by generational succession, we maintain that cultural stability across nations exerts an exogenous influence. Obversely, if generational succession exerts a statistically significant influence while country does not, we cite this as evidence of the influence that changing economic conditions has on modifications in value orientations.[1] Of course, it is possible that neither country nor generation could be responsible for the variance found in a particular attitude or belief, in which case the wisdom for its utility as an integral component in advancing the culture versus economic conditions debate can be questioned.

The Importance of Trust

The critical role that both trusting (by the one who trusts) and trustworthiness (of the one who is trusted) have on the economic enterprise has been discussed in Chapter 2. We asked our family respondents three questions around this issue, and their reactions are shown in Table 6.1. In Panel A, we show the mean level of response to a 10-point trust-ranking scale. It is clear that Reggio Maurizio exhibits the lowest overall trusting levels while Johnholm has the highest levels. Somewhat unexpected, if the existing literature is used as a guide, is the relatively high levels of trusting observed in San Arco—levels that mirror those in Raazpuram and are higher than those of both American and German respondents. While millennials have the highest trusting levels across generations in Christineberg, Reggio Maurizio, and Raazpuram, they have the lowest in Johnholm and Sherianne.

In Panels B and C of Table 6.1, we contrast responses to questions about learning trustworthiness and trusting in the home. While the former appears to receive universal acceptance in all but Christineberg and Raazpuram, the latter quality exhibits variability across country and over generations. In Christineberg, the trend in "yes" responses is positive across generations while in Reggio Maurizio, it is negative. In the other labor market areas, there

---

[1] We recognize that our use of intergenerational data here to help disentangle cultural impacts from those generated by economic activity does not guarantee complete orthogonality. While our three generations cover a wide variety of economic institutions (markets) and environments (labor supply and demand conditions within countries), they can also contain the influences of independently changing preferences and beliefs, a point made by Fernandez (2008) and Guiso, Sapienza, and Zingales (2008), among others. If the latter are significant, our obverse condition does not provide an uncontaminated estimate of the influence of economic circumstances. Strong intracountry generational effects, moreover, would be expected to attenuate cross country effects and therefore underestimate the total effect of intercountry culture.

Table 6.1 Indicators of Trusting Attitudes and Behavioral Intentions: Country and Generational Comparisons

	Generation Labor Market					
	Johnholm	Christineberg	Reggio Maurizio	San Arco	Sherianne	Raazpuram
Panel A: Most people can be trusted[a]						
Baby boomers	6.50	4.50	4.10	5.20	5.00	5.30
Generation Xers	7.30	4.30	2.00	5.90	4.80	5.40
Millennials	5.90	5.00	4.50	5.60	4.40	5.50
Overall	6.57	4.60	3.60	5.57	4.73	5.40
Panel B. Trustworthiness is a quality to be learned at home[b]						
Baby Boomers	100	66	100	100	100	70
Generation Xers	100	90	100	100	100	70
Millennials	100	80	100	100	100	70
Overall	100	79	100	100	100	70
Panel C: Trusting others is a quality to be learned at home[b]						
Baby boomers	90	63	89	90	90	60
Generation Xers	100	70	80	80	100	60
Millennials	90	80	44	80	80	50
Overall	93	71	71	83	90	57
N = 180						

[a]Scored on a scale from zero (not trusted) to 10 (trusted).
[b]Percentage answering "yes" to yes/no question.

appears to be stability at rather high levels, except in Raazpuram where the stability is moderate.

While descriptive data can provide insights into country and generational differences, they do not provide a formal statistical mechanism to test the relative impact of nation and generation on a component of value orientation. For this reason, we have conducted a series of multivariate regression analyses with measures of each of the eight components of value orientation serving as the dependent variable and country and generation categories used as regressors (independent variables). To facilitate the algebraic identification of these regression models the baby boom generation and liberal free market economies of Sherianne (U.S.) and Raazpuram (India) serve as reference categories. When the dependent variable was measured as continuous (e.g., the trust scale), we employed ordinary least squares regression (OLS); when the dependent variable was measured as a dichotomy or polytomy, we utilized binomial or multinomial logit. The detailed results of these regression analyses are listed in Appendix B.

With respect to the trust scale shown in Panel A of Table 6.1 our multivariate analyses show that Johnholm respondents demonstrate a statistically significant 1.5-unit higher level of trust compared to Sherianne and Raazpuram while Reggio Maurizio has a marginal effect that is nearly 1.5 units lower than the reference category, an effect that is also statistically significant. None of the other country effects are significant, nor are any of the generation effects. Hence, the multivariate results here closely mirror the inferences we could tentatively draw from the descriptive data. Inasmuch as there is limited variation in the question–response pattern depicted in Panel B—an almost unanimous consensus that "trustworthiness is a quality that is to be learned at home"—we turn our attention to the third measure of trust shown in Panel C. The results of a logistic regression of the "yes" or "no" dependent variable on country labor market and generation categories show a significant positive effect of Johnholm residence; however, none of the other country or generation independent variables are significant. Because the regression coefficients in a logit are linear in the log(odds), it is necessary to exponentiate a coefficient before interpretation is possible. In the case of Johnholm, this regression coefficient is 1.6 and its exponent is 4.95—that is, the odds of learning to trust others is nearly five times that of the reference countries, holding generation and other country variables constant.[2]

Our sample findings on trust are largely in accord with the country-specific literature we reviewed in Chapter 2. The trust deficit in Italy, especially southern Italy, has been documented by Guiso, Sapienza, and Zingales (2006), Bigoni et al. (2016, 2018), Tabellini (2008a), and Banfield and Fasano

---

[2] Since the logit model represents a nonlinear functional form, that is, the logit or (log[u/1−u]), marginal effects are not simple representations of the regression coefficients as they are in linear regression. There are generally two ways to express marginal effects in such models: the effect on the probability of the outcome and the effect of the transformed predictor on the odds (exp[B]). We have chosen the latter in this book because of its relatively seamless extension of the descriptive analyses we have undertaken. See, for example, Hosmer and Lemeshow (2000).

(1958), among others. Conversely, the trust surfeit in Sweden has also been the subject of considerable discussion (Esping-Andersen, 1985, 2002; Schumpeter, 1962; Hofstede, Hofstede, and Minkov, 2010, Gannon and Pillai, 2016; Hall and Soskice, 2001) as has the importance of trust in the creation of coordinated economic markets that appears to work well for business and labor.

Redistributive Justice

There is some controversy about the role that income redistributive justice plays in stimulating economic activity generally and engaging in work related behavior specifically. Recall the assertion by Ostry et al. (2014) representing the International Monetary Fund that wealth redistribution is necessary to promote a pro-growth economy. This has also been the position of OECD (Causa, de Serres, and Ruiz, 2015; Naquib, 2015). As we have seen, Sweden, with its GINI coefficient of 25.7, ranks lowest in inequality among our six-country study sample, and the United States (37.8) and India (47.9) rank the highest, with Germany, Spain, and Italy somewhere in the middle.

In Table 6.2, we present the responses of our sample to three measures designed to tap attitudes around income distribution. In Panel A, we see that the Swedish family members opine in a fashion that is virtually indistinguishable from that of Sherianne and Raazpuram. In contrast, respondents from Reggio Maurizio and San Arco, regardless of generation, are more likely to agree with the notion that everyone has a right to a minimal income. The Johnholm responses would be more of a surprise if Swedish labor force participation rates and the stigma of not leading a productive life are ignored. That generations within countries exhibit stable response patterns is unexpected given the apparent difficulties that millennials face in capitalist economies and their increased calls for government intervention (OECD, 2019; Schuck and Shore, 2019; Guillaud, 2013).

Panels B and C of Table 6.2 show sample responses to two yes/no questions about money redistribution in cases of people who cannot work and people who do not want to work. With respect to the former question, we see a broad consensus across labor markets and over generations that redistributing money to those who cannot work is a highly favored response. The one exception is Raazpuram, where each generation is split—here religiosity and the notion of predestination may come into consideration. In Panel

Table 6.2 Indicators of Redistribution Justice Attitudes and Behavioral Intentions: Country and Generational Comparisons

| | Generation Labor Market | | | | | |
	Johnholm	Christineberg	Reggio Maurizio	San Arco	Sherianne	Raazpuram
Panel A. Right to a minimal income[a]						
Baby Boomers	2.22	3.00	3.60	3.60	2.40	2.20
Generation Xers	2.30	3.11	3.90	3.10	2.20	2.20
Millennials	2.80	2.20	3.20	3.70	2.70	2.60
Overall	2.45	2.78	3.57	3.47	2.43	2.33
Panel B. Money should be given to those who cannot work.[b]						
Baby boomers	90	100	90	90	100	50
Generation Xers	90	70	90	100	90	50
Millennials	100	66	100	100	90	50
Overall	93	79	93	97	93	50
Panel C: Money should be given to those who do not want to work.						
Baby boomers	0	0	0	0	0	10
Generation Xers	0	20	0	10	0	20
Millennials	10	11	0	20	20	20
Overall	3	10	0	10	7	17
N = 180						

[a]Scored on a scale from zero (strongly disagree) to 10 (strongly agree).
[b]Percentage answering agree to agree/disagree question.

C, we also see broad consensus, but here it is disagreement with the statement that is pervasive. If there is an exception to this general opinion, it is among millennials; in Johnholm, San Arco, Sherianne, and Raazpuram, this younger generation demonstrates a slightly higher level of agreement than do baby boomers and Generation Xers.

Our multivariate findings (Appendix B) tend to be consistent with observations that can be made from the descriptive statistics. The OLS coefficients from the regression of "right to minimum income" (Table 6.2, Panel A) on labor market and generation are 1.18 for Reggio Maurizio and

1.08 for San Arco—over 1 unit of agreement higher than Sherianne and Raazpuram. They are also the only statistically significant coefficients in this regression model. The logistic regression of "cannot work" (Table 6.2, Panel B) shows that Reggio Maurizio and San Arco are more likely to agree to such redistribution, the former by a factor of 6 (exp[1.73]) and the latter by a factor of 11 (exp[2.47]) than in Raazpuram/Sherianne. Johnholm families also manifest a statistically significant level of agreement when compared with the reference category. In the logistic regression of "do not want to work," the only statistically significant effect we find is a generational one—millennials are nine times more likely than their grandparents (exp[2.24]) to favor giving money to this hypothetical group of people.

These findings around the redistribution of wealth indicate that the distinction between the "deserving" and "undeserving" remains quite real. Despite the small (yet statistically significant) effect of millennial approval of financial aid for "those not willing to work," there is a clear demarcation in every labor market except Raazpuram. If the data show that the "work ethic" is alive and well, it also points up a more nuanced interpretation of redistributive justice that depends to some extent on the prevailing economy and perhaps the unchanging economic conditions in a country. Respondents in both Reggio Maurizio and San Arco across three generations express stronger opinions concerning the right to a minimal income than other labor markets in the sample. Both Italy and Spain have experienced decades of slow economic growth after a period of economic expansion in the 1950s through early 1970s. Hence, in these labor markets—and, by extension, countries—respondents may well be reacting to wealth redistribution by taking into account persistent macrolevel failure.

Human Capital Formation through Education and Training

We have discussed the essential function that human capital development has in linking individuals to the labor force in Chapter 3. There we considered the personal and institutional choices that are made in countries concerning the provision of general and specialized education and training; the level of coordination among business, government, and unions; and the incentives for business-paid apprenticeship and opportunities for entrepreneurship and new business start-up. Also discussed was the emphasis a nation places on basic skills in math and science and the education/training systems' flexibility in meeting the demands of an increasingly global economy.

In Table 6.3, we describe the responses of our three-generational family members to queries about the importance of acquiring good mathematics skills, basic knowledge of science, and learning a second language. In Panel A, we display the percentage of respondents answering "yes" to a question about the importance of acquiring good math skills. Here we see a rather

Table 6.3 Indicators of Investing in Human Capital—Education and Training: Country and Generational Comparisons

	Generation Labor Market					
	Johnholm	Christineberg	Reggio Maurizio	San Arco	Sherianne	Raazpuram
Panel A. Importance of learning good mathematics skills[a]						
Baby boomers	67	78	90	90	80	80
Generation Xers	33	60	33	60	80	90
Millennials	50	60	67	50	70	80
Overall	50	66	63	67	77	83
Panel B. Importance of learning a second language[a]						
Baby boomers	67	50	100	100	70	70
Generation Xers	56	70	80	100	60	90
Millennials	70	70	67	100	90	80
Overall	64	63	82	100	73	80
Panel C Importance of learning basic science knowledge[a]						
Baby boomers	56	60	78	90	90	90
Generation Xers	44	60	50	90	70	100
Millennials	60	40	67	90	80	70
Overall	54	53	64	90	80	87
N = 177						

[a]Percentage answering agree to agree/disagree question.

sharp diminution in positive responses from baby boomers to Generation Xers and continuing through millennials in Johnholm, Christineberg, Reggio Maurizio, and San Arco. In Sherianne and Raazpuram, high levels of valuation are maintained across generations.

In Panel B of Table 6.3, we show the positive responses to a question about the importance of learning a second language. With the exception of the generational drop-off in Reggio Maurizio, there appears to be a trend in increasing valuations of this skill across countries. The proportion of millennials acknowledging the value of a second language is higher than baby boomers and Generation Xers in three out of six labor markets. In Panel C, respondents were asked to assess the importance of basic science skills in a curriculum of education and training. Along with math skills, some knowledge of fundamental science principles have been identified by economists as essential tools in an expanding information and STEM-based economy (Vogel, 2015; CEDEFOP, 2018b; Desilver, 2017). What is unexpected in these basic science distributions is the overall lower levels of importance assigned to basic science learning in Johnholm and Christineberg. As we have seen, both Sweden and Germany maintain school-to-work connections between businesses, government, and educational institutions, which facilitate youth entry into the labor market with skill sets that support high-end, value-added goods and services for export. The reason behind this apparent irony may lie in the question wording and its failure to distinguish applied and basic science—distinctions that are perhaps more tangible in Johnholm and Christineberg than they are in labor markets where varying forms of general education predominate.

The multivariate analyses of the human capital measures introduced in Table 6.3 indicate that generation is the most important factor when the subject is math skills. The odds that millennials value math are less than half (exp[−0.939]) those of their grandparents. The odds that Generation Xers value math are even lower (i.e., about one third). In our analyses of basic science skills, on the other hand, we find statistically significant country effects but none for generation. Johnholm and Christineberg respondents exhibit odds of favoring basic science learning that are less than one third (exp[−1.48]) those of Sherianne and Raazpuram, a finding that closely mirrors what is observed in the descriptive tabulations.

In summary, the findings around our (quite limited) set of human capital measures provide a mixed picture. Generally, baby boomers place higher value on acquiring math, a second language, and basic science skills, especially math skills. Given a global labor market driven by information and STEM, this is not a generational schism that is either expected or encouraging.

Belief in the Centrality of Work

Work centrality, also referred to rather loosely as work commitment, has been viewed as an essential ingredient for social integration and democratic capitalism (Deci and Ryan, 2000; Esser and Lindh, 2018; Hauff and Kirchner, 2015). Work supplies individuals with a sense of worth that can be manifest through extrinsic and/or intrinsic rewards, with millennials hypothesized to value the latter more than their parents or grandparents (Esser and Lindh, 2018; Hauff and Kirchner, 2015).

In our efforts to gauge the importance of work centrality in a multi-nation and multigenerational context, we examine the three variables that are listed in Table 6.4. Panel A shows the mean levels of response to a Likert scaled question about receiving money without having to work. The highest level of humiliation is found in Raazpuram and the lowest occurs in San Arco. The table also indicates that millennials are less likely than their parents or grandparents to express shame. The lower levels of humiliation in Christineberg, especially in Generation Xers and among millennials, are somewhat surprising.

The answers to a query about the priority of work appears in Panel B of Table 6.4. Here we see a rather sharp decline among millennials in Johnholm, San Arco, and Raazpuram in work priority—a decline that reflects a linear trend across generations. In Christineberg and Reggio Maurizio, millennials have a lower priority than do their parents. As was the case in Panel A, Christineberg respondents, regardless of generation, expressed the lowest levels of work priority. Lastly, in Panel C, we show the percentages of respondents who would continue to work even if money was not necessary to live comfortably. In Johnholm, San Arco, and Raazpuram, over two thirds of family members said they would continue to work; this percentage was 50 to 60 percent in Christineberg, Reggio Maurizio, and Sherianne.

If the reader turns to Appendix B, he or she will find the regression results from our multivariate analyses of work centrality. Millennials display a nearly one half-unit decrease in agreement (compared with their grandparents) with the statement that receiving money without working is humiliating, an

Table 6.4 Indicators of the Centrality of Work Attitudes and Behavioral
Intentions: Country and Generational Comparisons

	Generation Labor Market					
	Johnholm	Christineberg	Reggio Maurizio	San Arco	Sherianne	Raazpuram
Panel A. It is humiliating to receive money without having to work[a]						
Baby boomers	3.44	3.22	3.50	3.00	3.60	4.50
Generation Xers	3.40	2.78	4.00	2.80	2.60	4.40
Millennials	3.00	2.70	2.90	2.20	2.90	4.40
Overall	3.38	2.89	3.46	2.66	3.03	4.43
Panel B. Work should always come first[a]						
Baby boomers	4.22	2.56	2.90	3.80	3.10	3.70
Generation Xers	3.70	3.33	3.20	3.20	3.30	4.10
Millennials	2.30	2.20	2.50	2.20	3.00	2.80
Overall	3.38	2.68	2.86	3.07	3.13	3.53
Panel C. Would continue working even if you don't need the money[b]						
Baby Boomers	78	50	30	70	38	60
Generation Xers	80	50	50	60	80	80
Millennials	60	70	70	70	50	90
Overall	72	57	50	67	57	77
N = 180						

[a]Scored on a scale from zero (strongly disagree) to 5 (strongly agree).
[b]Percentage answering continue to continue/stop working question.

effect that is statistically significant. Residents of Christineberg and San Arco also indicate lower levels of agreement with this statement relative to Sherianne and Raazpuram, and these effects are also statistically significant. Millennials demonstrate a nearly nine tenths-unit decrease in agreement with the statement "Work should always come first"; the only other statistically significant effect is found in Christineberg where residence is associated with a nearly two-third-unit decrease in agreement relative to Sherianne and Raazpuram. The logistic regression of the work centrality measure "continue to work even if not an economic necessity" did not produce any statistically significant findings.

While our findings do not confirm the value differences across social democratic, liberal, and Mediterranean countries observed by Gallie (2019), we do find significant differences over generations. In this instance, our findings agree with those of Twenge et al. (2010), Ljunge (2011), and Van Den Broeck et al. (2019), among others, that millennials are more defined by the aphorism "I work to live" rather than by its converse "I live to work."

Labor Force Attachment

To gauge the level of commitment to labor force participation we asked respondents two questions, which appear in Table 6.5. In Panel A, family members were queried about their actual or projected involvement in

Table 6.5 Indicators of Attachment to Labor Force—Attitudes and Behavioral Intentions: Country and Generational Comparisons

	Generation Labor Market					
	Johnholm	Christineberg	Reggio Maurizio	San Arco	Sherianne	Raazpuram
Panel A. Percentage involved in paid work or retired at the time of Interview						
Baby boomers	90	95	80	60	40	60
Generation Xers	100	100	50	40	60	50
Millennials	50	50	30	10	40	50
Overall	80	82	53	37	47	53
Panel B. Hard work is a quality to be learned at home[a]						
Baby boomers	45	100	88	70	100	100
Generation Xers	78	90	90	70	100	100
Millennials	40	80	89	100	100	100
Overall	54	90	89	80	100	100
N = 177						

[a]Percentage answering "yes" to yes/no question.

full-time paid work. We see that millennials are less likely to report labor force attachment actions or intentions than their parents or grandparents. Certainly, some of this difference is a function of ongoing education and/ or training; however, in Reggio Maurizio and San Arco, lack of employment opportunities is an important contributor. The overall high proportions of respondents expressing actual or intentional labor force participation in Johnholm and Christineberg is expected, given the cultures of vocational and specific knowledge that predominate in these labor markets (Ulijn and Fayolle, 2004; Zimmermann et al., 2013; German Federal Ministry of Education, 2014; Esping-Andersen, 1985, 2002; Bergquist, 2016; Lahusen and Givigni, 2016).

In Panel B of Table 6.5, we give the percentage of respondents answering "yes" to the statement "Hard work is a quality to be learned at home." With the exception of Johnholm, respondents of all country groups overwhelmingly were in agreement. The baby boomers and millennials in Johnholm were less fervent than Generation Xers, begging an additional question (which was not asked) about where this value should be learned. Our conjecture is that the response would mostly likely be "in the labor force."

The lack of variation in the responses to the hard work question prevented any multivariate analyses of this measure; however, the variability in responses to the labor force attachment question did permit the estimation of a logistic regression. Two statistically significant effects were obtained: the odds of millennial labor force participation are less than a quarter ($\exp[-1.745]$) of those of their grandparents, while the odds are five times greater in Johnholm than they are in Sherianne or Raazuram. Millennial involvement in ongoing education or training could account for a portion of the difference; it is unlikely however that it would explain all the difference.

Risk-Taking Behavior

It would be difficult to deny the critical function of risk taking in the creation and maintenance of healthy market capitalism. In Table 6.6, we show three statements used to elicit responses around risk taking from our study sample. In Panel A, the mean scores on a 11-point risk taker scale are arrayed. Here we see that San Arco residents exhibit the highest score followed by Sherianne, Raazpuram, and Johnholm. As one would expect, millennials typically demonstrate a more risk-taking attitude than others in their family.

Table 6.6 Indicators of Risk Taking Attitudes and Behavioral Intentions: Country and Generational Comparisons

	Generation Labor Market					
	Johnholm	Christineberg	Reggio Maurizio	San Arco	Sherianne	Raazpuram
Panel A. Generally I am a risk taker						
Baby boomers	3.40	2.60	2.20	6.30	5.80	4.70
Generation Xers	6.30	4.66	6.50	6.00	6.10	6.30
Millennials	6.60	5.70	5.60	7.40	5.90	6.44
Overall	5.43	4.31	4.77	6.56	5.93	5.76
Panel B. Invest in savings bonds rather than stocks						
Baby boomers	30	67	44	90	33	100
Generation Xers	60	22	30	98	10	90
Millennials	44	44	20	70	50	70
Overall	45	44	31	79	30	86
Panel C. Bet on a sure thing rather than a long shot[b]						
Baby boomers	100	56	80	100	100	100
Generation Xers	90	56	60	70	40	60
Millennials	70	78	70	40	60	80
Overall	87	63	70	70	66	79
N = 180						

[a]Scored on a scale from zero (risk avoider) to 10 (risk taker).

[b]Percentage answering agree to agree/disagree question.

Our labor market rankings closely parallel those of the country rankings published by Bosma and Kelly (2018) in the National Entrepreneurial Context Index. In the National Entrepreneurial Context Index, India has a score of 5; the United States, 6; Spain, 16; Sweden, 18; Germany, 19; and Italy, 40. Our sample rankings also conform closely to those offered by Hofstede, Hofstede, and Minkov (2010) on their dimension of uncertainty avoidance with the exception of Spain, which is ranked high on avoiding risks. They also track very well, without exception, with the uncertainty avoidance rankings published by House et al. (2004).

In Panel B of Table 6.6, we ask respondents if they would rather invest in savings bonds than in the more risky stock market. In San Arco and Raazpuram, there is a general consensus among family members that a conservative investment strategy through savings bonds is preferred over the stock market. The volatility of stocks in India and Spain could be a factor in these cases, or these responses may stem from a more general mistrust of this institution in Raazpuram and San Arco. The relatively low levels of agreement in Sherianne, Johnholm, and Christineberg are anticipated given the strong economies in the United States, Sweden, and Germany but are not expected in Reggio Maurizio where the economy is more sluggish.

Responses to our third measure of risk-taking, "betting on a sure thing rather than a long shot" are shown in Panel C of Table 6.6. Large majorities of family members in all six labor markets agree with the "sure thing" option. Millennials in San Arco are the group who appear to be most likely to take a risk, which is consistent with the risk scale scores in Panel A.

In Appendix B, we provide the results from the multivariate examination of generational and local labor market effects. There are strong generational effects evident from the OLS regression of risk-taking on our country and generation categorical (dummy) variables. Millennial and Generation X respondents are more inclined than baby boomers to report themselves as risk takers. In the case of millennials, the extent is approximately 2 scale units, and for Generation Xers, 1.8 units—both are statistically significant. There are also significant labor market effects for Reggio Maurizio and Christineberg, with the former about 1 unit lower and the later 1½ units lower than the liberal capitalist reference category. Our logistic regression results for the savings bond–stocks decision indicate only one statistically significant result, for Reggio Maurizio. The odds in this labor market are only about a third (exp[−1.16]) of those respondents in the reference category. On the other hand, the odds of residents in San Arco are 2.5 times greater, but this effect is accompanied by an alpha-level error of 0.06. Lastly, the logistic regression on the sure thing versus the long shot choice reveals only statistically significant generational effects. For millennials, the odds of betting on a sure thing are less than a fourth (exp[−1.51]) of those of their grandparents, and those of their parents are even less—about a fifth, (exp[−1.66]).

Evidence of Social Capital

Along with trust, there is a good deal of research that has shown social capital in the form that engenders cooperation and bridging among
individuals is critical for economic growth and efficiency (Putnam,
1995, 2000; Guiso, Sapienza, and Zingales, 2004; Esser, 2008). In Table
6.7 we show scores of our sample on a scale of bridging capital and
sample responses to two measures of group cooperation. In Panel A, the
means listed represent the average number of voluntary organizations
that individuals belong to. The 15 items that comprised this additive
scale were reprised from the World Values Survey and included many

Table 6.7 Indicators of Cooperative Attitudes and Behavioral
Intentions: Country and Generational Comparisons

	Generation Labor Market					
	Johnholm	Christineberg	Reggio Maurizio	San Arco	Sherianne	Raazpuram
Panel A. Volunteering organization and activities score						
Baby Boomers	2.60	1.30	0.60	1.00	2.40	1.50
Generation X	2.60	1.60	1.00	2.00	2.90	0.90
Millennials	2.60	1.30	1.20	2.20	2.70	1.00
Overall	2.60	1.40	0.93	1.73	2.67	1.13
Panel B. Majority rule is best[a]						
Baby Boomers	70	80	40	70	57	60
Generation X	80	70	30	67	50	50
Millennials	67	67	33	10	80	30
Overall	72	72	34	48	62	47
Panel C. Best ideas come from people working together[a]						
Baby Boomers	70	90	80	100	90	90
Generation X	70	40	80	90	80	60
Millennials	80	89	70	90	70	70
Overall	80	79	77	93	79	73
N = 179						

[a]Percentage answering agree to agree/disagree question.

of the organizations listed by Putnam (2000, 2007) in his study of social relationships.[3]

In Panel A of Table 6.7, it is clear that Johnholm and Sherianne share the forefront of organizational membership. While the position of Johnholm is not surprising given Sweden's proclivity for coordination and cooperation, that of Sherianne is unexpected given Putnam's (1995) *Bowling Alone* thesis and similar critiques of Americans' more recent penchant of going it alone. Part of an explanation appears to lie in religiosity and related church-going of our Sherianne sample members.

Obversely, the lower organizational activity scores of San Arco, Christineberg, and Reggio Maurizio are congruous with the relatively low levels of institutional collectivism reported by House et al. (2004) and "embeddedness" in the work of Schwartz (1994). Recall McClelland's (1964) observation of a German value orientation where belief in the common-wealth trumps the need for affiliation (p. 73). Reggio Maurizio's position at the very bottom of the scale, moreover, could be anticipated if the accumu-lated research on suspicion and betrayal in southern Italy is accepted as con-vincing (see, e.g., Tabellini, 2008b, Bigoni et al., 2018; Guiso, Sapienza, and Zingales, 2004).

When family members were asked to answer with "agree" to "disagree" (Table 6.7, Panel B) with the statement "Majority rule is best," the responses form along the lines of Esping-Andersen typology (2002) with social dem-ocratic Johnholm and corporatist/continental Christineberg in agree-ment most often, followed by liberal market representatives Sherianne and Raazpuram, and Mediterranean Reggio Maurizio and San Arco, in agree-ment the least. One is also struck by the relative consistency in answers across generations with labor markets; San Arco is the exception with millennials expressing a view that is contrary to their parents or grandparents.

In Panel C of Table 6.7, we give the percentage distributions of "agree" responses to a statement asserting that the best ideas come from people working together. Over generations and cross labor markets, there is very strong support for this notion.

---

[3] The items included in the scale comprise memberships in social welfare services, religious or-ganizations, education/arts associations, trade unions, political parties, community action groups, human rights groups, conservation/environmental groups, professional associations, youth organi-zations, sports teams, women's groups, peace movements, animal rights groups, and health advocacy associations.

When we subject the three measures depicted in Table 6.7 to multivariate analysis, we find our Panel C measure is not subject to any statistically significant generational or labor market effects. This is also the case with our Panel B measure, although the signs of the labor market logit coefficients form a pattern, which is consistent with the descriptive data shown earlier. The regression analysis of organizational activity scale (Panel A), on the other hand, reveals that Reggio Maurizio respondents have an organizational engagement score that is nearly 1 unit (one organization) lower than the liberal market respondents while Johnholm respondents have a score that is 0.7 units higher. Christineberg family members also have a lower score than the reference groups, about one half unit, but this effect is not statistically significant.

The Need for Individual Achievement

Together with risk-taking behavior, individual achievement motivation occupies the ideological center of liberal market capitalism. In any number of cross-national studies, the United States is the undisputed leader in the need for individual achievement (Hofstede, Hofstede, and Minkov, 2010; McClelland, 1964, Collins, Hanges, and Locke, 2004). And, as we have noted in Chapter 2, individualism has been identified as an antidote to fatalism and the contraction in economic activity that it portends.

In Table 6.8 we provide the results of our descriptive analysis of the three measures of individual achievement motivation. Panel A recounts generational and labor market agreement with the statement "The best prepared people are the most successful." While the levels of agreement in Sherianne are, indeed, high, Christineberg and Raazpuram boast even higher levels. In each labor market, except Raazpuram, millennials report the lowest levels of agreement, and in San Arco, this disagreement is strikingly pronounced.

Does the best man or woman deserve to win? The proportions of family members who answered "agree" are given in Panel B of Table 6.8. Responses follow an Esping-Andersen categorization but do so in an unanticipated fashion. Sherianne and Raazpuram report the lowest levels of agreement while social democratic Johnholm and corporatist Christineberg have the highest. Mediterranean San Arco and Reggio Maurizio occupy the middle position with about three quarters of individuals in agreement. The lower

Table 6.8 Indicators of Individual Achievement and Motivation: Country and Generational Comparisons

| | Generation Labor Market | | | | | |
	Johnholm	Christineberg	Reggio Maurizio	San Arco	Sherianne	Raazpuram
Panel A. The best prepared people are most successful[a]						
Baby Boomers	70.0	89.0	70.0	80.0	67.0	100.0
Generation X	80.0	77.0	30.0	50.0	90.0	90.0
Millennials	50.0	75.0	60.0	30.0	60.0	100.0
Overall	67.0	81.0	53.3	53.3	72.5	96.5
Panel B. The best man/woman deserves to win[a]						
Baby Boomers	100.0	100.0	80.0	100.0	100.0	66.7
Generation X	80.0	50.0	50.0	60.0	60.0	50.0
Millennials	80.0	100.0	80.0	70.0	50.0	50.0
Overall	86.7	82.7	70.0	75.8	69.0	55.2
Panel C. Winning or losing is not important[a]						
Baby Boomers	90.0	50.0	100.0	100.0	89.0	90.0
Generation X	70.0	70.0	90.0	90.0	60.0	100.0
Millennials	60.0	67.0	70.0	80.0	69.0	93.3
Overall	73.0	62.0	87.0	90.0	73.0	93.3
N = 175						

[a]Percentage answering agree to agree/disagree question.

proportion of agreement to this item in Raazpuram, which may well be a reflection of religious philosophy, specifically an acknowledgment of the power of predestination. The lower proportion in Sherianne may stem from an explanation much closer to earth; namely, millennials' disaffection with a highly competitive economic system.

In Panel C of Table 6.8, family members were requested to either "agree" or "disagree" with the statement "Winning or losing is not important," it's how you play the game of life, the economic game, etc. Raazpuram residents, regardless of generation, expressed nearly unanimous agreement with this statement. The residents of San Arco and Reggio Maurizio also registered strong agreement. Only in Christineberg were agreement magnitudes some-what depressed, and this took place over all three generations.

Inasmuch as all three measures of individual achievement were meas-ured as simple dichotomies, we used logistic regression to test the simulta-neous impact of generation and labor market. For the achievement indicator "The best prepared people are most successful," we find statistically signif-icant effects for both generation and labor market. Millennials and their parents both have odds of agreement that are fractions of those communi-cated by baby boomers. In the instance of former, the odds are about a third $(\exp[-1.10])$, and for the latter, about two fifths $(\exp[-0.976])$. Consistent with our description of Panel A in Table 6.8, we find that Reggio Maurizio and San Arco have much lower odds of agreeing with the statement than do the families from Raazpuram or Sherianne (1/25, or $\exp[-3.32]$). The fami-lies of Johnholm are also less likely but in this labor market the odds decrease by 6.5 percent $(\exp[-2.73])$.

The results of the logistic regression regarding the statement "The best man/woman deserves to win" also reveals statistically significant generation and labor market impacts. Millennials and Generation Xers once again ex-hibit coefficients that suggests odds of agreement that are mere fractions of grandparents, specifically, one fourth $(\exp[-1.46])$ and one eighth $(\exp[-2.07])$, respectively. Families from Johnholm and Christineberg had significantly higher odds than families in the labor markets of Raazpuram and Sherianne, with Johnholm residents over four times higher odds of agreement and Christineberg residents over three times $(\exp[1.15])$ higher odds.

When we examine the statement "Winning or losing is not important" in a multivariate context we find limited generational and labor market effects. Millennials are less likely to agree with this notion than do their grandparents; the odds here are a little more than a third $(\exp[-1.02])$. The families of Christineberg are also less likely than the reference labor markets to express agreement, with odds that are also about a third $(\exp[-1.04])$.

In Table 6.9 we summarize our results around this set of eight attitude and belief components that have been linked conceptually and/or empiri-cally to the intention to engage in economic activity. Statistically significant effects are indicated in the table by (+) for an impact that is more positive than the reference category while a (−) is used to reference an impact that is more negative. Inasmuch as the reference category for labor market is liberal market capitalism country differences irrespective of generation

Table 6.9 Summary of Labor Market and Generational Effects Resulting From Multiple Regression Analyses (Statistically Significant Effects Only)

Attitude or belief component	Labor Market[a]				Generation[b]	
	John-holm	Christineberg	Reggio Maurizio	San Arco	Millennials	Generation X
Trusting attitude intention	+		−			
Redistributive justice			+	+	+	
Human Capital Investment	−	−			−	−
Centrality of work		−		−	−	
Labor Force Attachment	+				−	
Risk Taking		−		−	+	+
Cooperative Attitude/ intention	+		−			
Individual Achievement	+/-	−		−	−	−

[a]The reference categories for labor market comparisons are the liberal capitalist markets of Raazpuram and Sherianne.
[b]The reference category for generation comparisons is the baby boomer generation

amounts to an explicit test of the predictive utility of the Esping-Andersen (1990, 2002) typology. These country contrasts also have implications for the varieties of capitalism argument made by Hall and Soskice (2001). But more to the point of this book's main arguments, stability over generations within a specific country labor market adds weight to the thesis of cultural exogeneity as proposed by Fernandez and Fogli (2006), Gallie (2019), and Cook and Furstenberg (2002), among others. Conversely, significant differences between generations on belief and attitude components that transcend country-level differences would lend support in this study to Becker's (1996) idea of cultural endogeneity, since it would be difficult to claim that economic conditions in the six labor markets we have examined have not been witness to remarkable changes in economic opportunities, wages, prices, etc. over the three generations we have examined. Following the cultural pathways proposition of Cook and Furstenberg (2002) and Breen and Buchmann (2002), significant impacts of our study labor markets would suggest that vertical cultural transmission pathways remain operative while significant generational impacts could point up transmission pathways that have been blocked and/or redirected because of economic exigencies (recall Bisin and Verdier's, 2011, direct vertical socialization argument).

A review of Table 6.9 provides evidence that both cultural and economic factors may be at work in our sample of respondents. In both Johnholm and Reggio Maurizio, there are clusters of statistically significant effects that reveal a value orientation that transcends generation. Consistent with existing literature, the Swedes in this labor market embrace trusting attitudes and beliefs, labor force attachment, cooperative attitudes, and the belief in individual achievement. The (+/−) notion for the last component reflects some cynicism around the notion that the best prepared person is the most successful. In Reggio Maurizio too, a pattern consistent with the extant research prevails; it is one of low trust, low risk-taking, stunted cooperative attitudes/intentions, and shallow levels of achievement motivation.

Reggio Maurizio families, as would be expected, share some of the same beliefs and attitudes found in San Arco. In both labor markets, there is an appetite for income redistribution, which in San Arco is coupled with weak support for the centrality of work and for individual achievement.

The pattern of significant effects for Christineberg residents demonstrate uniformly lower levels than the reference group of liberal market capitalism. The less prominent risk-taking and individual achievement are anticipated in McClelland's (1964) German value formula (see also Gannon and Pillai, 2016). The lower intensity of human capital investment, which is shared by Johnholm, may simply be an artifact of question wording; that is, the questions about math and science did not stress the importance of applied knowledge, which, as we have discussed in Chapter 3, are of paramount import in both Sweden and Germany.

There is another possible explanation for the weaker commitment to human capital investment in Christineberg, however, and this is related to the weaker than expected support for the centrality of work. In Chapter 4 we discussed the concerns of the Association of German Chambers of Commerce and Industry in finding skilled and talented workers as Germans increasingly opt for general education options (Morath, 2019; CEDEFOP, 2018a,b). This however would be a generational argument and would not account for the uniformly lower levels over all three generations in Christineberg. As Gannon and Pillai (2016), among others, point out, German productivity per hours worked has been and remains among the highest in OECD countries, a condition that provides the typical German worker with the bona fides for limiting work as the principal component of personal identity.[4]

Table 6.9 does not show the effects of Sherianne or Raazpuram residents on our set of economic activity linked attitudes, beliefs, and behavioral intentions. As reference categories, their impact is captured in the regression intercept. Suffice it to say here that Sherianne families exhibited high levels of human capital investment, inclination to take risks, and the need for achievement, all of which are critical to success in capitalist economies with undeveloped governmental safety nets.

Pervasive generational effects are obvious in Table 6.9, with millennials expressing views that are often at odds with their grandparents. The youngest generation in our sample is less likely than baby boomers to support human capital investment, the centrality of work, attachment to the labor force, and individual achievement. They are more likely to favor redistributive justice, an indication that they believe the economy has not or will not function equitably (Guillaud, 2013; Brooks, 2013; Schuck and Shore, 2019). On measures of risk-taking our analysis reveals that both millennials and Generation Xers are more likely to take risks than baby boomers. Both generations define themselves as risk takers, and both indicate intentions to favor a long shot over a sure thing. Generation Xers are, like millennials, less in favor of human capital investment and individual achievement.

Previous research has not resulted in a body of congruous insights about the stability of basic values over generations. Research by Kalleberg and Marsden (2013, 2019) have found that millennials in the United States continue to value work and the reward that paid work can provide. Gallie (2019) and his associates in their European-based research have also found a high stability of work values over time. Another large American study by Twenge et al. (2010), however, finds that millennials place lower values on work centrality and their highest values on leisure. Moreover, nonsurvey analysis in Europe (Michau, 2013; Ljunge, 2011, Bergquist, 2016) provide some signs that market capitalism may be losing commitment among young adults (see also Saad, 2019). Our family results would appear to bolster the notion that the "spirit of capitalism" may be on the wane.

---

[4] It is worthwhile noting that the steady growth in German productivity since the mid-1970s has begun to decline in recent years. The possible connection to the movement of youth from vocational to general education tracks has been explored as one explanation for this phenomenon as has others, including changes in beliefs and attitudes about the centrality of work (OECD, 2019c).

In summary both culture and economic conditions appear to influence the attitudes and belief of our family members. Changes in economic opportunities, skill requirements, wages, and prices brought about by globalization have led to some breakdown in traditional value orientations, and it would appear some convergence around an altered way of experiencing capitalism (Hauff and Kirscher, 2015; Hancke, Rhodes, and Thatcher, 2007). The alteration, nevertheless, should not be interpreted as a metamorphosis, since on many beliefs, attitudes, and work-related intentions, there is substantial consistency over generations within countries.

Do Cultural Metaphors Matter?

In the conceptual model we introduced in Chapter 1 and expanded upon in Chapter 2, it was noted that while much of the book's focus would center upon measurable attitudes and beliefs (Chapter 6), and more challenging to measure job-related preferences (Chapter 7), we would additionally probe the feasibility of quantifying measures of "deep culture." The concept of the "cultural metaphor" was cited as a vehicle capable of succinctly capturing a culture's norms, preferences, beliefs, etc., with analogy that is vivid, compact, and realistic (Lakoff and Johnson, 1980; Ortony, 2001; Gannon and Pillai, 2016). Yet while the usefulness of metaphor has been touted as a fast-track approach to understanding national business culture (Gannon, 2009; Gannon and Pillai, 2016) and, more broadly, national symbolic meaning (Lakoff and Johnson, 1980, 1999), empirical tests of this utility are quite rare.

We began our work values and opinions interview schedule (Appendix A) with two questions designed to partially test Gannon and associates' widely promulgated "metaphorical journey" through national cultures. Figure 2.2 in Chapter 2 lists these metaphors and the countries they are thought to represent: the stuga or summer home (Sweden), a symphony (Germany), an opera (Italy), a bullfight (Spain), an athletic contest (United States), and a dance performance (India). If these metaphors accurately portray national culture, we would expect that family responses would gravitate toward the metaphor that Gannon and associates propose for their country of both origin and residence.

In Table 6.10, we show the response distributions for the item "Describes the way people you know get along with each other" (Panel A) and the way they should get along with each other (Panel B). The table is set up so

Table 6.10 Country Metaphors—Conceptual and Actual Response
Distributions

Country	Metaphor (Percentage)				
	Symphony	Athelete Contest	Opera	Dance	Summer Home
Panel A. Metaphor that describes the way people get along with each other					
Germany	6.7	50.0	23.0	14.0	7.0
United States	23.3	27.0	10.0	27.0	12.0
Italy	10.0	27.7	10.0	7.0	37.0
India	12.0	19.0	4.0	23.0	42.0
Sweden	27.0	17.0	0.0	27.0	30.0
Spain	7.0	23.0	13.0	17.0	40.0
Panel B. Metaphor that describes the way people <u>should</u> get along with each other					
Germany	20.0	6.7	10.0	26.7	36.7
United States	62.0	0.0	3.45	20.70	13.8
Italy	39.2	3.6	3.6	18.0	36.0
India	7.7	19.2	3.8	19.2	50.0
Sweden	36.0	14.2	4.0	32.1	14.3
Spain	50.0	6.7	6.7	6.7	30.0

N = 180

that percentages in each row add to 100, facilitating comparison across the columns. If these metaphors are indeed symbolic representations of national culture, one would expect to see a preponderance of responses concentrate along the table diagonal, with San Arco responses spread diffusely across metaphors inasmuch as they represent a counterfactual condition. In neither panel do we find such a pattern; instead, diffuse patterns emerge for family members across all six labor markets.

To provide a stronger test of this cultural metaphor hypothesis, we subjected the categories to a multinomial regression analysis.[5] The results of these regressions are provided in Appendix B. As we did in our binary logits, we simultaneously control for both country labor market and generation and employ Sherianne/Raazpuram and baby boomers as our reference categories.

---

[5] We should note that we show only the comparisons between each category (there are four) and the reference category (5 = athletic contest). For J = 5 categories, there exists J!/2!(J-2)! number of contrasts between categories (1 vs. 2, 1 vs. 3, etc.). Since virtually all of these nonreference comparisons were not statistically significant, they are not presented.

Inasmuch as our dependent variable in these multinomial logits has five categories, we cannot use the "other category" as the reference as we did in our binary logits. Here we have made the athletic contest, a metaphor associated by Gannon and his associates with the United States as the reference.

The results from these multinomial logits demonstrate that only two country labor markets have statistically significant contrasts. For Christineberg, the comparison between symphony versus athletic contest (−1.77), dance versus athletic contest (−1.38), and summer home versus athletic contest (−2.19) are significant and the exponentiation of these coefficients reveal odds that are only 0.17, 0.25, and 0.11, respectively, of selecting these options relative to viewing the world as an athletic event than they are for non-Germans. For Reggio Maurizio, the comparison between dance and athletic contest is statistically significant (−1.82) or odds of about 0.16 times as high as for non-Italians.

Not anticipated in the typology of Gannon metaphors is the possibility that these metaphorical meanings may be age-specific. For millennials, the summer home versus athletic contest comparison was significant (−1.82) indicating that their odds of viewing reality in this fashion are only 0.16 as high as their grandparents.

The reader will recall from Table 2.2 that we augmented the Gannon metaphor set with our own, more behavior-based grouping (also see Question 3 in the interview schedule). Using a journey through life (India) as our reference category, our multinomial logits show that with one exception (for San Arco on the contrast between difficult march versus journey), all the statistically significant effects are generational. Millennials have odds that are 0.12 (exp[−2.14]) of those of baby boomers when characterizing life as a difficult march rather than a journey. Their parents have odds of 0.20 (exp[−1.60]) or about a fifth of baby boomers. In the contrast between leisurely walk and journey, millennials and Generation Xers once again have lower odds than baby boomers; in this instance, these ratios are 0.05 (exp[−2.94]) and 0.12 (exp([−2.14]), respectively. It would appear from these results that baby boomers have had more experiences with the vicissitudes that complicate life's journey.

It would be safe to conclude from our brief incursion into the realm of metaphor that the deep meanings assigned by ordinary families in a nation may not be the same as those assigned by mid-level business managers working in the country or even academics who possess impressionistic, and perhaps romanticized, shorthand images.

7

National and Intergenerational Similarities and Differences in Stated Preferences

> *Our tastes greatly alter. The lad does not care for the child's rattle, and the old man does not care for the young man's whore.*
> —Samuel Johnson, *Boswell's Life of Johnson* (1791/1934)

In the opening chapter of the book, we provided a broad conceptual model of cultural value orientations and how this constellation of general attitudes and beliefs, norms, metaphors, and preferences, through vertical and oblique forms of generational transmission, impacts economic activity. There a distinction was made between specific attitudes and beliefs that have been linked quantitatively in the social science literature to outcomes like labor force attachment and employment-seeking intentions, and more general concepts including norms, meta-preferences, and metaphors, where the associations have been more qualitative or even anecdotal (see Figure 1.1). Most of the focus in the previous chapter centered on these specific beliefs and attitudes; additionally, the possible significance of cultural metaphors was examined.

We now turn our attention to the concept of utility preferences that are observable at the day-to-day transactional level (Becker, 1996; McFadden, 1975, 1986; Ben-Akiva and Lerman, 1994), their measurement and interpretation within a cross-national and transgenerational context. Our perspective on preferences as an integral component of value orientation is influenced by Becker's (1996) theoretical work and its extension by cultural economists, especially Bisin and Verdier (2011), Fernandez (2008), Guiso, Sapienza, and Zingales (2008), and McFadden (1975, 1986). This intellectual debt is manifest in two ways: (a) while conceding that preferences are often consequences of historical events and economic conditions and in this respect are endogenous, but by also acknowledging that preferences become exogenous factors when parents promulgate "priors" (Guiso, Sapienza, and Zingales, 2008) and/or serve as active agents in the choice of their own or their

Caught in the Cultural Preference Net. Michael J. Camasso and Radha Jagannathan, Oxford University Press (2021).
© Oxford University Press. DOI: 10.1093/oso/9780190672782.003.0007

children's values and preferences (Bisin and Verdier, 2011) and (b) acknowledging that preferences serve as a linchpin between beliefs and attitudes, on the one hand, and behavioral intentions and economic activity, on the other. We attribute this latter insight to McFadden's seminal work on stated and revealed preferences. In Figure 7.1, we provide the reader with a path diagram that depicts the pivotal position of preferences in the individual decision process. This model recognizes that personal beliefs and attitudes are the precursors of behavioral intentions or the probability of acting on a belief or attitude (Fishbein and Ajzen, 1975). However the model also identifies, as does McFadden (1975), the mediating role played by a rational agent's meta preferences (Becker, 1996) in prioritizing decision alternatives based on each alternative's relative utility in advancing the agent's personal interests. These meta preferences, in turn, trigger stated preference responses (McFadden, 1975) and/or behavioral intention (Fishbein and Ajzen, 1975), which then stimulate market action. From the vantage point of Figure 7.1, beliefs and attitudes are instrumental variables, transmitting their effects through individual preferences.

In their 2000 article, "Measuring Trust," Glaeser et al., (2000) comment on what they see as the limitations of standard attitudinal/belief survey questions to study impact of human and social capital, advocating for a research approach that combines surveys with attitude/belief linked experiments. They conclude:

> Experiments measure preferences, behavioral propensities and other individual attributes much more convincingly than surveys, since experiments provide direct observations of behavior. By connecting experiments and surveys, we can determine the socioeconomic correlates

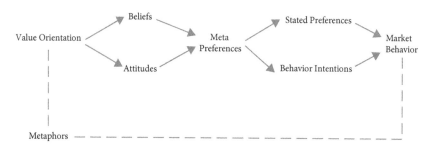

Figure 7.1 Path diagram illustrating the mediating role played by preferences in the value orientation–market behavior relationship.

of hard-to-measure individual attributes, and test the validity of survey measures of these attributes. (p. 841)

This recommendation has gone largely unheeded in the cultural economics literature with a few notable exceptions.[1] Perhaps the most prominent of these exceptions is the research conducted by Maria Bigoni and her associates on social capital in Italy (Bigoni et al., 2016, 2018). We briefly discussed Bigoni et al. (2016, 2018) in Chapters 2 and 5 and this research team's isolation of a "deep trait" in Italian culture they referred to as the "preference for betrayal aversion." Like Glaeser et al. (2000), Bigoni et al. (2018) perform a "trust game"[2] experiment on a subject pool of university students, which, of course, limits the generalizability of these studies. An earlier Bigoni et al. (2016) trust game experiment, which recruited 618 participants from the general population of Cuneo, Firenza, Crotone, and Ragusa in Italy, has much broader implications for the study of value orientations and economic activity. Unfortunately, these researchers do not examine their data for age or generational differences. This same limitation applies to trust experiments conducted by Cappelen et al. (2015) who simultaneously utilized sample of students and individuals from the Norwegian general population. As might be expected, Cappelen et al.'s student and representative adult samples differed in fundamental ways, with students exhibiting less value for reciprocity, equity, and other prosocial behavior, leading these authors to conclude, not surprisingly, that "experiments with student subjects might not be informative about the social preferences in society at large" (p. 1324).

The type of experiment we will describe in this chapter has been labeled variously as discrete choice experiments (DCEs; World Health Organization, 2012), stated preference experiments (Camasso and

---

[1] Cappelen et al. (2015) note that the standard approach to the study of social preferences in economics is to conduct experiments on students in a laboratory setting, usually on campus. In their review of papers published on social preferences in the top five economics journals, these researchers found that only 4 out of 24 papers published report from experiments on nonstudent samples and only two of these papers report from experiments performed outside a college/university lab setting.

[2] The trust game and its variants the investment game, the dictator game, the centipede game, and others follow the same basic two-stage structure. Berg, Dickhaut, and McCabe (1995) describe how a simple game is played. Subjects in lab room A decide how much of their $10.00 show-up fee to send to an anonymous counterpart in lab room B. Subjects in lab room A are informed that each dollar they choose to send will be tripled by the time it reaches lab room B. The counterpart subjects in lab room B then decide how much of the tripled money to keep and how much to send back to their counterparts in lab room A. The unique Nash equilibrium prediction for this game with perfect information is to send zero money back. However, in many cases, this prediction is rejected, and varying amounts of money are indeed sent back to lab room A. The conditions under which the reciprocity on trust equilibrium obtains motivates a great deal of this game research.

Jagannathan, 2001), or conjoint analysis (Phillips, Johnson, and Maddala, 2002). To our knowledge, this is the first time that a DCE has been utilized in a cross- cultural, multigenerational context. It is useful to describe this—or, for that matter, any—discrete choice experiment as a five-step process comprising (a) a defining of choice attributes, (b) the assignment of attribute levels, (c) the creation of choice scenarios, (d) determining the number of choice sets, and (e) estimation of individuals' utility differences on these choice sets (Louviere, Hensher, and Swait, 2000; Camasso and Jagannathan, 2001; Phillips, Maddala, and Johnson, 2002). We will now guide the reader through the structure of our experiment and the construction of the DCE instrument used to collect respondent choices. A copy of this instrument appears in its entirety in Appendix A, Section 2 of the family interview schedule.

Defining Attributes

Examining the previous research on labor supply and the decision criteria used by individuals to seek employment, change jobs, or remain on the labor force sidelines, we selected five features (attributes) that ranked as most consequential: type of job, salary, skill set required, level of job prestige, and job setting. All of these attributes, with the possible exception of salary, were touched upon in our Chapter 6 discussions. To be clear, this list is not exhaustive, nor was it meant to be. The accumulating research on DCEs has shown that with too many attributes individuals will not consider all the information available but instead adopt simple decision-making strategies like always choosing a government job (World Health Organization, 2012). In previous work by these authors, we have used as many as 13 decision attributes (Camasso and Jagannathan, 2001) with some applications employing as few as 2 and some as many as 24 (World Health Organization, 2012; Phillips, Johnson, and Maddala, 2002; de Bekker-Grob et al., 2012). The consensus for applications to workforce issues in samples that contain low- and middle-income respondents range from five to eight. Our selection of five attributes reflects the multigenerational nature of our labor market samples, striking a balance between the costs of the experiment to the families and the potential research benefits and limiting the number to features that are amenable to change.

Attribute Levels

Attribute levels can be defined as either categorical or continuous. One advantage of continuous attributes is that they allow for the estimation of trade-offs. For example, if salary is included in an attribute set, it is possible to determine how much money an individual is willing to give up for improvements in other aspects of a job such as social prestige. In this experiment, we treat salary as continuous, and the other four attributes, as categorical, each with three levels. The decision to limit the levels to this number of possibilities takes into consideration the nature of our multigenerational sample, its large elderly component, and what the literature indicates are realistic levels of potentially actionable decision options (World Health Organization, 2012; Phillips, Johnson, and Maddala, 2002; de Bekker-Grob et al., 2012). A description of the five decision attributes and their values used create our stated preference instrument are presented in Table 7.1. The values selected for the four categorical attributes reflect important choices in today's globalized job market. As government job opportunities dwindle, individuals will be compelled to seek employment in the private sector or to engage in entrepreneurial activity. Globalization will also increase the need

Table 7.1 Attributes and Attribute Levels used in the Preference Experiment

Attribute	Levels (Choices)
Salary	€35,000/€50,000/€ 75,000[a]
Job skill set	Job requires native language only [reference]
	Job requires native language and English
	Job requires native language, English and math
Job prestige	Job is honored/valued by parents [reference]
	Job is honored/valued by society
	Job is honored/valued by self
Type of job	Government job [reference]
	Private sector/business
	Self-employment
Job skill set	Work alone [reference]
	Work with 1–3 people
	Work in large team

[a]In the United States and India, these amounts were converted to U.S. dollars and Indian rupees, respectively.

for an expanded skill set, especially numeracy (Economist Intelligence Unit, 2014) and English, the world's business language. Job setting has taken an increased significance with the efficiency and productivity of small teams gaining increased prominence in the business/management literatures (Wu, Wang and Evans, 2019; Hardy, 2005; Wang and Evans, 2019). Finally, the selection of the three levels of job prestige (i.e., honored by self, by parent, or by society) represented our intention to measure the element of social capital in the job selection decisions. Specifically, this attribute and its levels address the bonding–bridging capital and individualism–collectivism considerations discussed in Chapters 2, 3, and 6.

Creation of Choice Scenarios and Choice Tasks

Using the attributes and levels depicted in Table 7.1, our next step in the DCE was to construct a series of hypothetical job choices with distinctive combinations of these attributes and levels. Given that we had five attributes each with three levels, it was possible to create (3^5) or 243 possible job choice scenarios. If respondents were asked to choose among these scenarios two at a time (i.e., Job1 vs. Job2), they would be faced with [(243 * 242)/2] or 29,403 choice tasks. Of course, this is not practical, and the typical DCE relies on fractional factorial experimental designs to maintain the experiment's integrity while greatly reducing the scenarios and choice tasks. As we have in our previous work with DCEs, we employed the Detailed Master Plans for fractional factor designs catalogued by Hahn and Shapiro (1966). Under these plans, an experiment with five attributes that each has three levels can be conducted with 32 paired scenarios or 16 choice tasks. We reproduce one of these choice tasks in Figure 7.2; all 16 tasks are provided to the reader in Appendix A. Our design only allows us to estimate orthogonal main effects for attributes; interactions between these design variables are assumed to be negligible.[3]

---

[3] The goal of the fractional factorial design is to reduce the number of paired comparisons to the smallest necessary to efficiently estimate utility weights (i.e., step 5 of the experimental process). Efficient fractional factorial designs are evaluated on several criteria: orthogonality or low correlations among the levels of any two attributes; balance or attribute levels appear in choice sets an equal number of times; and minimal overlap or the minimalization of choice sets while attribute levels do not vary. We designed our experiment with these criteria in mind. For more on these conditions, see World Health Organization (2010); Phillips, Maddala, and Johnson (2002), and McFadden (1986).

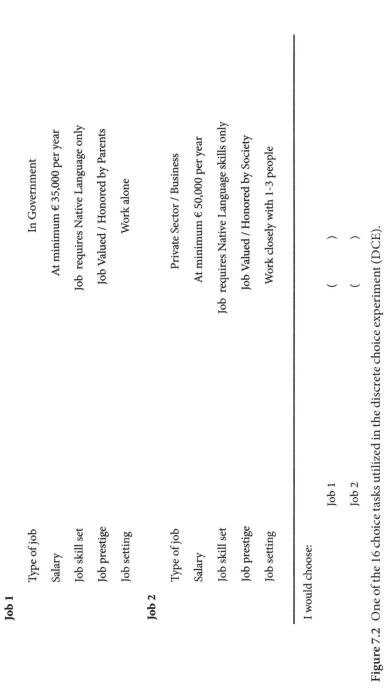

DCZ - CTB1

Job 1

Type of job	In Government
Salary	At minimum € 35,000 per year
Job skill set	Job requires Native Language only
Job prestige	Job Valued / Honored by Parents
Job setting	Work alone

Job 2

Type of job	Private Sector / Business
Salary	At minimum € 50,000 per year
Job skill set	Job requires Native Language skills only
Job prestige	Job Valued / Honored by Society
Job setting	Work closely with 1-3 people

I would choose:

Job 1   (   )

Job 2   (   )

Figure 7.2 One of the 16 choice tasks utilized in the discrete choice experiment (DCE).

Estimating Family Members' Utility Parameters

Unlike in Chapter 6, where our analysis of respondent attitudes, beliefs, and metaphors was based on 180 individuals (30 family members × 6 country labor markets), the analysis of the stated job preferences here was based on 5,760 observations (180 individuals × 16 choice scenarios × 2 options for each scenario). In the first instance, the individual is the unit of analysis and the individual's characteristics (his or her generation, country of residence, gender, religiosity, etc.) are explanatory variables, used to explain individual's attitudes, beliefs, etc. In the second instance, the choice (Job1 vs. Job2) is the unit of analysis and the characteristics of choice, that is, the attributes (salary, job type, etc.) are the explanatory variables used to explain the individual's utility preference(s). As Hoffman and Duncan (1988) remark, an analysis of the "chooser" can provide us with useful information "about which individuals make which choices" because of attitudes, beliefs, etc.; however, such analysis are not well suited to "testing hypothesis about why these choices are made" (p. 418). A statistical estimation model that preserves the structure of the individual's decision-making process is the random utility approach associated with Daniel McFadden (1975, 1986), more commonly known as conditional logit discrete choice model (CLGT).

The choice probabilities in the CLGT can be estimated using the equation[4]

$$\text{Prob}\left(Y = j\right) = \frac{\exp\left(\sum_{k=1}^{K} a_k \, Z_{jk}\right)}{\sum_{j=1}^{J} \exp\left(\sum_{k=1}^{K} a_k \, Z_{jk}\right)}$$

---

[4] Note that this estimation model differs in several important ways from the binary and multinomial logit model (MNLGT) employed in Chapter 6. There $\text{Prob}\left(Y = j\right) = \dfrac{\exp\left(\sum_{k=0}^{K} \beta_{jk} \, X_k\right)}{1 + \sum_{j=1}^{J-1} \exp\left(\sum_{k=0}^{K} \beta_{jk} \, X_k\right)}$

where in this case $j = 1, 2 \ldots J-1$ represents the response categories of the dependent variable and K the number of explanatory variables X. In cases where $J = 2$, the multinominal reduces to a binary logit. β_{jk} represent the parameter estimates of which there are $(J-1)(K+1)$. For example, in our metaphor regressions in Chapter 6, the number of parameter estimates including identifying intercepts was ([5−1] [6+1]) or 28 (Appendix B).

As Hoffman and Duncan (1988) and McFadden (1986) point out, CLGT and MNLGT specifications differ with respect to the preferability of a structural model (CLGT) over a reduced-form model (MNLGT) to explain human behavior and the more direct relevance of an approach that focuses on actual decisions (CLGT) for policy changes rather than approaches that focus on characteristics of the decision maker (MNLGT).

where $j = 1, 2$ for Job1 or Job2; Z is a variable with two subscripts, k distinguishes the attributes (five in this experiment), and j distinguishes the attribute levels; a represents the parameter estimates for the impact of an attribute and level on the probability of job choice.

We estimated CLGT models for all decisions made, irrespective of labor market or generation, a model for each generation irrespective of labor market (N = 3), another for each labor market regardless of generation (N = 6), and a series of regressions specific to both generation and labor market (N = 18). For all these regression models, we estimated two specifications—one that included only the choice attributes and their levels and a second that augmented the first with the appropriate labor market, generation, and/or individual fixed effects. These individual controls include gender, income, education, and levels of religiosity. The inclusion of these individual controls and fixed effects to our CLGT estimation transforms these models into a mixed specification where characteristics of the decision maker are constant across the various (16) scenarios.

Results From Our Choice Analysis

The coefficients and standard errors from the conditional logit regression for all six labor markets and three generations are presented in Table 7.2. An examination of the sign and statistical significance of the coefficients reveal that salary, working in a job that is honored either by oneself or by society (compared to one that is honored by the parent), and working in small or large teams (as opposed to working alone) increase an individual's utility for a job; conversely, working in the private sector or self-employment (compared to working for the government) and the necessity of possessing additional human capital skills (math and second language, compared to native language only) decreases the job's utility in this sample.

As we have seen in Chapter 6, a more precise way of looking at the impacts of predictor variables is to compute the marginal effect of each variable on the odds of a particular choice. For example, by exponentiating the coefficient for "job honored by self" in the model controlling for fixed effects (Model 2; $e^{0.441}$), we find that the typical sample respondent is 1.55 or approximately 1½ times more likely to select a job that has this feature, relative to a job honored by the parent. On the other hand, the odds of a respondent choosing self-employment are ($e^{0.304}$) or decreased by a factor of 0.738 or about 26% ($[e^b - 1] * 100$), compared to working for the government. Inasmuch as the salary

Table 7.2 CLGT Regressions: All Labor Markets and All Generations Combined

Choice Variables	Model 1	Model 2[a]
Salary	0.00002 **	0.00002**
	(0.000003)	(0.000003)
Govt. Job [reference]		
Private Job	−0.361**	−0.172
	(0.131)	(0.165)
Self-employment	−0.412**	−0.304**
	(0.114)	(0.131)
Native language only [REFERENCE]		
Native language + English + Math	−0.225**	−0.279**
	(0.072)	(0.087)
Native language + English	−0.252**	−0.282**
	(0.083)	(0.096)
Job honored by parents [reference]		
Job honored by society	0.223**	0.256**
	(0.083)	(0.100)
Job honored by self	0.375**	0.441**
	(0.098)	(0.123)
Work alone [Reference]		
Work in large team	0.176*	0.221*
	(0.091)	(0.116)
Work with 1–3 people	0.145	0.269*
	(0.117)	(0.147)
n	5,462	4,310

[a]Model 2 includes fixed effects for countries and generations and also for controls for sex, income, and religiosity

**P-value < 0.05; *P-values < 0.1.

attribute is measured as a continuous variable the coefficient indicates how much of the job's utility increases by having one extra euro (or its equivalent) per year, and for this sample the increase in odds are ($e^{0.00002}$) or 1.00002 per euro. Thus for a 10,000 euro increase in salary, the odds of selecting a job would increase by ($e^{0.00002 \times 10,000}$) or 1.22 (or 22 percent higher).

In Table 7.3, we provide the generation-specific CLGT results for millennials, Generation Xers, and baby boomers. Here we see that salary is important for both millennials and Generation Xers but not for baby boomers. Salary, of course, manifests its utility as a pivotal extrinsic value (i.e., a tangible source of income and security). Its significance for the two younger generations but not for baby boomers runs not only counter to the findings of Kalleberg and Marsden (2013) and Gallie (2019), who report

Table 7.3 CLGT Regressions: All Labor Markets Combined by Generations

Choice Variables	Millennials		Generation X		Baby Boomers	
	Model 1	Model 2[a]	Model 1	Model 2[a]	Model 1	Model 2[a]
Salary	0.00002**	0.00002**	0.00002**	0.00003**	0.00001**	0.000007
	(0.000007)	(0.000006)	(0.000005)	(0.000007)	(0.000004)	(0.000005)
Govt. job [reference]						
Private job	−0.010	−0.069	−0.278	0.227	−0.690**	−0.547**
	(0.241)	(0.310)	(0.230)	(0.313)	(0.229)	(0.275)
Self-employment	0.0002	−0.101	−0.408**	−0.156	−0.775**	−0.569**
	(0.241)	(0.250)	(0.196)	(0.229)	(0.213)	(0.230)
Native language only [reference]						
Native language + English + Math	−0.280	−0.258	−0.268**	−0.505**	−0.151	−0.150
	(0.176)	(0.219)	(0.121)	(0.158)	(0.099)	(0.110)
Native language + English	−0.339**	−0.325*	−0.154	−0.221	−0.278*	−0.335**
	(0.156)	(0.194)	(0.119)	(0.162)	(0.162)	(0.166)
Job honored by parents [reference]						
Job honored by society	0.140	0.247	0.217*	0.140	0.309**	0.346**
	(0.160)	(0.187)	(0.133)	(0.171)	(0.149)	(0.175)
Job honored by self	0.332*	0.437*	0.193	0.245	0.600**	0.596**
	(0.194)	(0.229)	(0.168)	(0.242)	(0.165)	(0.197)
Work alone [reference]						
Work in large team	0.504**	0.655**	0.083	0.028	0.010	0.063
	(0.209)	(0.270)	(0.130)	(0.186)	(0.150)	(0.177)
Work with 1–3 people	0.553**	0.725**	−0.118	−0.139	0.101	0.284
	(0.236)	(0.304)	(0.182)	(0.261)	(0.199)	(0.232)
n	1,838	1,328	1,834	1,418	1,790	1,564

[a]Model 2 includes country fixed effects and controls for sex, income and religiosity.

**P-values < 0.05; *P-values < 0.1.

stability and importance across generations, but it also runs counter to the prediction of Hauff and Kirchner (2015) and Esser and Lindh (2018), among others, that millennials devalue a job's extrinsic rewards more than their parents. The pattern with our sample is closer in consonance with the findings of Twenge et al. (2010) who observe in their large U.S. sample that the older generation(s) are less driven by salary than millennials.

On a second extrinsic value in our attribute set, however (i.e., type of job) the pattern for salary is reversed. Baby boomers have significantly less utility for a job in the private sector or for self-employment than they do for a more secure government position. Seniors have odds that decrease by a factor of 0.58, i.e., $(e^{-0.547})$ or, in other words, the odds of selecting a private sector job over a government job decline by 42 percent. For self-employment versus a government job, the decrease in the odds is nearly identical ($e^{-0.569}$) or 0.57.

Jobs can provide utility through a panoply of intrinsic or intangible rewards including flexibility of work hours, independence, opportunity for creativity, etc. (Rainsford, Maloney, and Popa, 2019; Esser and Lindh, 2018; Kraaykamp, Cemalcilar, and Tosun, 2019). In our choice set, we included an attribute specifying which locus (e.g., parents, society, or oneself) provided the individual with the most intrinsic reward or honor. Two of these attribute levels, honored by self and honored by society have appeared quite often on lists of intrinsic rewards (Twenge et al., 2010; Kalleberg and Marsden, 2019; Esser and Lindh, 2018).

In Table 7.3, we see that a job honored by oneself has significant utility for both millennials and baby boomers, but not for Generation Xers. This may simply be a function of a person's stage in the life cycle and reflect the latter's role as the main breadwinner—necessity arising from the need to take care of one's family usually trumps focus on self and broad society. In the overall sample of millennials, a job honored by oneself increases the odds of choosing the job by ($e^{0.437}$) or has 1.55 times the odds of a job that is honored by the parent. The odds of selection for baby boomers increase by ($e^{0.596}$) or 1.8 times. Baby boomers also find utility in jobs that have societal honor rather than parental honor: the increased odds here are ($e^{0.346}$) or 1.41, a little more than 40 percent.

In addition to intrinsic and extrinsic rewards, our choice scenarios contain two measures of human capital; the first, job skill set, attempts to tap into the technical side of the concept while the second, job setting, endeavors to measure the impact of "soft skills" utilization on the job decision. While we covered the importance of acquiring technical skills in Chapter 3 (i.e., the so-called hard or cognitive skills), our discussion of "soft" or relationship skills for successful labor force attachment has received somewhat less attention by us as a human capital input per se. Defined variously as self-discipline, persistence, reliability, perseverance, trustworthiness, ability to work with others, and sensitivity to other's feelings and ideas (Carneiro and Heckman, 2003; Cunha, Heckman, and Schennach, 2010; Ibarraran et al., 2014; Attanasio, 2015), soft skills have been found to exhibit dynamic complementarities and interactions with technical skill learning. Recall our earlier examination of the implications of cooperation, social capital, and trust for efficient economic activity in Chapters 2, 4, and 6.

As is evident from Table 7.3, the only statistically significant regression coefficients around working with a team of people occurs among the millennial subsample. Their preference for a job where work is done in a large team rather than working alone increases by ($e^{0.655}$) or 1.93 (93 %); this preference increases for a job in a more intimate work environment by ($e^{0.725}$) or 2.06. With respect to hard or technical skills—namely, mathematics and a second language—jobs requiring these skills were not preferred by any age group. For both millennials and baby boomers, the decrease in utility for a job requiring both native language and English was approximately ($e^{-0.3}$) or 0.74, about 26 percent. Generation Xers expressed disutility for a job requiring a second language and math skills, ($e^{-0.505}$) or a factor of 0.6. Recall from Chapter 6 that beliefs in the importance of skills in mathematics for millennials and Generation Xers were significantly more negative than they were for grandparents, a result that appears to be reprised in the utility analysis. Needless to say, this finding augurs badly for a labor market where numeracy has greatly increased in value (The Economist Intelligence Unit, 2014; Cunha, Heckman, and Schennach, 2010) and where a rapidly increasing number of employers grumble about the poor technical preparation of job applicants (CEDEFOP, 2018b; Morath, 2019; Rinne and Schneider, 2017).

Labor Market–Specific Choice Analysis

In the series of CLGT analyses that follow, we provide our results from labor market–specific regressions. We also present generation-specific results from within these (country) labor markets. The objective of these analyses is to discern if job preferences do indeed mediate the relationship between economic activity and value orientations, orientations that as we have seen, have helped shape national beliefs and attitudes around labor force participation and market behavior; have influenced both the supply and demand for labor; and have been transmitted from one generation to the next. Distinctive decision-making patterns based on intrinsic versus extrinsic job reward and/ or hard and soft skill utilities can provide a more fine-grained insight into this mediation process.

Table 7.4 CLGT Regressions: Johnholm Labor Market

Choice Variables	Overall		Millennials		Generation X		Baby Boomers	
	Model 1	Model 2[a]	Model 1	Model 2[b]	Model 1	Model 2[b]	Model 1	Model 2[b]
Salary	0.00002	-0.00002	-0.00001	-0.00001	Model cannot be estimated—		-0.00003*	-0.00003
	(0.00001)	(0.00001)	(0.00002)	(0.00002)	not much variability in choices		(0.00001)	(0.00002)
Govt. job [reference]					across choice sets			
Private job	0.289	0.622	0.336	0.363			-2.619**	-2.479
	(0.695)	(0.785)	(1.441)	(1.451)			(1.275)	(1.707)
Self-employment	-0.588	-0.477	0.361	0.366			-2.395**	-2.546**
	(0.478)	(0.541)	(0.962)	(0.972)			(0.697)	(0.917)
Native language only [reference]								
Native language + English + Math	0.142	0.144	1.118	1.125			1.293*	1.498
	(0.364)	(0.387)	(0.844)	(0.845)			(0.804)	(0.984)
Native language + English	-0.466	-0.508	-1.732**	-1.756**			-1.115	-1.315
	(0.385)	(0.410)	(0.805)	(0.823)			(0.816)	(0.955)
Job honored by parents [reference]								
Job honored by society	-0.177	-0.201	-1.464**	-1.498**			1.189*	1.316*
	(0.358)	(0.383)	(0.723)	(0.760)			(0.623)	(0.703)
Job honored by self	0.565	0.449	0.946	0.945			2.124**	2.237**
	(0.483)	(0.510)	(1.487)	(1.496)			(0.705)	(0.630)
Work alone [reference]								
Work in large team	1.193**	1.282**	3.313**	3.354**			1.836*	2.096
	(0.466)	(0.492)	(0.933)	(0.930)			(1.137)	(1.338)
Work with 1–3 people	1.362**	1.621**	2.981**	3.029**			0.730	1.170*
	(0.420)	(0.437)	(0.977)	(0.996)			(0.509)	(0.623)
n	672	670	240	240			192	190

[a]Model 2 includes fixed effects for generations and controls for sex, income and religiosity.

[b]Controls for sex, income, and religiosity.

**P-values < 0.05; *P-values < 0.1.

Job Decisions in Johnholm

Table 7.4 contains the CLGT regression coefficients for millennials and baby boomers in Johnholm. Insufficient variation in the Generation X sub-sample precluded us from drawing any statistical inferences for this group. Extrinsic rewards, salary, and job security were not significant factors in the decision-making of young Swedes. For baby boomers, salary was likewise not significant, but the disutility for self-employment was substantial in this age group—($e^{-2.546}$) or a factor of 0.078. The odds of seniors selecting such a job relative to governmental work declined by 92 percent.

There is a wide gulf between millennials and baby boomers on the value of intrinsic rewards with the latter preferring jobs that had both consequence for self and for society. Jobs honored by self increased the odds of choosing such a job by ($e^{2.237}$) or a factor of nine times and a job honored by society increased these odds by ($e^{1.316}$) or a factor of 3.7 times, compared to a job that is honored by the parent. Millennials, conversely, showed an aversion for socially honored jobs, is ($e^{-1.498}$) or 0.22, which made them 78 percent less likely to select a job based on this criterion.

Technical skill development was a consideration for millennials but not for their grandparents. Learning English and using it on the job was not of value and, in fact, decreased the appeal of the job by ($e^{-1.756}$) or by about 83 percent. Soft skill utilities were quite high for millennials and were to a lesser extent also of value for baby boomers. Working in a small group increased millennial odds of choosing a job by ($e^{3.029}$) or by a factor of 20 and working in a large group by ($e^{3.354}$) or by a factor of 28, compared to a job where they would be working alone. For baby boomers, working in a small group raised their utility by ($e^{1.17}$) or 3.2 times compared to working alone.

Job Decisions in Christineberg

It would be fair to conclude from the CLGT regression results in Table 7.5 that the intrinsic reward and soft skill attributes extended to our Christineberg families were not significant factors in their stated job preferences. Salary, too, was not a consideration once covariates like gender, religiosity, and income are controlled for statistically. In point of fact, none of our attribute set apparently figured into the decision process of the baby boomers or

Table 7.5 CLGT Regressions: Christineberg Labor Market

Choice Variables	Overall		Millennials		Generation X		Baby Boomers	
	Model 1	Model 2[a]	Model 1	Model 2[b]	Model 1	Model 2[b]	Model 1	Model 2[b]
Salary	0.00002*	0.00002	0.000008	0.000003	0.00002	0.00003	0.00002	0.00002
	(0.00001)	(0.00001)	(0.00002)	(0.00001)	(0.00002)	(0.00002)	(0.00002)	(0.00002)
Govt. job [reference]								
Private job	0.167	0.263	−0.626**	−0.744*	0.432	0.804	0.648	0.667
	(0.315)	(0.350)	(0.324)	(0.401)	(0.676)	(0.822)	(0.512)	(0.527)
Self-employment	−0.004	0.059	−0.061	−0.095	−0.050	0.206	0.068	0.068
	(0.219)	(0.237)	(0.386)	(0.479)	(0.353)	(0.327)	(0.420)	(0.434)
Native language only [reference]								
Native language + English + Math	−0.159	−0.239	0.041	−0.019	−0.293	−0.505	−0.238	−0.242
	(0.207)	(0.233)	(0.480)	(0.558)	(0.328)	(0.376)	(0.298)	(0.307)
Native language + English	−0.341	−0.440*	−0.756*	−1.122**	0.052	0.057	−0.373	−0.386
	(0.238)	(0.263)	(0.471)	(0.499)	(0.362)	(0.436)	(0.444)	(0.462)
Job honored by parents [Reference]								
Job honored by society	−0.058	0.006	−0.148	−0.295	−0.071	0.206	0.016	0.019
	(0.213)	(0.216)	(0.354)	(0.422)	(0.348)	(0.259)	(0.485)	(0.501)
Job honored by self	0.280	0.414	0.153	0.231	0.377	0.677	0.304	0.316
	(0.241)	(0.259)	(0.314)	(0.368)	(0.447)	(0.465)	(0.545)	(0.562)
Work alone [reference]								
Work in large team	0.213	0.243	0.642	0.859	−0.027	−0.155	0.035	0.036
	(0.265)	(0.300)	(0.600)	(0.723)	(0.178)	(0.195)	(0.573)	(0.590)
Work with 1–3 people	0.299	0.373	0.806	1.136	−0.059	−0.150	0.183	0.188
	(0.332)	(0.379)	(0.704)	(0.810)	(0.339)	(0.422)	(0.733)	(0.757)
n	956	892	320	288	318	286	318	318

[a]Model 2 includes country fixed effects and controls for sex, income and religiosity.

[b]Controls for sex, income, and religiosity.

** P-values < 0.05; * P-values < 0.1.

Generation Xers from Christineberg if the criterion of statistical significance is used.

This is not the case for millennials, however, where the type of job and job skill set exert an influence on decision-making. Examining the regression coefficients associated with the selection of a job in the private sector reveals that while parents and grandparents were positively (although not significantly so) predisposed to such work, millennials in Christineberg demonstrate a dramatic reversal in proclivity. Their utility for private sector jobs is decreased by ($e^{-0.744}$) or ([1 − 0.475] * 100) or by 52 percent. The millennials of Christineberg also have lower utilities for jobs that require both German and English of ($e^{-1.12}$) or about 67 percent compared to a job that only required German. This is rather surprising since most millennials in Germany are fluent in English. Moreover, this finding is consistent with the lower levels of importance assigned to math and basic science by Christineberg millennials (Table 6.3 in Chapter 6).

Job Choices in Reggio Maurizio

It is rather unambiguous from the coefficients in Table 7.6 that salary is an important consideration for the families of Reggio Maurizio; we find statistically significant coefficients for salary across all generations. The transgenerational odds are about ($e^{0.00002}$) or 1.00002 per euro; hence, with a 1,000 euro salary increase the odds of job selection would rise by ($e^{0.00002 \times 1000}$) or about 2 percent. Job security, the other extrinsic reward, does not manifest itself across generations and is significant only for Generation X family members. The prospect of self-employment decreases the odds of Reggio Maurizio parents choosing a job by ($e^{-0.619}$) or 0.54 (or by 46 percent) relative to a government job.

In addition to salary, job security appears to be a factor in job choice, at least in the case of Generation X. Self-employment lowers the value of a job of Reggio Maurizio parents by ($e^{-0.619}$) or 0.538 (46 percent). But the attribute most critical to job choice was the necessity to acquire technical skills to perform the work. Overall, and among youth and their parents, jobs demanding a second language and mathematics were especially spurned. The disutility for millennials was ($e^{-1.018}$) or 0.36; for Generation Xers, it was similar. Interestingly, the millennials of Reggio Maurizio expressed affinity for

Table 7.6 CLGT Regressions: Reggio Maurizio Labor Market

Choice Variables	Overall		Millennials		Generation X		Baby Boomers	
	Model 1	Model 2[a]	Model 1	Model 2[b]	Model 1	Model 2[b]	Model 1	Model 2[b]
Salary	0.00003** (0.000007)	0.00002** (0.000006)	0.00005** (0.00002)	0.00005 (0.00004)	0.00002 (0.00001)	0.00003** (0.00001)	0.00002** (0.000006)	0.00002* (0.000006)
Govt. job [reference]								
Private job	−0.290 (0.360)	−0.429 (0.471)	0.120 (0.949)	0.097 (2.097)	0.566 (0.428)	0.565 (0.612)	−0.987 (0.645)	−1.087 (0.707)
Self-employment	−0.248 (0.306)	−0.505 (0.398)	−0.130 (0.727)	−0.461 (1.973)	0.193 (0.539)	−0.619* (0.332)	−0.475 (0.541)	−0.543 (0.622)
Native language only [reference]								
Native language + English + Math	−0.372** (0.167)	−0.428** (0.188)	−0.711** (0.093)	−1.018** (0.326)	−0.692* (0.432)	−1.066** (0.510)	−0.085 (0.251)	−0.015 (0.281)
Native language + English	−0.141 (0.276)	0.234 (0.290)	0.093 (0.373)	1.423* (0.782)	−0.264 (0.488)	0.388 (0.330)	−0.423 (0.613)	−0.010 (0.508)
Job honored by parents [reference]								
Job honored by society	0.188 (0.285)	0.363 (0.369)	−0.200 (0.492)	1.002 (0.839)	−0.067 (0.768)	−0.476 (1.275)	0.377 (0.396)	0.482 (0.433)
Job honored by self	0.252 (0.251)	0.375 (0.307)	−0.249 (0.590)	1.273 (0.984)	0.238 (0.852)	−0.770 (1.236)	0.428 (0.285)	0.522* (0.308)
Work alone [reference]								
Work in large team	0.069 (0.336)	−0.009 (0.301)	−0.052 (0.378)	−0.094 (0.140)	0.505 (0.370)	0.541 (0.458)	−0.085 (0.432)	−0.103 (0.494)
Work with 1–3 people	−0.299 (0.318)	−0.331 (0.434)	−0.119 (0.408)	−0.065 (1.343)	−1.116 (0.736)	−1.185 (1.036)	0.020 (0.557)	−0.010 (0.643)
n	958	670	320	128	318	254	320	288

[a]Model 2 includes fixed effects for generations and controls for sex, income, and religiosity.

[b]Controls for sex, income, and religiosity.

**P-values < 0.05; *P-values < 0.1.

jobs that required English but not math skills. Such a job increased the odds of selection by ($e^{1.423}$) or a factor of four.

Besides salary, the only other job attribute that exerted a significant impact for grandparents was a position that was honored by oneself. Baby boomers selected a job with this feature ($e^{0.522}$) or by a factor of 1.7 times more often than a job that was valued by their parent.

Job Choices in San Arco

When we examine the job choice coefficients of San Arco residents in Table 7.7, ignoring generational differences we see a profile that suggests the avoidance of private sector work and that eschews positions requiring mathematics or a second language. This profile is impressionistic, however, since these attributes lose significance when covariates are entered into the CLGTs. Unlike in Reggio Maurizio where young people and their parents find disincentives in jobs requiring both math and a second language, in San Arco it is the baby boomers who find low utility in jobs requiring a second language. The odds of a grandparent choosing this kind of job is ($e^{-1.436}$) or a decrease by a factor of 0.24 (or 76 percent). Grandparents additionally place a negative value on salary, the only time this happens at statistically significant levels in our CLGT regression analysis.

Intrinsic rewards and soft skill utilization do not appear to exert much of an influence on the job decisions in San Arco. In the one instance where this is not true (i.e., working with small teams), parents find this feature to be a characteristic that is to be avoided; the odds of job selection decline by ($e^{-0.917}$) or by a factor of about 0.4—or by almost 60 percent. The general devaluation of intrinsic rewards across generations mirrors the CLGT findings from Reggio Maurizio and is also what would be expected in labor markets with high unemployment and depressed economic activity (Esser and Lindh, 2018; Hauff and Kirschner, 2015).

Job Choices in Sherianne

Salary is an important component in the job consideration of millennials and their parents in Sherianne. For each extra dollar, the odds of job selection increase by ($e^{0.00008}$) or 1.00008; for example, a $10,000 increase

Table 7.7 CLGT Regressions: San Arco Labor Market

Choice Variables	Overall		Millennials		Generation X		Baby Boomers	
	Model 1	Model 2[a]	Model 1	Model 2[b]	Model 1	Model 2[b]	Model 1	Model 2[b]
Salary	0.000001	−0.0000001	0.000002	0.000002	0.000007	0.00004	−0.000008	−0.00002*
	(0.000006)	(0.0000008)	(0.00002)	(0.00002)	(0.00001)	(0.00002)	(0.000008)	(0.00001)
Govt. job [reference]								
Private job	−0.494*	−0.461	−0.376	−0.392	−0.344	−0.139	−0.823	−1.296
	(0.280)	(0.334)	(0.483)	(0.506)	(0.468)	(0.618)	(0.588)	(0.991)
Self-employment	−0.121	−0.024	−0.223	−0.232	0.044	0.156	−0.156	0.071
	(0.238)	(0.276)	(0.204)	(0.215)	(0.543)	(0.727)	(0.471)	(0.668)
Native language only [reference]								
Native language + English + Math	−0.377**	−0.233	0.017	0.014	−0.685**	−0.478	−0.344	−0.198
	(0.186)	(0.185)	(0.401)	(0.417)	(0.324)	(0.328)	(0.276)	(0.332)
Native language + English	−0.582**	−0.641**	−0.447	−0.466	−0.576*	−0.618	−0.958**	−1.436**
	(0.161)	(0.189)	(0.306)	(0.322)	(0.335)	(0.395)	(0.389)	(0.555)
Job honored by parents [reference]								
Job honored by society	0.136	0.074	0.317	0.332	0.229	0.048	−0.239	−0.448
	(0.169)	(0.186)	(0.395)	(0.415)	(0.264)	(0.267)	(0.248)	(0.392)
Job honored by self	0.104	0.074	−0.312	−0.328	−0.153	−0.128	0.814	0.845
	(0.250)	(0.293)	(0.473)	(0.493)	(0.403)	(0.560)	(0.530)	(0.618)
Work alone [reference]								
Work in large team	0.066	0.110	0.625	0.658	−0.213	−0.387	0.029	0.280
	(0.231)	(0.268)	(0.598)	(0.627)	(0.327)	(0.402)	(0.381)	(0.505)
Work with 1–3 people	0.032	0.061	0.877	0.914	−0.506	−0.917*	0.019	0.518
	(0.288)	(0.321)	(0.611)	(0.633)	(0.471)	(0.546)	(0.435)	(0.511)
n	960	832	320	288	320	256	320	288

[a]Model 2 includes fixed effects for generations and controls for sex, income, and religiosity.

[b]Controls for sex, income, and religiosity.

**P-values < 0.05; *P-values < 0.1.

Table 7.8 CLGT Regressions: SherriAnne Labor Market

Choice Variables	Overall		Millennials		Generation X		Baby Boomers	
	Model 1	Model 2[a]	Model 1	Model 2[b]	Model 1	Model 2[b]	Model 1	Model 2[b]
Salary	0.00004**	0.00004**	0.00008**	0.00008**	0.00008**	0.00009**	0.0000001	0.00000009
	(0.00001)	(0.00001)	(0.00003)	(0.00003)	(0.00003)	(0.00003)	(0.00001)	(0.00001)
Govt. job [reference]								
Private job	0.152	0.121	-0.621	-0.665	0.946	0.973	-0.119	-0.127
	(0.309)	(0.317)	(0.794)	(0.791)	(0.777)	(0.815)	(0.434)	(0.464)
Self-employment	-0.014	-0.021	-0.314	-0.340	-0.115	-0.110	0.004	0.007
	(0.239)	(0.249)	(0.439)	(0.453)	(0.501)	(0.530)	(0.386)	(0.414)
Native language only [reference]								
Native language + English + Math	-0.340	-0.341	-0.446	-0.454	-0.564	-0.578	-0.089	-0.097
	(0.305)	(0.314)	(1.031)	(1.073)	(0.549)	(0.570)	(0.319)	(0.339)
Native language + English	-0.158	-0.221	0.684	0.609	-1.147**	-1.202**	-0.257	-0.286
	(0.253)	(0.262)	(0.649)	(0.706)	(0.270)	(0.280)	(0.442)	(0.468)
Job honored by parents [reference]								
Job honored by society	0.609*	0.577*	1.793**	1.739**	0.591	0.595	0.299	0.320
	(0.331)	(0.336)	(0.545)	(0.583)	(0.520)	(0.535)	(0.497)	(0.532)
Job honored by self	0.932**	0.908**	2.258**	2.204**	0.461	0.473	0.881	0.949
	(0.457)	(0.470)	(0.654)	(0.678)	(0.633)	(0.672)	(0.852)	(0.911)
Work alone [reference]								
Work in large team	-0.201	-0.207	0.934	0.938	-1.655*	-1.693*	-0.202	-0.221
	(0.319)	(0.327)	(1.496)	(1.535)	(0.881)	(0.891)	(0.390)	(0.413)
Work with 1–3 people	0.480	0.530	1.605	1.646	-1.54*	1.570*	1.322**	1.409**
	(0.449)	(0.460)	(1.923)	(1.952)	(0.952)	(0.972)	(0.553)	(0.637)
n	958	894	320	288	318	286	320	320

[a]Model 2 includes fixed effects for generations and controls for sex, income, and religiosity.

[b]Controls for sex, income, and religiosity.

**P-values < 0.05; *P-values < 0.1.

on salary would increase the odds by ($e^{0.00008 \times 10,000}$) or about 122 percent. It is also evident from Table 7.8 that job type and security associated with each type did not influence the decisions of any group of Sherianne residents.

What is striking about the data in Table 7.8 is the importance that intrinsic rewards had on the decision making of millennials. The odds of selecting a job that was honored by the individual improved by ($e^{2.204}$) or a factor of nine times and a job with societal prestige increased the odds by ($e^{1.739}$) or by a factor of almost six times relative to a job honored by their parents. This is the first evidence we have that millennials place more utility in these attributes than their parents or grandparents and supports the evidence referenced by Deci and Ryan (2000) and Van den Broeck et al. (2019), among others. Quantitative analyses tend to report little transgenerational differences with more variation attributed to country differences (Twenge et al., 2010; Gallie, 2019; Esser and Lindh, 2018).

The impacts of hard and soft skill requirements on job choice in Sherianne was confined to parents and grandparents. Baby boomers expressed a preference for jobs requiring small work groups over working alone. The odds of picking this type of job increased by ($e^{1.409}$) or a factor of four times. The children of baby boomers did not share their parents' appreciation for this type of job; their utility decreased by ($e^{-1.57}$) or about 80 percent ([0.208 – 1[* 100). Generation Xers in Sherianne did not value work in large groups either, and their odds of choosing a job with this attribute level decreased by ($e^{-1.693}$) or 82 percent.

Taking on a job that required Generation Xers to learn a language in addition to English was not valued by these individuals. The odds of choosing this type of job decreased by ($e^{-1.202}$) or 0.3 (or by 70 percent). Salary, and salary alone, appears to have the principal incentive for Sherianne parents. As the primary breadwinners in the family, this finding is not unexpected, and it is consistent with results reported by other American researchers (see, e.g., Kalleberg and Marsden, 2013; Twenge et al., 2010).

Job Choices in Raazpuram

Because of insufficient variability in the baby boomer subsample, our discussion of job choices in Raazpuram are limited to millennials and their parents. In Table 7.9, we show the CLGT regression coefficients and their standard

Table 7.9 CLGT Regressions: Raazpuram Labor Market

Choice Variables	Overall		Millennials		Generation X		Baby Boomers	
	Model 1	Model 2[a]	Model 1	Model 2[b]	Model 1	Model 2[b]	Model 1	Model 2
Salary	0.00002** (0.00006)	0.00003** (0.00008)	0.00003* (0.00002)	0.00004* (0.00002)	0.00001 (0.00001)	0.00002 (0.00002)	Not much variability across choice sets Models do not produce standard errors	
Govt. job [reference]								
Private job	-1.544** (0.356)	-1.786** (0.408)	-0.277 (0.666)	-0.293 (0.733)	-2.446** (0.999)	-2.736** (0.950)		
Self-employment	-1.520** (0.405)	-1.756** (0.480)	0.327 (0.565)	0.371 (0.608)	-2.376** (0.928)	-2.671** (0.896)		
Native Language only [reference]								
Native language + English + Math	-0.191 (0.128)	-0.223 (0.151)	-0.513** (0.266)	-0.572** (0.302)	0.183 (0.185)	0.202 (0.205)		
Native language + English	0.154 (0.156)	0.180 (0.182)	-0.402 (0.268)	-0.453* (0.276)	0.474 (0.351)	0.514 (0.367)		
Job honored by parents [reference]								
Job honored by society	0.451** (0.157)	0.521** (0.191)	0.443 (0.398)	0.492 (0.462)	0.280 (0.296)	0.311 (0.316)		
Job honored by self	0.348** (0.158)	0.402** (0.191)	0.709** (0.364)	0.791* (0.430)	-0.388 (0.484)	-0.436 (0.537)		
Work alone [reference]								
Work in large team	0.044 (0.158)	0.055 (0.179)	0.288 (0.309)	0.312 (0.345)	-0.138 (0.439)	-0.154 (0.489)		
Work with 1–3 people	-0.353 (0.222)	-0.394 (0.259)	0.339 (0.431)	0.367 (0.467)	-0.445 (0.510)	-0.506 (0.560)		
n	958	958	318	318	320	320		

[a]Model 2 includes fixed effects for generations and controls for sex, income, and religiosity.

[b]Controls for sex, income, and religiosity.

**P-values < 0.05; *P-values < 0.1.

errors. The pattern of significant coefficients indicates that while millennials focus their attention on salary, their parents are more concerned about security when picking a job. The odds of a Generation Xer in Raazpuram choosing a private sector job decline by ($e^{-2.736}$) and by ($e^{-2.671}$) when it is self-employment, by over 90 percent in both circumstances, relative to a much more stable government job.

As we saw in Sherianne, millennials in Raazpuram place high value on intrinsic rewards when choosing a job, specifically positions that they view as self-fulfilling rather than those that their parents value. The odds here increase by ($e^{0.791}$), or more than double. Millennials do not show a job preference based on teamwork (soft skill) but do demonstrate a rather strong aversion for jobs requiring learning a business language other than English (i.e., one of the two official business languages in India) and mathematics. The odds of selecting this type of job declined by ($e^{-0.572}$) or 0.56 (44 percent). Even jobs that required only a second language other than English were devalued by a factor of ($e^{-0.453}$) or 0.64 (36 percent).

Experimental Summary

Our unique application of a stated preference experiment in a six-nation, three-generation context was conducted with the objective of moving cultural analysis (including our own) beyond the measurement of beliefs and attitudes and the descriptions of the "chooser" they provide. We sought to expand our knowledge about why individuals make the labor market decisions they make and to discern if this decision-making process is a product of national culture and its generational transmission. We will have more to say about this in Chapter 8, but before we undertake that discussion, we would like to summarize what we believe we have learnt from the application. First, there are clear differences in the decision criteria employed by respondents in country labor markets, and these differences are often generational. For millennials, irrespective of country, the extrinsic rewards provided by a job are positively valued, most typically salary (three samples) but also security (Table 7.10). Intrinsic rewards appear to be less important and in Johnholm they serve as a disincentive.

A second conclusion that can be drawn about millennials is their aversion to learning mathematics and/or a second language to secure a job. With the exception of Sherianne youth, the millennials of Johnholm, Christineberg, Reggio Maurizio, San Arco, and Raazpuram expressed significant disutility

Table 7.10 Summary of Labor Market and Generational Effects Resulting From the Conditional Logistic Regression Analyses—Statistically Significant Effects Only

Generation	Johnholm	Christineberg	Reggio Maurizio	San Arco	Sherianne	Raazpuram
Millennials	(–) HS (–) IV (+) SS	(+) EV (security) (–) HS	(+) EV (salary) (–) HS	(–) HS	(+) EV (salary) (+) IV	(+) EV (salary) (+) IV (–) HS
Generation Xers			+ EV (salary) (–) HS	(–) HS (–) SS	(+) EV (salary) – (HS) – (SS)	(+) EV Salary (+) EV Security (–) SS
Baby boomers	(+) EV (security) (+) IV (+) SS		(+) EV Salary (+) IV	(+) HS	(+) SS	

Notes: EV = extrinsic value; IV = intrinsic value; HS = hard skill; SS = soft skill.

for these kinds of jobs, and only in Johnholm were soft skills a positive factor in job selection.

For Generation X, in three of six of our markets (Reggio Maurizio, Sherianne, and Raazpuram), salary was a significant attribute when making a job choice. In Raazpuram, government jobs offering security was also an influential characteristic. Hard and soft skill utilization did not influence the decisions for parents in Johnholm or Christineberg and exhibited negative value in Reggio Maurizio, San Arco, and Raazpuram. In both San Arco and Sherianne either hard or soft skill job components proved to be significant.

Finally, among baby boomers extrinsic rewards had a significant impact in Johnholm and Reggio Maurizio. Intrinsic rewards were also important considerations within these two groups of seniors. In the only instance of a positive attribute affecting job choices in San Arco, grandparents found the acquisition of technical skills to increase their preference for a job—this is in sharp contrast to their children and grandchildren. The soft skills required to work in groups was valued by seniors in Johnholm and Sherianne but nowhere else.

8

Cultural Preference Nets

The Good, Not So Good, and Just Plain Dysfunctional

> *Few nations have been able to reach intellectual refinement and es-*
> *thetic sensitivity without sacrificing so much in virility and unity that*
> *their wealth presents an irresistible temptation to impecunious bar-*
> *barians. Around every Rome hover the Gauls; around every Athens*
> *some Macedon.*
>
> —Will Durant, *The Life of Greece* (1939)

In our introductory chapter, we laid out three research objectives that organized our efforts to isolate culture's consequences for labor force attachment in
six capitalist democracies. Specifically, we focused on these questions:

1. Do some national cultures hold on to value orientations that are more
   successful than others in promoting economic opportunity?
2. Does the transmission of these value orientations demonstrate a stability or persistence, irrespective of economic conditions, or are they
   simply the result of these exogenous conditions?
3. If value orientations are not simply the result of economic conditions,
   do they exert their influence through stated preferences and behavioral
   intentions, central concepts in virtually all explanations of economic
   behavior?

In posing these questions, we have sought to advance the perennial discussion around the relative importance of culture in shaping our economic
intentions and choices. This is a discussion which gained initial prominence with the publication of Max Weber's work on the spirit (culture) of
capitalism (Weber, 1904/1958) and which has lost very little rigor over the
past 100 years. Our juxtapositions of the work done by Bourdieu (1986)
and by Becker (1996) as well as our review of the research being conducted
in the expanding subfield of cultural economics (Bisin and Verdier, 2011;

Caught in the Cultural Preference Net. Michael J. Camasso and Radha Jagannathan, Oxford University Press (2021).
© Oxford University Press. DOI: 10.1093/oso/9780190672782.003.0008

Fernandez, 2008) are indications of the intensity with which the subject continues to be examined.

In this eighth and final chapter, we close with several sets of conclusions that point up both the possibilities and constraints that national cultures exert on economic choices. We organize these observations and conclusions under five headings: cultural consequences for personal beliefs and attitudes, consequences for preferences and their utility maximization, ramifications for labor market structure, the fraying of the preference net, and cultural consequences for globalization.

Personal Beliefs and Attitudes

The descriptive and multivariate analyses in Chapter 6 revealed that in our samples of 60 multigenerational families cultural as well as economic factors appear to influence the attitudes and beliefs of our respondents. The chapter's summary table (Table 6.9) clearly shows the stability in beliefs and attitudes across generations in our Swedish and Italian families. Consistent with existing studies in the two countries (e.g., Sweden: Esping-Andersen, 1985, 2002; Hall, 2007; Schumpeter, 1962; Richardson and Van Den Berg, 2006; Pastore, 2018; Italy: Putnam, Leonardi, and Raffaella, 1993; Bigoni et al., 2016; Tabellini, 2008a,b; Guiso, Sapienza, and Zingales, 2006, 2008), we find country effects while statistically controlling for the impact of generational differences. When compared to the liberal market reference category comprised of the United States and India, Swedes, regardless of generation, demonstrate higher levels of trust, commitment to labor force attachment, and cooperative attitudes and intentions. They also show a somewhat stronger penchant for individual achievement, but this difference is less pronounced.

When our Italian families are compared to the two liberal market countries, they manifest significantly lower levels of trust, less of an appetite for risk-taking, less cooperation, and less desire for individual achievement. Along with our Spanish families, Italians in our sample favor policies that allow for the reduction of income differences between the rich and poor. Italians also share with Spanish respondents less of a drive for individual achievement than do respondents in the United States and Indian samples.

The attitudes and beliefs expressed by our German families around risk-taking and the need for individual achievement when contrasted with respondents from liberal market countries are more negative; this is expected given prior research (McClelland, 1964; Weber, Hsu, and Sokolowska, 1998; House et al., 2004; Hofstede, Hofstede, and Minkov, 2010). The negative attitudes of our German respondents around human capital investment and work centrality were not expected, but these findings could simply reflect the basis of comparison (i.e., the highly work-centered value orientations of America and India).

Notwithstanding these patterns of stable beliefs and attitudes within countries, our analysis also pointed up generational differences that cut across all six countries. Controlling for country differences, millennials, in particular, show signs of breaking from the value orientations in their countries. This younger generation is more likely than their parents and grandparents to favor wealth redistribution and less likely to share pro-capitalist beliefs around human capital investment, the centrality of work, commitment to labor force attachment, and individual achievement. Our research is consistent with the work of others (Michau, 2008; Hauff and Kircher, 2015; Hancke, Rhodes, and Thatcher, 2007; Saad, 2019; Ljunge, 2011; Bergquist, 2016; Twenge et al., 2010) who have reported that millennials do not embrace capitalism with the same vigor as their parents and grandparents.

Conclusion

There is substantial evidence that points to the stability of labor-related attitudes and beliefs that cuts across generations and preserves national identities; however, this stability is under assault by economic conditions and oblique forms of value transmission as evidenced by the diminution in these attitudes and beliefs among millennials.

Preferences and Job Utility

In Chapter 7, we extended our analysis beyond cultural beliefs and attitudes to utility preferences, which many economists have linked directly to behavioral intentions and actual behavior (Becker, 1996; McFadden, 1975, 1986; Bisin and Verdier, 2011). Writing from a narrow economist perspective, Becker (1996) acknowledges that "preferences both influence economic outcomes and are in turn influenced by the economy" (p. 18). Our six-nation, multigenerational experiment is an effort to extend the discussion beyond this non-recursive relationship to preferences and cultural value orientations.

One can infer from the work on cultural transmission by Bigoni et al. (2018), Bisin and Verdier (2011), Fernandez (2008), and others that preferences are characterized by a persistence that is not found to the same degree in attitudes or beliefs. This issue is far from settled as the work of Kahneman et al. (1999) and Kahneman and Tversky (1979) and others in the field of cognitive economics demonstrate.

Our stated preference experiment focused on the features of a job that resulted in the greatest utility for our family members. Our features were a mixture of extrinsic and intrinsic work values and sets of hard (cognitive) and soft (noncognitive) skills. In our Italian, Indian, and U.S. samples, we find transgenerational stability with respect to the value placed on the extrinsic factors of job salary and security. Such stability in extrinsic work value has been reported by other researchers (Kalleberg and Marsden, 2013, 2019; Gallie, 2019; Cook and Furstenberg, 2002; Baron, Cobb-Clark, and Erkal, 2008). In Italy and Spain, we also found some evidence for the disutility of hard skills (e.g., second language, math skills) across two of the three generations. For Sweden and Germany, however, we found no evidence to suggest consistency in the decision criteria used by the family member to indicate job preferences.

The Swedish sample, in point of fact, reveals a sharp discontinuity between millennials and their grandparents on the type of job that maximizes utility. For baby boomers, jobs that possess security and provide intrinsic value in the form of a position valued by society are to be pursued; for millennials, jobs honored by society are eschewed as are jobs requiring an investment in hard skills. One feature of stability in the Swedish sample is the preference for jobs in settings that require working in teams—large or small. This penchant for cooperation has been documented throughout the book, and not surprisingly, it is once again revealed at the microlevel of stated preference.

Cross-cutting any of the transgenerational stability we are able to observe within countries, there are fissures evident indicating that millennials, generally, are making employment decisions using decision criteria that differ from their parents and grandparents. In five out of six nations (the exception is the United States), jobs requiring math skills and/or a second language lower that job's utility for younger individuals. Millennials also favor jobs that offer extrinsic rewards in Sweden, Germany, Italy, India, and the United

States; intrinsic rewards are attractive only in the United States and India. Our findings around extrinsic rewards are consistent with those of Twenge et al. (2010), Michau (2008), Kalleberg and Marsden (2013), and Saad, 2019.

Given the importance of numeracy and language in an accelerating global economy (The Economist Intelligent Unit, 2014; DeSilver, 2017; Cunha, Heckman, and Schennach, 2010), the reader might find it puzzling why skills thought by economists to be essential are held in low regard by millennials. Some of the explanation might reside in the weakening popularity of market capitalism (Saad, 2019; Michau, 2008; Esser and Lindh, 2018). An additional determinant might be the increasing popularity, even in Sweden and Germany, of general education tracks and colleges that require more than basic math and science. One result of the educational migration has been the increasing difficulties in developing and hiring skilled technicians and tradesmen and women (CEDEFOP, 2018a; Rinne and Schneider, 2017; Bergquist, 2016; Morath, 2019).

Conclusion

Our stated preference experiment reveals that there is some stability in the decision criteria used by families in four of our country samples. Inferences about continuities in family member job decisions need to be tempered by two generational differences that cut across countries: the disutility of hard skills and the high value placed in extrinsic rewards by millennials. These latter findings do not allow us to rule out the impact of economic opportunity as well as cultural value orientation as the antecedents of job preferences.

Labor Market Structures

A crisis like the 2020 COVID-19 pandemic will undoubtedly once again point up the features of national labor markets that are their most significant vulnerabilities. In this book, we organized our sampling frame around the four principal structures identified by Esping-Andersen (2002). The typology of liberal market economies and coordinated market economies, later expanded to include mixed-market economies (MMEs) by Hall and Soskice (2001) and Hancke, Rhodes, and Thatcher (2007), also figured prominently in our research design. As we have attempted to show throughout this book, labor market structures are the result of preferences that have cultural as well as economic antecedents.

Our country selection allowed us to compare family responses in countries with highly flexible labor markets (United States, India) with those of families in rigid labor markets (Sweden, Germany, Italy, and Spain). National labor markets are the result of choices and the institutionalization of the choices around wage setting, hiring and firing protocols, working conditions, fringe benefits, the length of employer–employee contracts including no contract work, job qualifications, skill levels, and even the adoption of efficient production methods. All these elements are subject to the Bourdieu paradox.

The value orientations that make flexible labor markets possible provide employees with the freedom to set wages/salaries, hire/fire employees, change worker hours, and even cut pay in times of crisis. Separation and/or termination of employees can be undertaken without costly severance pay, compensation packages, lawsuits, or guarantees of transfers or outplacement. As Zimmermann et al. (2013), Pastore (2018), and other labor economists have shown, flexible markets are more often than not associated with higher country gross domestic product and lower rates of long-term unemployment.

Liberal market economies and their flexible labor market arrangements are not the preference of most capitalist democracies where there is real concern about employee security and working conditions. In our samples from coordinated market economies (Sweden and Germany) and MMEs (Italy and Spain) government and, to a lesser extent, labor unions have placed restrictions on firing/termination, probationary periods, outsourced production, and even the substitution of capital for labor (Allard, 2010; Pastore, 2018). These restrictions and other measures including large severance payments, long notice periods, and subsidies to workers for retraining and continuing education have resulted in the formation of rigid labor markets, which in times of crisis can prevent businesses from downsizing due to weak demand for their products or services. Without sufficient cost-cutting, businesses may have to declare bankruptcy or close if regulations prevent them from dismissing employees.

As we discussed in Chapter 4, Germany has introduced flexibility into its otherwise rigid labor market by providing workers through apprenticeships or through its strong vocational education and training (VET) system with the necessary skills to move between job sectors and respond rapidly to innovative technology (Cahuc et al., 2013; Eichhorst and Rinne, 2016). In

Sweden, the rigidity of its labor markets are circumvented with a panoply of VET programs post–high school, that are tightly coordinated with business interests, both legacy and innovative (Carcillo, Hyee, and Keane, 2016; Richardson and Van Den Berg, 2006).

The MMEs of Italy and Spain have not been as successful as Germany and Sweden in introducing pliancy into their labor markets. These countries along with France, Greece, and several others in Europe have chosen to combat rigidity by creating a dual or segmented labor market: one set of rules and guarantees for workers with long-term work contracts and/or union protections and another set for an ever-growing temporary, short-term contract labor force. In France, Askenazy (2019) has documented the steady rise of short-term temporary work contracts over that past 20 years, now reaching the point where nearly half of the labor force works under this condition of continuous uncertainty. He also notes that only about 20 percent of these short-term agreements last for a month or more with the median duration only about eight days. Much the same is occurring in the dual labor markets of Italy and Spain with the added consequence of a growing shadow economy replete with even fewer worker protections (Marino and Nunziata, 2017). Cahuc et al. (2013) present evidence that segmented labor markets substitute long-term unemployment for youth with cyclical forms of unemployment and underemployment.

The effects of rigid markets that have been remedied by the creation of a segmented labor force, however, appear to engender consequences that extend far beyond pay and protection differentials. Allard (2010) points to research linking rigid labor markets to low fertility rates as women (and their spouses) postpone childbearing until one or both secure a permanent work contract. She also discusses the stifling effect that rigid markets can have on innovation especially if protections around seniority force companies to fire their newest and/or youngest workers.

Conclusion

The preference for flexible or rigid labor markets, the institutionalization of that preference, and the remedies utilized to introduce flexibility during times of economic downturn or crisis are rooted in a nation's value orientation in addition to on-the-ground economic conditions. Market structures and the fixes for structural failures resonate the stocks of trust, cooperation, commitment to human capital formation, risk-taking, and need for individual achievement that reside in the people of that nation, qualities that are relatively enduring features of national identity.

Fraying of the Traditional Preference Net

In Chapter 5, we introduced the reader to the often-competing forms of cultural transmission that Bisin and Verdier (2011) have labeled direct, vertical socialization, and oblique horizontal socialization. The latter form can be effectuated through economic and political institutions, but the typical transfer mechanism is education, especially higher education. In our analysis of preferences, attitudes, and beliefs, we have presented evidence that millennials make decisions and express viewpoints around economic questions that often are at variance with older family members. One manifestation of these differences is the diminution of religiosity in our youngest generation; another is the more widespread pursuit of general education and college as a means of escaping the world of "dirty jobs."

A distaste or even contempt for individuals who make their living through the application of technical or vocational skills in European democracies can be traced as far back as the ancient Greeks. Landes (2000) states that Greek luminaires and philosophers coined the term *banausic* to identify the artisan, ship owners, traders, farmers, and other ordinary folk who were believed to lack the education, culture, and refinement necessary to participate fully in Greek life. If McClelland (1964), Lefebvre (1962), and Durant (1963), among others, are correct and French culture reviews itself as the direct descendant of the classical Greek and Roman civilizations, it becomes easier to understand an education "pour l'ordinaire."

To help the reader assess if the banausic legacy in France is a figment of the author's hyperbole, we offer these reviews by OECD. The first done in 1984 (OECD, 1984) sums up the French educational system in this way:

> Its main purpose seems to have been to select and train for the most important jobs in the country. The criteria of selection have predominantly been the talent for abstraction, the ability to simplify complex problems while leaving room for their complexities, and an overall knowledge of French history, philosophy and culture. . . . One of the mainsprings of this system has been to let the best of each generation remain as long as possible in

general education. The vocational training of this elite should therefore begin very late. It could then take place in special institutions, such as les Grandes Ecoles or on-the-job: e.g., public administration in the Foreign Service. (pp. 57–58)

This report then goes on to cite vocational training as second-class education (p. 93) delivered with inadequate tools, broken equipment, meager supplies, and instructors with limited knowledge of the labor market or workplace.

In 2017, OECD once again evaluated the French vocational system (OECD, 2017) and drew these conclusions:

The popularity of the vocational track in secondary education is on decline in France. The number of students in vocational education at the upper secondary school decreased by 9 percent in the period 1995-2015 and the upper secondary level apprenticeship declined by about 2.5 percent.... Overall many students in vocational education specialize in sectors and occupations that are declining, and limited options are available for entering into emerging fields. (p. 66)

This report continues on to point up the poor image of vocational education among employers, students, and parents; the insufficient skill levels of many vocational instructors and the limited knowledge that many of these same instructors have of the workplace or the labor market. These conditions, the authors conclude, have helped France earn the dubious distinction "as one of the few EU countries where the employment rate of vocational, non-tertiary graduates is worse than that of general non-tertiary graduates" (p. 68).

In each of the six democracies, millennials are pursuing educational pathways that favor the acquisition of general knowledge but neglect hands-on experience and skill development. Based on our description of apprenticeship and VET in Italy and Spain (Chapter 3), conditions in these countries appear to be even less desirable than they are in France. The push to attend college under the Obama administration has done little to redeem VET in the United States from poor reputation and stagnant and low student participation rates. In India, we saw a growing problem of graduates and postgraduates from universities who do not possess skills necessary for employment in the growing sectors of the economy (Tara and Kumar, 2017; Zimmermann et al., 2013). Even in Germany the banausic stigma may be taking hold with more students each year following the Gymnasium track and fewer attending Realschule or Hauptschule (OECD, 2019c; Fazekas and Field, 2013). Much the same phenomenon is unfolding in Sweden (Kuczera and Jeon, 2019; Kuczera et al., 2008).

General trends in overeducation, underskilling and skill–education mismatches have appeared to help fortify old forms of intellectual elitism and fuel new forms as competition among the ever-increasing number of tertiary school graduates. In the United States, social scientists have uncovered the rise of a new upper class, part of whose pedigree is defined by attendance at one of America's elite colleges and universities. Charles Murray (2012) points to a narrow set of elite actors with strong connections to Ivy League universities (and a small handful of selective public institutions) who exert a disproportionate impact on affairs of state, the economy, and technology. Murray maintains that the United States is experiencing a new form of residential segregation where the interaction of high cognitive ability and graduation from elite colleges live in relative isolation from the rest of the country. Communities defined by this elite cognitive culture (e.g., The Upper East side in New York City; the Mainline in Philadelphia; Northwest Washington, DC; North Shore, Chicago; Lower Marin County, San Francisco) exhibit a value orientation that De Tocqueville would probably find alien. Murray (2012) sums it up this way:

> The culture of the new upper class carries with it an unmistakable whiff of a we're better than the rabble mentality. The daily yoga and jogging that keep them whippet-thin are not just healthy things for them to do; people who are overweight are less admirable as people. Deciding not to recycle does not reflect just an alternative opinion about whether recycling makes sense; it is inherently irresponsible. Smokers are not to be worried about, but to be held in contempt. (p. 84)

David Brooks (2000) documented the emergence of this new upper class a full decade before Murray did. He referred to them as "Bobos," an acronym for "bourgeois bohemians," exemplified by the elite school educated banker, outfitted in a $3,000 Armani suit and a pair of Nike sneakers. While this portmanteau has never really caught on in the United States, it has maintained popularity in France to describe the country's newer generation of free-spirit capitalist elite. Brooks (2013) has gone on to describe a dynamic that has been activated by the creation of this new educated elite class and the meritocracy that underpins it. Like Murray, he sees wealth, creativity, and power becoming clustered in a few geographic areas, mostly on the United States east and west coasts. Additionally, however, he concludes that the segregation acts as a powerful deterrent to wealth redistribution that cannot be remedied by tax increases because income disparities are primarily a downstream effect of the human capital and geographical disparities.

Even Germany has sought to create a system of elite universities, but since the inception of the endeavor in 2004 under the Schroder regime, questions have been raised about its real purpose (i.e., to create academically elite institutions or to create institutions for the already elite; Hessler, 2004). This initiative was renewed recently and extended through 2026 with press coverage generally lauding the attempt to replicate the United States Ivies and Britain's Oxford and Cambridge (see, e.g., German Center for Research and Innovation, 2019). Whether here, as in the United States and France, this endeavor will create similar patterns of class formation and isolation remains to be seen.

Conclusion

The preference for general education vis-à-vis vocational education and training among Millennials, which promises to accelerate for Generation Z, poses a significant threat to a nation's capacity to develop domestically, complex, value-added goods and services with high earnings margins and export potential. Coupled with the advent of an elite upper class of intellectuals concentrated geographically and sectorally in the IT, communications, professional, and scientific services, there is a mounting danger of "feudal capitalism" or what Kuttner and Stone (2020) call "neo-feudalism," that is, capitalism controlled solely by elites with limited input from a disappearing middle class.

Cultural Consequences for Globalization

The cultural preference nets that we have examined in this book reveal the value orientations, or as McClelland (1964) terms, the value formulae, that individuals and countries organize not only their economic activities around but their identities as well. Metaphorically speaking, these nets both structure and constrain national character. There are many social scientists, politicians, governmental and nongovernmental officials, and intellectuals who believe they do too good of a job in buttressing national character and in so doing produce insularity, xenophobia, primordialism, and even fascism. Albert Einstein is quoted as saying "Nationalism is an infantile sickness. It is the measles of the human race" (Dukos and Hoffman, 1979, p. 38).

The obvious alternative to nationalism is globalism, cosmopolitanism, postnationalism, and modernism. According to modernization theory, the convergence of values due to global economic forces will cause nation-states to melt away (Hauff and Kirchner, 2015). Current events—the election of Donald Trump, Brexit, the rise of conservative-leaning governments in a half dozen other European countries, border closings for immigration control, and now coronavirus—however would seem to indicate that nationalism is far from deceased. Calhoun (2007) notes that despite being the source of many evils, national cultures have been responsible for a great deal of what we call civilization and have produced history's "most enduring and suc-cessful experiments in large-scale democracy" (p. 4).

While the many sins of nationalism have been documented—wars, ethnic cleansing, tariffs, territorial conquests, etc.—the economic and societal issues that accompany globalization are being felt with ever-increasing frequency. In principle, the weakening of the bonds of nationally organized capitalism should result in a concomitant reduction in prejudices and stereotyping, which, in turn, should reduce barriers to trade, cooperation, and innovation and propagate a new source of solidarity. Globalization has surely increased these person-to-person connections, but it has also done so much more by greatly enhancing the influence of multinational corporations and interna-tional governmental bodies whose actions have had the unintended outcome of increasing the very nationalism globalism was designed to extinguish.

In 1989, the MIT Commission of Industrial Productivity (Dertouzos, Solow, and Lester, 1989) produced an industry-by-industry report on the state of American manufacturing in a changing world economy. The Commission asserted that the United States was losing its competitive edge and that this was most evident in manufacturing performance. Curing the weaknesses in manufacturing was seen as essential for five reasons: (a) it is not realistic for the economy to rely on the export of services to pay for imports of manufactured goods because of the total value added differen-tial of manufactured goods compared to services; (b) by ceding high-wage manufacturing industries to other countries, what is to stop high-wage serv-ices that provide inputs to manufacturing—design, engineering, accounting, payroll, finance, insurance, etc. from following? (c) U.S. capital investment is mobile internationally and would follow the opportunities overseas; (d) manufacturing firms account for virtually all of the research and development done by American industry and generate most of the technological innovations adopted both inside and outside their own industry; and (e) a manufacturing base is fundamental to a nation's national security.

The United States engaged in two actions—the ratification of the North American Free Trade Agreement (NAFTA) in January 1994 and the admission of China into the World Trade Organization (WTO) in December 2001—that accelerated this manufacturing loss. Both of these actions were proclaimed as measures that would open markets to American exports while providing consumers with quality imports at low prices. Barlett and Steele (1996) show that the immediate impact of NAFTA was to convert a $688 million surplus with Mexico (1994) into a $16.2 billion trade deficit in 1995. The treaty has been responsible for substantially increasing the import of manufacturing goods while exporting American manufacturing jobs overseas. With China's entry into WTO under developing nation status, the United States trade deficit with that country rose from $83 billion in 2001 to as high as $419 billion in 2018 before declining to $345 billion in 2019. These deficits according to the Economic Policy Institute (Scott, 2017) have cost America 3.4 million jobs, largely in the manufacturing industries.

As we witnessed in our stated preference experiment, a major consideration in job choice is salary. In Sweden, Germany, and, until very recently, the United States, the best way to create good-paying jobs for workers without advanced college degrees is to facilitate the export of manufactured goods and related services. The MIT Commission report (Dertouzos, Lester, and Solow, 1989) described a good company as "not one that pays low wages; it is a firm that has productivity to pay high wages, so that it can hire skilled individuals to operate sophisticated new machinery" (p. 17). Barlett and Steele (1996) are a bit more forceful:

> A society built on the economic principle that the lowest price is all that matters is quite different from a society built on a principle that everyone who wants to work should receive a living wage. The former society—label it the bottom line society—will be filled with retail clerks, warehouse helpers and shippers earning little more than minimum wage. The latter with skilled tradesmen, craftsmen and professional workers earning $20 an hour or more. (p. 26)

Global trade, the multinational corporations that conduct it, and the political institutions that facilitate it ignore the preferences of the American worker with the result being the election of Donald Trump. His message of "Bring American companies back," "Make product in the United States," "Make America great again" and similar shibboleths of nationalism strike many in America's elite upper class as simplistic, even banausic. Opinion polls show that the Trump message does not resonate very well with Bobos, but this could change with a more broad-based outsourcing that affects upper management and professional/scientific jobs.

The global practices of multinational corporations are not the only source for populist recoil—international governing bodies like the International Court of Justice, the World Health Organization, the aforementioned WTO, and the European Union, to name a few, have either through their actions or passivity provoked considerable nationalist backlash. Brexit provides an outstanding case of how cultural preferences, specifically legal preferences, help pave the way to a renewed nationalism.

Writing in the *International and Comparative Law Quarterly*, Legrand (1996) pursued the argument that European legal systems are not converging and are unlikely to do so because of deeply ingrained cultural structures replete with their country-specific epistemologies, mythologies, and histories that cannot be bridged by international legal directives or courts of law. Teubner (2001) advances this argument by detailing the complications and confusion that an EU legal instruction requiring the criterion of "good faith" to be incorporated in British contract law. He explains that in the English common law tradition the notion of bona fides is "clearly at odds with the more rule-oriented, technical, concrete, but loosely systematized British style of legal reasoning" (p. 421). Teubner (2001) goes on to note that general concepts of law like "good faith," "legitimate expectation," "proportionality," and other abstract concepts are at the heart of German law and, in the British legal mind, are specimens of German-style dogmatization.

While legal incompatibilities and continental inclusions on British democracy may have furnished the cultural predispositions for Brexit, it was the globalist orientation of the British Labour Party that served as the precipitating factor. In the December 2019 general election the Labour Party, which had steadfastly opposed leaving the EU, lost in a landslide, securing the Conservative Party's mandate to exit. In writing Labour's epitaph, the trade union activist, Paul Embery (2019) recounts how the party of working-class voters had succumbed to the leadership of "Toytown revolutionaries," British Bobos out of touch with its blue-collar base. Embery writes:

> They failed to grasp that working-class voters desire something more than just economic security; they want cultural security too. They want politicians to respect their way of life and their sense of place and belonging; to elevate real-world concepts such as work, family and community over nebulous constructs like diversity, equality and inclusivity. . . . In the end Labour was losing a culture war that it didn't even realize it was fighting.

Conclusion

Although they show some signs of fraying, the cultural preference nets that we have examined remain resilient. We agree with Calhoun's (2007) assessment that national cultures are not likely to be put to an end by globalization; quite the contrary, they are likely to reinvigorate if globalization engenders anxiety or threatens established value orientations. According to Calhoun (2007) national culture "still matters, still troubles many of us, but still organizes something considerable in who we are . . . seeking to bypass nationalism in pursuit of a rational universalism may reflect equally dangerous illusions" (p. 171).

We would like to end with a small note on the viability of cultural metaphors. It is extremely appealing to have a shorthand mechanism for distilling the essence of a national culture. Notwithstanding the apparent success that Gannon and his associates (Gannon and Pillai, 2016) have had using this approach with managers primarily in business settings, our experience around metaphor efficacy with family members indicates that a good deal more research is needed to establish validity. In our opinion, this validity can only be reached when we uncover metaphors that the general population lives by, to borrow a phrase from Lakoff and Johnson (1980). And perhaps after enough of this research has accumulated, we may find that there are no shortcuts to any place worth going.

Work Values and Opinions
Interview Schedule

Introduction and Consent to Participate

We invite you to participate in a survey that is part of an important research study. This research is conducted by Rutgers University in the United States along with participants from the University of Catania, Italy. We are trying to improve our understanding of youth attitudes toward employment and economic self-sufficiency.

You are one of a small number of people selected to provide opinions and information that will be of great value to business, industry, and government. We would like to get those opinions from you, your parents, and grandparents.

It is important that you answer each question as thoughtfully and candidly as possible. This survey is not a test—there are no right or wrong answers. We realize that some of the questions ask for personal information about you and your family. We can assure you that **your answers are completely confidential**—you as an individual will never be identified. The answers you give will be grouped with the answers of all the other respondents for the purposes of statistical analysis.

The first part of the survey contains questions that ask you about how you see the world, your views on employment, economic self-sufficiency, trust, risk taking, etc., along with some biographical details about you. The second part of the survey contains a set of 16 job choices. In each of these job choices, we describe two jobs and ask you to select the job that you would prefer to have.

The entire survey should take you approximately 30 to 40 minutes to complete. Your participation in this research is completely voluntary—if you do not wish to answer any questions, you do not have to do so. You can stop answering questions anytime you wish.

When you complete the survey, you will be paid 25 euros for your help with this important research. For us to have a record that shows that we paid you, we need your signature and contact information at the bottom of this page.

We thank you very much for your participation. Your help is invaluable.

Your address: _____

_____

Your email address: _____

Your phone number: _____

Your signature: _____

Section 1

In this section of the survey, we would like to know about how you see the world and how you view work and employment.

Q1. Which of these events best describes the way people you know get along with each other? Please select only one answer.

1. A Symphony   ☐ 1
2. An Athletic Contest   ☐ 2
3. An Opera   ☐ 3
4. A Dance Performance   ☐ 4
5. A Quiet Summer Vacation   ☐ 5

Q1a. If not any of these, how would you describe it? _____

_____

_____

Q2. Which of these events best describes the way people you know should get along with each other? Please select only one answer.

1. A Symphony   ☐ 1
2. An Athletic Contest   ☐ 2
3. An Opera   ☐ 3
4. A Dance Performance   ☐ 4
5. A Quiet Summer Vacation   ☐ 5

Q2a. If not any of these, how would you describe it? _____

_____

_____

Q3. Complete the sentence "Life is _____." Please select only one answer.

1. An Investigation   ☐ 1
2. An Exciting Pursuit   ☐ 2
3. A Difficult March   ☐ 3
4. A Journey   ☐ 4
5. A Leisurely Walk   ☐ 5

Q3a. If not any of these, how would you describe it? _____

_____

_____

Q4. Do you Agree or Disagree with these statements. Please select only one answer for each statement.

1. Everyone should be treated equally in the eyes of law   ☐A   ☐D
2. Everyone should have enough money to live comfortably   ☐A   ☐D
3. If some people do not have enough money to live comfortably,
    the more fortunate should give them enough money to do so.   ☐A   ☐D
4. Money should be given to the less fortunate who cannot work.   ☐A   ☐D
5. Money should be given to the less fortunate who do not want
    to work.   ☐A   ☐D

Q5. Do you Agree or Disagree with these statements. Please select only one answer for each statement.

1. Personal happiness is a worthy goal in life. ☐A ☐D
2. No one player is more important than the team. ☐A ☐D
3. Majority rule is best. ☐A ☐D
4. The best ideas come from groups of people working together. ☐A ☐D
5. Great people make history. ☐A ☐D
6. History makes great people. ☐A ☐D

Q6. Do you Agree or Disagree with these statements. Please select only one answer for each statement.

1. The best man or woman deserves to win. ☐A ☐D
2. Winning or losing is not important, it's how you play the game. ☐A ☐D
3. More gets done when people cooperate. ☐A ☐D
4. The best prepared people are the most successful. ☐A ☐D

Q7. Do you Agree or Disagree with these statements. "If given the choice, I would . . ." Please select only one answer for each statement.

1. Ride a roller-coaster and not a merry-go-round. ☐A ☐D
2. Invest in Savings Bonds and not Stocks. ☐A ☐D
3. Speed through a yellow light rather than slow down. ☐A ☐D
4. Bet on the sure thing rather than the longshot. ☐A ☐D

Q8. Do you Agree or Disagree with these statements. Please select only one answer for each statement.

1. Rome was not built in a day. ☐A ☐D
2. Houses made of stone are better than houses made of wood ☐A ☐D
3. A home mortgage is the only purchase you should make
   on-time payment. ☐A ☐D
4. Put off today what you can do tomorrow. ☐A ☐D
5. It is a good idea to put at least 10 percent of earnings on
   a rainy day fund. ☐A ☐D

Q9. Do you Agree or Disagree with these statements. Please select only one answer for each statement.

1. Spontaneity is always a good thing. ☐A ☐D
2. Letting "steam off" is good for your health. ☐A ☐D
3. Most rules were made to be broken. ☐A ☐D
4. It is best not to say the first thing that comes into your head. ☐A ☐D
5. Not having sex before marriage is old fashioned. ☐A ☐D
6. Having a child outside of marriage is not big deal. ☐A ☐D

Q10. How important to you are the following benefits when looking for a job?

	Not at All Important	Somewhat Important	Very Important
1. A health insurance plan	1	2	3
2. A retirement plan such as profit sharing or pension			
3. A bonus plan			
4. Stock options or other stock ownership			
5. Paid vacation			
6. Paid sick time			
7. Flexible work schedule			
8. Opportunities for advancement			
9. Provision of housing			
10. Provision of transportation			
11. Negotiable pay scale			

Q11. Which of the following descriptions applies to what you have been doing for the last month? Select all that apply.

1. In paid work (or away temporarily) (employee, self-employed, working for your family business) ☐
2. In education (not paid for by employer) even if on vacation ☐
3. Unemployed and actively looking for a job ☐
4. Unemployed, wanting a job but not actively looking for a job ☐
5. Permanently sick or disabled ☐
6. Retired ☐
7. In community or military service ☐
8. Doing housework, looking after children or other persons ☐
9. Other _____ ☐

Q12. Please rate yourself on the following statement: My current financial situation allows me to . . .

		1 No, not at all	2 Occasionally	3 Sometimes	4 Most of the time	5 Yes, all of the time
1.	Meet my obligations	☐	☐	☐	☐	☐
2.	Do what I want to do, when I want to do it	☐	☐	☐	☐	☐
3.	Pay my own way without borrowing from family or friends	☐	☐	☐	☐	☐
4.	Afford to have a reliable car	☐	☐	☐	☐	☐
5.	Afford to have decent housing	☐	☐	☐	☐	☐
6.	Buy the kind and amount of food I like	☐	☐	☐	☐	☐
7.	Afford to take trips	☐	☐	☐	☐	☐
8.	Buy "extras" for my family and myself	☐	☐	☐	☐	☐
9.	Pursue my own interests and goals	☐	☐	☐	☐	☐
10.	Get health care for myself and my family	☐	☐	☐	☐	☐
11.	Put money in a savings account	☐	☐	☐	☐	☐
12.	Stay on a budget	☐	☐	☐	☐	☐
13.	Make payments on my debts	☐	☐	☐	☐	☐
14.	Afford decent child care (leave blank if you don't have children)	☐	☐	☐	☐	☐

Q13. Here is a list of qualities which children can be encouraged to learn at home. Which do you consider to be especially important? Please check Yes or No.

	Yes	No
a. Good manners	☐	☐
b. Independence	☐	☐
c. Hard work	☐	☐
d. Feeling of responsibility	☐	☐
e. Imagination	☐	☐
f. Tolerance and respect for other people	☐	☐
g. Thrift, saving money and things	☐	☐
h. Determination, perseverance	☐	☐
i. Religious faith	☐	☐
j. Unselfishness	☐	☐
k. Obedience	☐	☐
l. Love	☐	☐
m. Justice	☐	☐
n. Prudence	☐	☐
o. Courage	☐	☐
p. Temperance	☐	☐
q. Trustworthiness	☐	☐
r. Trusting others	☐	☐
s. Good mathematics skills	☐	☐
t. Learning a second language	☐	☐
u. Public speaking	☐	☐
v. Basic science knowledge	☐	☐
w. Learning historical facts	☐	☐

Q14. If you were to get enough money to live as comfortably as you would like for the rest of your life, would you continue to work or would you stop working?

Continue to work ☐
Stop working ☐
Don't know ☐

Q15. On a scale from 0 to 10 would you say that in general you are a person who tends to avoid taking risks or are you fully prepared to take risks?

0	1	2	3	4	5	6	7	8	9	10
I tend to avoid risks										I am fully prepared to take risks
☐	☐	☐	☐	☐	☐	☐	☐	☐	☐	☐

Q16. To what extent do you agree or disagree with the following statements?

	4 Strongly agree	3 Somewhat agree	2 Somewhat disagree	1 Strongly disagree
a. I often set a goal but later choose to pursue a different one	☐	☐	☐	☐
b. I have difficulty maintaining my focus on projects that take more than a few months to complete	☐	☐	☐	☐
c. New ideas and projects sometimes distract me from previous ones	☐	☐	☐	☐
d. I always finish whatever I begin	☐	☐	☐	☐
e. Setbacks discourage me	☐	☐	☐	☐
f. I am hard working	☐	☐	☐	☐
g. I am confident that I can deal efficiently with unexpected events	☐	☐	☐	☐
h. Usually I do more than I am asked to do	☐	☐	☐	☐
i. My life is determined by my own actions	☐	☐	☐	☐

Q17. There are many reasons why people think that work is important. Please read the following and tell us how much you agree or disagree with them.

	1 Strongly disagree	2 Disagree	3 Neither agree nor disagree	4 Agree Strongly	5 agree
a. To fully develop your talents you need to have a job.	☐	☐	☐	☐	☐
b. It's humiliating to receive money without having to work.	☐	☐	☐	☐	☐
c. If welfare benefits are too high there is no incentive to find	☐	☐	☐	☐	☐
d. Work is a duty toward society.	☐	☐	☐	☐	☐
e. Work should always come first even if it means less spare time.	☐	☐	☐	☐	☐
f. Everyone should have the right to a minimum income even if they are not working.	☐	☐	☐	☐	☐
g. A husband's job is to earn money; a wife's job is to look after the home and family	☐	☐	☐	☐	☐

Q18. How many times in the last twelve months have you:

	Never	1-2 times	3-5 times	More than 5 times
a. Attended a ballet, classical music concert, the theatre or an opera	☐	☐	☐	☐
b. Visited museums or galleries	☐	☐	☐	☐
c. Finished reading a book	☐	☐	☐	☐

Q19. Generally speaking, would you say that most people can be trusted, or that you can't be too careful in dealing with people? Please indicate on a score of 0 to 10, where 0 means you can't be too careful and 10 means that most people can be trusted.

0		1	2	3	4	5	6	7	8	9	10
you can't be too careful											trusted
☐		☐	☐	☐	☐	☐	☐	☐	☐	☐	☐

Q20. Please look carefully at the following list of voluntary organizations and activities and say which, if any, you belong to.

	Yes	No
Social welfare services for elderly, handicapped or deprived people	☐	☐
Religious or church organizations	☐	☐
Education, arts, music or cultural activities	☐	☐
Trade unions	☐	☐
Political parties or groups	☐	☐
Local community action on issues like poverty, employment, housing, racial inequality	☐	☐
Third world development or human rights	☐	☐
Conservation, the environment, ecology	☐	☐
Professional associations	☐	☐
Youth work (e.g. scouts, guides, youth clubs, etc.)	☐	☐
Sports or recreation	☐	☐
Women's groups	☐	☐
Peace movement	☐	☐
Animal rights	☐	☐
Voluntary organizations concerned with health	☐	☐
Other groups_____(please specify)	☐	☐
None	☐	☐

We would now like to ask you about your education and employment experiences. We also ask about your parents and grandparents and their education.

Q21.   What is your date of birth? What is the highest grade in school that you completed? What was your major or program of study? Do you have any vocational or technical training?

Name	Sex	DOB	Age	Highest year of education completed	Program of study (College Major)	Vocational Training? (yes/no)
RESPONDENT	F					
	M					
FATHER	M					
MOTHER	F					
GRANDFATHER	M					
GRANDMOTHER	F					

Q22.   Your work history:

JOB	CURRENT JOB	PREVIOUS JOB #1	PREVIOUS JOB #2	PREVIOUS JOB #3
Where do/ did you work? (Name of employer)				
Are/were you self-employed?				
How long were you at this job? (from when to when)				
How many hours per week did you work at this job?				
What were your hourly/weekly wages at this job?				
What type of business or in-dustry did you work in?				
What type of work did you do?				
Did you receive health insur-ance benefits from this job?				
Why did you leave your pre-vious jobs?				

Q23. Do you consider yourself as belonging to any particular religion or denomination?

Yes	☐ 1
No	☐ 2

Q24. If you said Yes to Q15, please indicate which religion:

Roman Catholic	☐ 1
Protestant	☐ 2
Eastern Orthodox	☐ 3
Other Christian Denomination	☐ 4
Jewish	☐ 5
Islamic	☐ 6
Buddhist	☐ 7
Hindu	☐ 8
Other	☐ 9

Q25. Regardless of whether you belong to a particular religion, how religious would you say you are?

0	1	2	3	4	5	6	7	8	9	10	97
Not at all religious										Very religious	No answer
☐	☐	☐	☐	☐	☐	☐	☐	☐	☐	☐	☐

Q26. What is your current marital status?

1 Married
2 Divorced
3 Separated
4 Widowed
5 Single (Never married)

Q27. Where were you born?

_____

Q28. If you add up the income from all sources, which number describes your personal annual total net income? If you don't know the exact figure, please give an estimate:

Less than [15,000 euros per year]	☐ 1
Between [15,001 and 25,000 euros per year]	☐ 2
Between [25,001 and 35,000 euros per year]	☐ 3
Between [35,001 and 45,000 euros per year]	☐ 4
Between [45,001 and 55,000 euros per year]	☐ 5
Between [55,001 and 65,000 euros per year]	☐ 6
Between [65,001 and 75,000 euros per year]	☐ 7
Over [75,000 euros per year]	☐ 10
Don't know	☐ 98

Q29. In politics people sometimes talk of "left" and "right". Where would you place yourself on the scale below, where 0 means left and 10 means right?

left	1	2	3	4	5	6	7	8	9	right
☐	☐	☐	☐	☐	☐	☐	☐	☐	☐	☐

Thank you for your help

Now please proceed with the second part of the survey that contains 16 hypothetical job scenarios, and for each one, place a check on the job you would choose.

Section 2

DCZ—CTB1

Job 1

Type of job	In Government
Salary	At minimum €35,000 per year
Job skill set	Job requires Native Language only
Job prestige	Job Valued/Honored by Parents
Job setting	Work alone

Job 2

Type of job	Private Sector/Business
Salary	At minimum €50,000 per year
Job skill set	Job requires Native Language skills only
Job prestige	Job Valued/Honored by Society
Job setting	Work closely with 1–3 people

I would choose:
Job 1	( )
Job 2	( )

SGP- CTB1

Job 1

Type of job	In Government
Salary	At minimum €50,000 per year
Job skill set	Job requires Skills in Native Language, English and Math
Job prestige	Job Valued/Honored by Society
Job setting	Work alone

Job 2

Type of job	Self-Employed
Salary	At minimum €75,000 per year
Job skill set	Job requires Skills in Native Language and English
Job prestige	Job Valued/Honored by Society
Job setting	Work closely with a large team of people

I would choose:
Job 1	( )
Job 2	( )

EPV- CTB1

Job 1

Type of job	In Government
Salary	At minimum €50,000 per year
Job skill set	Job requires Native Language skills only
Job prestige	Job Valued/Honored by Parents
Job setting	Work closely with a large team of people

Job 2

Type of job	Self-Employed
Salary	At minimum €50,000 per year
Job skill set	Job requires Skills in Native Language and English
Job prestige	Job Valued/Honored by Society
Job setting	Work closely with a large team of people

I would choose:

Job 1	( )
Job 2	( )

MVE- CTB1

Job 1

Type of job	Self-Employed
Salary	At minimum €35,000 per year
Job skill set	Job requires Native Language skills only
Job prestige	Job Valued/Honored by Society
Job setting	Work alone

Job 2

Type of job	Private Sector/Business
Salary	At minimum €50,000 per year
Job skill set	Job requires Skills in Native Language and English
Job prestige	Job Valued/Honored by Society
Job setting	Work closely with a large team of people

I would choose:

Job 1	( )
Job 2	( )

POS- CTB1

Job 1

Type of job	In Government
Salary	At minimum €50,000 per year
Job skill set	Job requires Skills in Native Language, English and Math
Job prestige	Job Valued/Honored by Parents
Job setting	Work alone

Job 2

Type of job	Private Sector/Business
Salary	At minimum €50,000 per year
Job skill set	Job requires Native Language skills only
Job prestige	Job Valued/Honored by Me
Job setting	Work closely with a large team of people

I would choose:

Job 1	( )
Job 2	( )

CXP- CTB1

Job 1

Type of job	Self-Employed
Salary	At minimum €50,000 per year
Job skill set	Job requires Native Language skills only
Job prestige	Job Valued/Honored by Society
Job setting	Work closely with a large team of people

Job 2

Type of job	Self-Employed
Salary	At minimum €50,000 per year
Job skill set	Job requires Native Language skills only
Job prestige	Job Valued/Honored by Society
Job setting	Work closely with 1–3 people

I would choose:

Job 1	( )
Job 2	( )

POG- CTB1

Job 1

Type of job	In Government
Salary	At minimum €35,000 per year
Job skill set	Job requires Native Language skills only
Job prestige	Job Valued/Honored by Parents
Job setting	Work alone

Job 2

Type of job	Self-Employed
Salary	At minimum €75,000 per year
Job skill set	Job requires Skills in Native Language and English
Job prestige	Job Valued/Honored by Me
Job setting	Work closely with 1–3 people

I would choose:

Job 1	( )
Job 2	( )

CPS- CTB1

Job 1

Type of job	Self-Employed
Salary	At minimum €50,000 per year
Job skill set	Job requires Skills in Native Language, English and Math
Job prestige	Job Valued/Honored by Parents
Job setting	Work alone

Job 2

Type of job	Self-Employed
Salary	At minimum €75,000 per year
Job skill set	Job requires Native Language skills only
Job prestige	Job Valued/Honored by Society
Job setting	Work closely with 1–3 people

I would choose:

Job 1	( )
Job 2	( )

LDK- CTB1

Job 1

Type of job	In Government
Salary	At minimum €35,000 per year
Job skill set	Job requires Native Language skills only
Job prestige	Job Valued/Honored by Society
Job setting	Work closely with a large team of people

Job 2

Type of job	Self-Employed
Salary	At minimum €50,000 per year
Job skill set	Job requires Skills in Native Language and English
Job prestige	Job Valued/Honored by Me
Job setting	Work closely with 1–3 people

I would choose:

Job 1	()
Job 2	()

PSE- CTB1

Job 1

Type of job	Self-Employed
Salary	At minimum €50,000 per year
Job skill set	Job requires Skills in Native Language, English and Math
Job prestige	Job Valued/Honored by Parents
Job setting	Work alone

Job 2

Type of job	Private Sector/Business
Salary	At minimum €50,000 per year
Job skill set	Job requires Skills in Native Language and English
Job prestige	Job Valued/Honored by Me
Job setting	Work closely with 1–3 people

I would choose:

	Job 1	()
	Job 2	()

IDS- CTB1

Job 1

Type of job	Self-Employed
Salary	At minimum €35,000 per year
Job skill set	Job requires Skills in Native Language, English and Math
Job prestige	Job Valued/Honored by Parents
Job setting	Work closely with a large team of people

Job 2

Type of job	Private Sector/Business
Salary	At minimum €75,000 per year
Job skill set	Job requires Skills in Native Language and English
Job prestige	Job Valued/Honored by Society
Job setting	Work closely with a large team of people

I would choose:

	Job 1	()
	Job 2	()

ALE- CTB1

Job 1

Type of job	In Government
Salary	At minimum €50,000 per year
Job skill set	Job requires Native Language skills only
Job prestige	Job Valued/Honored by Parents
Job setting	Work closely with a large team of people

Job 2

Type of job	Private Sector/Business
Salary	At minimum €75,000 per year
Job skill set	Job requires Native Language skills only
Job prestige	Job Valued/Honored by Me
Job setting	Work closely with a large team of people

I would choose:

	Job 1	( )
	Job 2	( )

SPD- CTB1

Job 1

Type of job	Self-Employed
Salary	At minimum €35,000 per year
Job skill set	Job requires Native Language skills only
Job prestige	Job Valued/Honored by Society
Job setting	Work alone

Job 2

Type of job	Self-Employed
Salary	At minimum €75,000 per year
Job skill set	Job requires Native Language skills only
Job prestige	Job Valued/Honored by Me
Job setting	Work closely with a large team of people

I would choose:

Job 1	( )
Job 2	( )

MSN- CTB1

Job 1

Type of job	In Government
Salary	At minimum €35,000 per year
Job skill set	Job requires Skills in Native Language, English and Math
Job prestige	Job Valued/Honored by Society
Job setting	Work closely with a large team of people

Job 2

Type of job	Private Sector/Business
Salary	At minimum €75,000 per year
Job skill set	Job requires Skills in Native Language
Job prestige	Job Valued/Honored by Society
Job setting	Work closely with 1–3 people

I would choose:

Job 1	( )
Job 2	( )

XST- CTB1

Job 1

Type of job	Self-Employed
Salary	At minimum €35,000 per year
Job skill set	Job requires Skills in Native Language, English and Math
Job prestige	Job Valued/Honored by Parents
Job setting	Work closely with a large team of people

Job 2

Type of job	Self-Employed
Salary	At minimum €50,000 per year
Job skill set	Job requires Native Language skills only
Job prestige	Job Valued/Honored by Society
Job setting	Work closely with a large team of people

I would choose:

Job 1	()
Job 2	()

ROC- CTB1

Job 1

Type of job	Self-Employed
Salary	At minimum €50,000 per year
Job skill set	Job requires Native Language skills only
Job prestige	Job Valued/Honored by Society
Job setting	Work closely with a large team of people

Job 2

Type of job	Private Sector/Business
Salary	At minimum €75,000 per year
Job skill set	Job requires Skills in Native Language and English
Job prestige	Job Valued/Honored by Me
Job setting	Work closely with 1–3 people

I would choose:

Job 1	()
Job 2	()

Regression Results Supporting Chapter 6 Discussion

Trust

```
. reg Q19_trustotherpeople Millennial GenX Reg_Maurizio SanArco
Johnholm Christineberg if small_n==1 ;
```

Source	SS	df	MS		
Model	146.922222	6	24.487037		
Residual	1053.98889	173	6.09242132		
Total	1200.91111	179	6.70900062		

```
Number of obs =       180
F(6, 173)     =      4.02
Prob > F      =    0.0009
R-squared     =    0.1223
Adj R-squared =    0.0919
Root MSE      =    2.4683
```

Q19_trusto~e	Coef.	Std. Err.	t	P>t	[95% Conf. Interval]
Millennial	.05	.4506448	0.11	0.912	-.8394697 .9394697
GenX	-.1166667	.4506448	-0.26	0.796	-1.006136 .772803
Reg_Maurizio	-1.466667	.5519249	-2.66	0.009	-2.55604 -.3772932
SanArco	.5	.5519249	0.91	0.366	-.5893735 1.589373
Johnholm	1.5	.5519249	2.72	0.007	.4106265 2.589373
Christineberg	-.4666667	.5519249	-0.85	0.399	-1.55604 .6227068
_cons	5.088889	.4113805	12.37	0.000	4.276918 5.90086

Reference categories are Baby Boomers for the generations and Sherianne and Raazpuram for labor markets.

```
. logit Q13r_trustingothers Millennial GenX Reg_Maurizio SanArco
Johnholm Christineberg if small_n==1 ;

Iteration 0:   log likelihood = -92.330008

Iteration 1:   log likelihood = -87.872465

Iteration 2:   log likelihood = -87.638519

Iteration 3:   log likelihood = -87.63742

Iteration 4:   log likelihood = -87.63742


Logistic regression                          Number of obs   =       173
                                             LR chi2(6)      =      9.39
                                             Prob > chi2     =    0.1530
Log likelihood = -87.63742                   Pseudo R2       =    0.0508
```

```
Q13r_trustingothers ¦  Coef.    Std. Err.    z     P>z   [95% Conf. Interval]
        Millennial¦ -.5290918  .4518451  -1.17  0.242   -1.414692  .3565083
              GenX¦  .0586292  .4826655   0.12  0.903    -.8873778 1.004636
       Reg_Maurizio¦ -.085093  .5146932  -0.17  0.869   -1.093873  .9236872
           SanArco¦  .6250503  .5741974   1.09  0.276     -.500356 1.750457
          Johnholm¦ 1.602111   .7932345   2.02  0.043       .0474  3.156822
      Christineberg¦ -.0652359 .5150076  -0.13  0.899   -1.074632  .9441605
             _cons¦ 1.164766   .4064297   2.87  0.004     .3681782 1.961354
```

Reference categories are Baby Boomers for the generations and
Sherianne and Raazpuram for labor markets.

Redistributive Justice

. reg Q17f_minimumincomeright Millennial GenX Reg_Maurizio SanArco
Johnholm Christineberg if small_n==1 ;

```
    Source ¦    SS        df      MS        Number of obs  =     177
-----------+----------------------------   F(6, 170)      =    5.19
     Model¦ 44.8375791    6   7.47292985   Prob > F       =  0.0001
  Residual¦ 244.733042   170  1.43960613   R-squared      =  0.1548
-----------+----------------------------   Adj R-squared  =  0.1250
     Total¦ 289.570621   176  1.64528762   Root MSE       =  1.1998
```

```
Q17f_minim~t ¦  Coef.    Std. Err.    t     P>t   [95% Conf. Interval]
Millennial    ¦ .0122582  .220984    0.06  0.956  -.4239679   .4484844
GenX          ¦ -.0587169 .2218853  -0.26  0.792  -.4967221   .3792884
Reg_Maurizio  ¦ 1.183333  .2682915   4.41  0.000   .6537215   1.712945
SanArco       ¦ 1.083333  .2682915   4.04  0.000   .5537215   1.612945
Johnholm      ¦ .0654765  .2713937   0.24  0.810  -.4702592   .6012122
Christineberg ¦ .4013901  .2746425   1.46  0.146  -.1407589    .943539
_cons         ¦ 2.39882   .2010166  11.93  0.000  2.002009    2.79563
```

Reference categories are Baby Boomers for the generations and
Sherianne and Raazpuram for labor markets.

.logit Q45_givemoney_donotwanttowork Millennial GenX Reg_Maurizio
SanArco Johnholm Christineberg if small_n==1 ;

note: Reg_Maurizio != 0 predicts failure perfectly
      Reg_Maurizio dropped and 30 obs not used

```
Iteration 0:     log likelihood = -46.230354
Iteration 1:     log likelihood = -42.49429
Iteration 2:     log likelihood = -41.863986
Iteration 3:     log likelihood = -41.853716
Iteration 4:     log likelihood = -41.853713
```

```
Logistic regression                      Number of obs   =       147
                                         LR chi2(5)      =      8.75
                                         Prob > chi2     =    0.1193
Log likelihood = -41.853713              Pseudo R2       =    0.0947
```

Q45_givemoney_ donotwanttowork	Coef.	Std. Err.	z	P>z	[95% Conf. Interval]	
Millennial	2.247875	1.085012	2.07	0.038	.1212911	4.374458
GenX	1.67249	1.117597	1.50	0.135	-.5179599	3.862939
Reg_Maurizio	0 (omitted)					
SanArco	-.18559	.7464965	-0.25	0.804	-1.648696	1.277516
Johnholm	-1.380195	1.105116	-1.25	0.212	-3.546183	.7857935
Christineberg	-.1164837	.7483972	-0.16	0.876	-1.583315	1.350348
_cons	-3.626398	1.053927	-3.44	0.001	-5.692057	-1.560739

Reference categories are Baby Boomers for the generations and Sherianne and Raazpuram for labor markets.

```
. logit Q44_givemoney_cannotwork Millennial GenX Reg_Maurizio
SanArco Johnholm Christineberg if small_n==1 ;

Iteration 0:   log likelihood = -77.460452
Iteration 1:   log likelihood = -69.856506
Iteration 2:   log likelihood = -69.043124
Iteration 3:   log likelihood = -69.031377
Iteration 4:   log likelihood = -69.031341
Iteration 5:   log likelihood = -69.031341


Logistic regression                      Number of obs   =      = 178
                                         LR chi2(6)      =     16.86
                                         Prob > chi2     =    0.0098
Log likelihood = -69.031341              Pseudo R2       =   =0.1088
```

Q44_givemoney_ cannotwork	Coef.	Std. Err.	z	P>z	[95% Conf. Interval]	
Millennial	-.1380849	.5475693	-0.25	0.801	-1.211301	.9351311
GenX	-.3742306	.5291224	-0.71	0.479	-1.411291	.6628302
Reg_Maurizio	1.737152	.7872229	2.21	0.027	.1942236	3.280081
SanArco	2.466214	1.057614	2.33	0.020	.3933283	4.5391
Johnholm	1.737152	.7872229	2.21	0.027	.1942236	3.280081
Christineberg	.43974	.5424546	0.81	0.418	-.6234515	1.502931
_cons	1.083118	.439124	2.47	0.014	.222451	1.943785

Reference categories are Baby Boomers for the generations and Sherianne and Raazpuram for labor markets.

Educational Training

```
.logit Q13s_goodmathskills Millennial GenX Reg_Maurizio SanArco
Johnholm Christineberg if small_n==1 ;

Iteration 0:    log likelihood = -109.31514
Iteration 1:    log likelihood = -101.61932
Iteration 2:    log likelihood = -101.45402
Iteration 3:    log likelihood = -101.45398
Iteration 4:    log likelihood = -101.45398
```

```
Logistic regression                     Number of obs  =      174
                                        LR chi2(6)     =    15.72
                                        Prob > chi2    =   0.0153
Log likelihood = -101.45398             Pseudo R2      =   0.0719
```

Q13s_goodmathskills	Coef.	Std. Err.	z	P>z	[95% Conf. Interval]	
Millennial	-.9398189	.4411838	-2.13	0.033	-1.804523	-.0751145
GenX	-1.060656	.4413376	-2.40	0.016	-1.925661	-.1956498
Reg_Maurizio	-.8880015	.5234385	-1.70	0.090	-1.913922	.1379192
SanArco	-.7180518	.5137996	-1.40	0.162	-1.725081	.2889769
Johnholm	-1.436396	.5093279	-2.82	0.005	-2.434661	-.438132
Christineberg	-.7496436	.5161003	-1.45	0.146	-1.761182	.2618945
_cons	2.119191	.4538185	4.67	0.000	1.229723	3.008659

Reference categories are Baby Boomers for the generations and
Sherianne and Raazpuram for labor markets.

```
.  logit Q13t_learnsecondlanguage Millennial GenX Reg_Maurizio
SanArco Johnholm Christineberg if small_n==1 ;

note: SanArco != 0 predicts success perfectly
      SanArco dropped and 30 obs not used

Iteration 0:    log likelihood = -85.726845
Iteration 1:    log likelihood = -83.536349
Iteration 2:    log likelihood = -83.513983
Iteration 3:    log likelihood = -83.513976
```

```
Logistic regression                     Number of obs  =      146
                                        LR chi2(5)     =     4.43
                                        Prob > chi2    =   0.4899
Log likelihood = -83.513976             Pseudo R2      =   0.0258
```

Q13t_learnsecondlanguage	Coef.	Std. Err.	z	P>z	[95% Conf. Interval]	
Millennial	.2543394	.4661855	0.55	0.585	-.6593674	1.168046
GenX	.0196314	.4548797	0.04	0.966	-.8719164	.9111791
Reg_Maurizio	.3396297	.5808729	0.58	0.559	-.7988602	1.47812
SanArco	0	(omitted)				
Johnholm	-.6091614	.4996346	-1.22	0.223	-1.588427	.3701044
Christineberg	-.644762	.4872247	-1.32	0.186	-1.599705	.3101809
_cons	1.101832	.4001941	2.75	0.006	.3174659	1.886198

Reference categories are Baby Boomers for the generations and Sherianne and Raazpuram for labor markets.
.logit Q13v_basicscience Millennial GenX Reg_Maurizio SanArco Johnholm Christineberg if small_n==1 ;

```
Iteration 0:   log likelihood = -105.03251
Iteration 1:   log likelihood = -94.629773
Iteration 2:   log likelihood = -94.246344
Iteration 3:   log likelihood = -94.244648
Iteration 4:   log likelihood = -94.244648
```

Logistic regression				Number of obs	=	176
				LR chi2(6)	=	21.58
				Prob > chi2	=	0.0014
Log likelihood = -94.244648				Pseudo R2	=	0.1027

Q13v_basicscience	Coef.	Std. Err.	z	P>z	[95% Conf. Interval]	
Millennial	-.5399659	.4451556	-1.21	0.225	-1.412455	.3325231
GenX	-.4605541	.4474247	-1.03	0.303	-1.33749	.4163822
Reg_Maurizio	-1.027249	.527711	-1.95	0.052	-2.061544	.0070453
SanArco	.5911012	.7020458	0.84	0.400	-.7848833	1.967086
Johnholm	-1.474774	.5165002	-2.86	0.004	-2.487096	-.4624527
Christineberg	-1.49188	.5071596	-2.94	0.003	-2.485894	-.4978651
_cons	1.961525	.4529471	4.33	0.000	1.073765	2.849285

Reference categories are Baby Boomers for the generations and Sherianne and Raazpuram for labor markets.

Work Centrality

. reg Q17b_moneywithoutwork Millennial GenX Reg_Maurizio SanArco Johnholm Christineberg if small_n==1 ;

Source	SS	df	MS		Number of obs	=	177
					F(6, 170)	=	3.80
Model	35.7135707	6	5.95226178		Prob > F	=	0.0014
Residual	266.568915	170	1.56805244		R-squared	=	0.1181
					Adj R-squared	=	0.0870
Total	302.282486	176	1.71751412		Root MSE	=	1.2522

Q17b_money~k	Coef.	Std. Err.	t	P>t	[95% Conf. Interval]	
Millennial	-.4791839	.2306319	-2.08	0.039	-.934455	-.0239127
GenX	-.2138694	.2315725	-0.92	0.357	-.6709973	.2432585
Reg_Maurizio	-.2666667	.2800047	-0.95	0.342	-.8194006	.2860673
SanArco	-1.066667	.2800047	-3.81	0.000	-1.619401	-.5139327
Johnholm	-.3460569	.2832424	-1.22	0.223	-.905182	.2130683
Christineberg	-.8316131	.286633	-2.90	0.004	-1.397432	-.2657947
_cons	3.964351	.2097927	18.90	0.000	3.550217	4.378485

Reference categories are Baby Boomers for the generations and Sherianne and Raazpuram for labor markets.

```
. reg  Q17e_workpriority  Millennial  GenX  Reg_Maurizio  SanArco
Johnholm Christineberg if small_n==1 ;
```

Source	SS	df	MS
Model	46.1272171	6	7.68786952
Residual	283.612896	170	1.66831115
Total	329.740113	176	1.87352337

```
Number of obs   =      177
F(6, 170)       =     4.61
Prob > F        =   0.0002
R-squared       =   0.1399
Adj R-squared   =   0.1095
Root MSE        =   1.2916
```

Q17e_workp~y	Coef.	Std. Err.	t	P>t	[95% Conf. Interval]	
Millennial	-.8768836	.2378907	-3.69	0.000	-1.346484	-.4072834
GenX	.0906709	.238861	0.38	0.705	-.3808446	.5621864
Reg_Maurizio	-.4666667	.2888175	-1.62	0.108	-1.036797	.1034639
SanArco	-.2666667	.2888175	-0.92	0.357	-.8367973	.3034639
Johnholm	.0550139	.2921571	0.19	0.851	-.5217091	.6317369
Christineberg	-.6328043	.2956545	-2.14	0.034	-1.216431	-.0491774
_cons	3.595404	.2163957	16.61	0.000	3.168235	4.022573

Reference categories are Baby Boomers for the generations and Sherianne and Raazpuram for labor markets.

```
. logit workanyway Millennial GenX Reg_Maurizio SanArco Johnholm
Christineberg if small_n==1 ;

Iteration 0:    log likelihood = -116.37146
Iteration 1:    log likelihood = -112.78749
Iteration 2:    log likelihood = -112.77702
Iteration 3:    log likelihood = -112.77702


Logistic regression                  Number of obs   = = 177
                                     LR chi2(6)      =   7.19
                                     Prob > chi2     = 0.3037
Log likelihood = -112.77702          Pseudo R2       = = 0.0309
```

workanyway	Coef.	Std. Err.	z	P>z	[95% Conf. Interval]	
Millennial	.5957884	.3893862	1.53	0.126	-.1673945	1.358971
GenX	.5179344	.3867289	1.34	0.180	-.2400403	1.275909
Reg_Maurizio	-.7182197	.4639195	-1.55	0.122	-1.627485	.1910459
SanArco	-.0130843	.4817003	-0.03	0.978	-.9571996	.931031
Johnholm	.2497088	.5046528	0.49	0.621	-.7393926	1.23881
Christineberg	-.4452398	.4665246	-0.95	0.340	-1.359611	.4691317
_cons	.3459598	.3564728	0.97	0.332	-.3527141	1.044634

Reference categories are Baby Boomers for the generations and Sherianne and Raazpuram for labor markets.

Labor Force Attachment

```
. logit lfstat_new Millennial GenX Reg_Maurizio SanArco Johnholm
Christineberg if small_n==1 ;

Iteration 0:   log likelihood = -124.75538
Iteration 1:   log likelihood = -106.22946
Iteration 2:   log likelihood = -106.12035
Iteration 3:   log likelihood = -106.12008
Iteration 4:   log likelihood = -106.12008


Logistic regression                     Number of obs   =        180
                                         LR chi2(6)      =      37.27
                                         Prob > chi2     =     0.0000
Log likelihood = -106.12008             Pseudo R2       =     0.1494
```

lfstat_new	Coef.	Std. Err.	z	P>z	[95% Conf. Interval]	
Millennial	-1.745513	.4269563	-4.09	0.000	-2.582332	-.9086936
GenX	-.4607038	.3937893	-1.17	0.242	-1.232517	.3111091
Reg_Maurizio	.3032541	.4781092	0.63	0.526	-.6338228	1.240331
SanArco	-.6252296	.4917822	-1.27	0.204	-1.589105	.3386458
Johnholm	1.716989	.560894	3.06	0.002	.6176567	2.816321
Christineberg	-.4630816	.4853991	-0.95	0.340	-1.414446	.4882831
_cons	.5670917	.3579431	1.58	0.113	-.1344638	1.268647

Reference categories are Baby Boomers for the generations and
Sherianne and Raazpuram for labor markets.

Risk-Taking

```
. reg Q15_takingrisks Millennial GenX Reg_Maurizio SanArco Johnholm
Christineberg if small_n==1 ;
```

Source	SS	df	MS		Number of obs = 178
					F(6, 171) = 7.02
Model	253.146038	6	42.1910064		Prob > F = 0.0000
Residual	1027.15171	171	6.00673517		R-squared = 0.1977
					Adj R-squared = 0.1696
Total	1280.29775	177	7.23332064		Root MSE = 2.4509

Q15_taking~s	Coef.	Std. Err.	t	P>t	[95% Conf. Interval]	
Millennial	2.11116	.4493782	4.70	0.000	1.224117	2.998203
GenX	1.797028	.4494115	4.00	0.000	.9099195	2.684137
Reg_Maurizio	-1.094493	.5495935	-1.99	0.048	-2.179354	-.0096319
SanArco	.7055068	.5495935	1.28	0.201	-.3793545	1.790368
Johnholm	-.4278265	.5495935	-0.78	0.437	-1.512688	.6570348
Christineberg	-1.53377	.5559476	-2.76	0.006	-2.631174	-.4363664
_cons	4.558431	.4096523	11.13	0.000	3.749804	5.367057

Reference categories are Baby Boomers for the generations and
Sherianne and Raazpuram for labor markets.

```
. logit  Q72_savingbondsVSstocks  Millennial  GenX  Reg_Maurizio
SanArco Johnholm Christineberg if small_n==1 ;

Iteration 0:    log likelihood = -118.93045
Iteration 1:    log likelihood = -109.53846
Iteration 2:    log likelihood = -109.50654
Iteration 3:    log likelihood = -109.50654
```

```
Logistic regression                  Number of obs    =        172
                                     LR chi2(6)       =      18.85
                                     Prob > chi2      =     0.0044
Log likelihood = -109.50654          Pseudo R2        =     0.0792
```

Q72_ savingbondsVSstocks	Coef.	Std. Err.	z	P>z	[95% Conf. Interval]	
Millennial	-.4787853	.399055	-1.20	0.230	-1.260919	.3033481
GenX	-.5275756	.3984889	-1.32	0.186	-1.308599	.2534483
Reg_Maurizio	-1.162139	.4853458	-2.39	0.017	-2.113399	-.2108786
SanArco	.9884977	.5328808	1.86	0.064	-.0559295	2.032925
Johnholm	-.5802091	.4625854	-1.25	0.210	-1.48686	.3264416
Christineberg	-.5908915	.4737911	-1.25	0.212	-1.519505	.3377221
_cons	.7007949	.3652202	1.92	0.055	-.0150235	1.416613

Reference categories are Baby Boomers for the generations and Sherianne and Raazpuram for labor markets.

```
. logit  Q74_surethingVSlongshot  Millennial  GenX  Reg_Maurizio
SanArco Johnholm Christineberg if small_n==1 ;

Iteration 0:    log likelihood = -102.80814
Iteration 1:    log likelihood = -93.747823
Iteration 2:    log likelihood = -93.343469
Iteration 3:    log likelihood = -93.341665
Iteration 4:    log likelihood = -93.341665
```

```
Logistic regression                  Number of obs    =        175
                                     LR chi2(6)       =      18.93
                                     Prob > chi2      =     0.0043
Log likelihood = -93.341665          Pseudo R2        =     0.0921
```

Q74_ surethingVSlongshot	Coef.	Std. Err.	z	P>z	[95% Conf. Interval]	
Millennial	-1.506749	.5175447	-2.91	0.004	-2.521118	-.49238
GenX	-1.660053	.5148256	-3.22	0.001	-2.669092	-.6510131
Reg_Maurizio	-.1594252	.5154367	-0.31	0.757	-1.169662	.8508121
SanArco	-.1594252	.5154367	-0.31	0.757	-1.169662	.8508121
Johnholm	.92692	.6263636	1.48	0.139	-.3007301	2.15457
Christineberg	-.5072796	.5193063	-0.98	0.329	-1.525101	.510542
_cons	2.18378	.5067652	4.31	0.000	1.190539	3.177022

Reference categories are Baby Boomers for the generations and Sherianne and Raazpuram for labor markets.

Cooperation

```
. reg putnam_cooperation Millennial GenX Reg_Maurizio SanArco
Johnholm Christineberg if small_n==1 ;
```

Source	SS	df	MS		Number of obs	= 180
					F(6, 173)	= 4.35
Model	49.5555556	6	8.25925926		Prob > F	= 0.0004
Residual	328.688889	173	1.89993577		R-squared	= 0.1310
					Adj R-squared	= 0.1009
Total	378.244444	179	2.11309745		Root MSE	= 1.3784

putnam_coo~n	Coef.	Std. Err.	t	P>t	[95% Conf. Interval]	
Millennial	.2666667	.2516569	1.06	0.291	-.2300465	.7633798
GenX	.2666667	.2516569	1.06	0.291	-.2300465	.7633798
Reg_Maurizio	-.9666667	.3082155	-3.14	0.002	-1.575014	-.3583198
SanArco	-.1666667	.3082155	-0.54	0.589	-.7750136	.4416802
Johnholm	.7	.3082155	2.27	0.024	.0916531	1.308347
Christineberg	-.5	.3082155	-1.62	0.107	-1.108347	.1083469
_cons	1.722222	.2297303	7.50	0.000	1.268787	2.175657

Reference categories are Baby Boomers for the generations and Sherianne and Raazpuram for labor markets.

```
. logit Q53_majorityrule Millennial GenX Reg_Maurizio SanArco
Johnholm Christineberg if small_n==1 ;
```

```
Iteration 0:   log likelihood = -120.03772
Iteration 1:   log likelihood = -112.15298
Iteration 2:   log likelihood = -112.11925
Iteration 3:   log likelihood = -112.11924
```

Logistic regression		Number of obs	=	175
		LR chi2(6)	=	15.84
		Prob > chi2	=	0.0147
Log likelihood = -112.11924		Pseudo R2	=	0.0660

Q53_majorityrule	Coef.	Std. Err.	z	P>z	[95% Conf. Interval]	
Millennial	-.6645165	.3932032	-1.69	0.091	-1.435181	.1061476
GenX	-.2338528	.3915483	-0.60	0.550	-1.001273	.5335677
Reg_Maurizio	-.8439765	.4747468	-1.78	0.075	-1.774463	.0865101
SanArco	-.2462883	.4588179	-0.54	0.591	-1.145555	.6529783
Johnholm	.7910364	.4948563	1.60	0.110	-.1788642	1.760937
Christineberg	.7910364	.4948563	1.60	0.110	-.1788642	1.760937
_cons	.4770917	.3528703	1.35	0.176	-.2145213	1.168705

Reference categories are Baby Boomers for the generations and Sherianne and Raazpuram for labor markets.

```
. logit Q54_bestideasGroups Millennial GenX Reg_Maurizio SanArco
Johnholm Christineberg if small_n==1 ;

Iteration 0:       log likelihood = -88.233508
Iteration 1:       log likelihood = -84.822375
Iteration 2:       log likelihood =-84.65281
Iteration 3:       log likelihood = -84.652221
Iteration 4:       log likelihood = -84.652221
```

Logistic regression		Number of obs	=	178
		LR chi2(6)	=	7.16
		Prob > chi2	=	0.3061
Log likelihood = -84.652221		Pseudo R2	=	0.0406

Q54_bestideasGroups	Coef.	Std. Err.	z	P>z	[95% Conf. Interval]	
Millennial	-.5979892	.4983974	-1.20	0.230	-1.57483	.3788518
GenX	-.6728397	.4927578	-1.37	0.172	-1.638627	.2929478
Reg_Maurizio	.0155241	.5329094	0.03	0.977	-1.028959	1.060007
SanArco	1.47776	.7957848	1.86	0.063	-.0819498	3.037469
Johnholm	.2148773	.553109	0.39	0.698	-.8691964	1.298951
Christineberg	.1663712	.5550121	0.30	0.764	-.9214324	1.254175
_cons	1.621968	.4536661	3.58	0.000	.7327992	2.511138

Reference categories are Baby Boomers for the generations and
Sherianne and Raazpuram for labor markets.

Individual Achievement Motivation

```
. logit Q64_preparedpeople Millennial GenX Reg_Maurizio SanArco
Johnholm Christineberg if small_n==1 ;

Iteration 0:       log likelihood = -89.354996
Iteration 1:       log likelihood = -76.007027
Iteration 2:       log likelihood = -74.77476
Iteration 3:       log likelihood = -74.728175
Iteration 4:       log likelihood = -74.728126
Iteration 5:       log likelihood = -74.728126
```

Logistic regression		Number of obs	=	= 146
LR chi2(6)		=	=	29.25
Prob > chi2		=	=	0.0001
Log likelihood = -74.728126		Pseudo R2	=	=0.1637

Q64_ prepared people	Coef.	Std. Err.	z	P>z	[95% Conf.	Interval]
Millennial	-1.109838	.50807	-2.18	0.029	-2.105637	-.1140394
GenX	-.9765753	.5075311	-1.92	0.054	-1.971318	.0181673
Reg_Maurizio	-3.320066	1.089048	-3.05	0.002	-5.45456	-1.185572
SanArco	-3.320066	1.089048	-3.05	0.002	-5.45456	-1.185572
Johnholm	-2.730283	1.094837	-2.49	0.013	-4.876125	-.584441
Christineberg	-1.975006	1.138311	-1.74	0.083	-4.206055	.2560425
_cons	4.163866	1.088661	3.82	0.000	2.03013	6.297602

Reference categories are Baby Boomers for the generations and Sherianne and Raazpuram for labor markets.

. logit Q61_bestmanwins Millennial GenX Reg_Maurizio SanArco Johnholm Christineberg if small_n==1 ;

Iteration 0:   log likelihood = -102.13245
Iteration 1:   log likelihood = -89.534688
Iteration 2:   log likelihood = -88.735415
Iteration 3:   log likelihood = -88.730612
Iteration 4:   log likelihood = -88.730612

Logistic regression   Number of obs   =   176
                                        LR chi2(6)   =   26.80
                                        Prob > chi2   =   0.0002
Log likelihood = -88.730612   Pseudo R2   =   0.1312

Q61_ bestmanwins	Coef.	Std. Err.	z	P>z	[95% Conf.	Interval]
Millennial	-1.463987	.5586066	-2.62	0.009	-2.558836	-.3691384
GenX	-2.078983	.5482024	-3.79	0.000	-3.15344	-1.004526
Reg_Maurizio	.3651836	.5125734	0.71	0.476	-.6394418	1.369809
SanArco	.7309512	.539706	1.35	0.176	-.3268531	1.788756
Johnholm	1.479571	.625455	2.37	0.018	.2537013	2.70544
Christineberg	1.154957	.5883215	1.96	0.050	.0018685	2.308046
_cons	1.823023	.5121002	3.56	0.000	.8193255	2.826721

Reference categories are Baby Boomers for the generations and Sherianne and Raazpuram for labor markets.

. logit Q62_importanceofwinning Millennial GenX Reg_Maurizio SanArco Johnholm Christineberg if small_n==1 ;

Iteration 0:   log likelihood = -90.978365
Iteration 1:   log likelihood = -84.556365
Iteration 2:   log likelihood = -84.229007
Iteration 3:   log likelihood = -84.227741
Iteration 4:   log likelihood = -84.227741

```
Logistic regression                    Number of obs   =        178
                                       LR chi2(6)      =      13.50
                                       Prob > chi2     =     0.0357
Log likelihood = -84.227741            Pseudo R2       =     0.0742
```

Q62_ importanceofwinning	Coef.	Std. Err.	z	P>z	[95% Conf. Interval]	
Millennial	-1.024721	.491593	-2.08	0.037	-1.988226	-.0612165
GenX	-.4926857	.5113691	-0.96	0.335	-1.494951	.5095792
Reg_Maurizio	.3995551	.6394069	0.62	0.532	-.8536593	1.65277
SanArco	.7306805	.7005741	1.04	0.297	-.6424194	2.10378
Johnholm	-.4837189	.5395969	-0.90	0.370	-1.541309	.5738715
Christineberg	-1.041188	.5186758	-2.01	0.045	-2.057774	-.0246026
_cons	2.041686	.4864825	4.20	0.000	1.088198	2.995174

Reference categories are Baby Boomers for the generations and Sherianne and Raazpuram for labor markets.

Cultural Metaphors

```
. mlogit Q1_getalong Millennial GenX Reg_Maurizio SanArco Johnholm
Christineberg if small_n==1, base(2) ;

Iteration 0:    log likelihood = -270.89954
Iteration 1:    log likelihood = -239.99515
Iteration 2:    log likelihood = -238.05798
Iteration 3:    log likelihood =-237.7994
Iteration 4:    log likelihood = -237.75191
Iteration 5:    log likelihood = -237.74721
Iteration 6:    log likelihood =-237.7462
Iteration 7:    log likelihood = -237.74599
Iteration 8:    log likelihood = -237.74594
Iteration 9:    log likelihood = -237.74593


Multinomial logistic regression       Number of obs   =      176
                                       LR chi2(24)     =    66.31
                                       Prob > chi2     =   0.0000
Log likelihood = -237.74593            Pseudo R2       =   0.1224
```

```
Q1_getalong   Coef.      Std. Err.    z      P>z    [95% Conf. Interval]
Symphony
    Millennial  -.5033692  .6650267 -0.76  0.449   -1.806798    .8000592
          GenX   .2916629  .6373094  0.46  0.647    -.9574406   1.540766
   Reg_Maurizio -1.024596  .7809386 -1.31  0.190   -2.555207    .506016
       SanArco  -.9781725  .9102874 -1.07  0.283   -2.762303    .8059581
      Johnholm   .7314722  .7131084  1.03  0.305    -.6661946   2.129139
  Christineberg -1.775055  .8666196 -2.05  0.041   -3.473598    -.076512
         _cons  -.1932668  .5884064 -0.33  0.743   -1.346522    .9599885

      Athletic  (base outcome)

         Opera
    Millennial -1.229714  .7126823 -1.73  0.084   -2.626546    .1671173
          GenX  -.5144997  .6626783 -0.78  0.438   -1.813325    .7843259
   Reg_Maurizio -.0530263  .8764122 -0.06  0.952   -1.770763   1.66471
       SanArco   .6895737  .8588655  0.80  0.422    -.9937718   2.372919
      Johnholm -13.53216  699.7815  -0.02  0.985   -1385.079   1358.014
  Christineberg  .3894856  .7428368  0.52  0.600   -1.066448   1.845419
         _cons  -.6294506  .6702967 -0.94  0.348   -1.943208    .6843068

Dance
    Millennial  1.005481  .6734343  1.49  0.135    -.3144259   2.325388
          GenX   .8492326  .7100204  1.20  0.232    -.5423818   2.240847
   Reg_Maurizio -1.824473  .8636767 -2.11  0.035   -3.517248    -.1316976
       SanArco  -.4576878  .7053111 -0.65  0.516   -1.840072    .9246965
      Johnholm   .395352   .692814   0.57  0.568    -.9625386   1.753243
  Christineberg -1.381455  .6870457 -2.01  0.044   -2.72804     -.0348704
         _cons  -.6870536  .6551609 -1.05  0.294   -1.971145    .5970382

Summer_Vac
Millennial     -1.828123  .556938  -3.28  0.001   -2.919702    -.7365446
GenX            -.9061284  .5226673 -1.73  0.083   -1.930537    .1182807
Reg_Maurizio    -.036229   .5987758 -0.06  0.952   -1.209808   1.13735
SanArco         .5077194  .6357224  0.80  0.424    -.7382735   1.753712
Johnholm        .4453193  .6984907  0.64  0.524    -.9236974   1.814336
Christineberg  -2.19289   .8624109 -2.54  0.011   -3.883185    -.5025961
_cons           .9130311  .4783172  1.91  0.056    -.0244534   1.850516
```

Reference categories are Baby Boomers for the generations and
Sherianne and Raazpuram for labor markets.

```
. mlogit Q2_shouldgetalong Millennial GenX Reg_Maurizio SanArco
Johnholm Christineberg if small_n==1, base(2) ;

Iteration 0:   log likelihood = -241.66002
Iteration 1:   log likelihood = -228.47735
Iteration 2:   log likelihood = -227.87468
Iteration 3:   log likelihood = -227.87071
Iteration 4:   log likelihood = -227.87071


Multinomial logistic regression      Number of obs   =      171
                                      LR chi2(24)     =      27.58
                                      Prob > chi2     =      0.2782
Log likelihood = -227.87071           Pseudo R2       =      0.0571
```

Q2_shouldg~g	Coef.	Std. Err.	z	P>z	[95% Conf.	Interval]
Symphony						
Millennial	-1.244049	.8696352	-1.43	0.153	-2.948503	.4604049
GenX	-.7514033	.8979815	-0.84	0.403	-2.511415	1.008608
Reg_Maurizio	1.043863	1.16245	0.90	0.369	-1.234497	3.322223
SanArco	.6288564	.9093152	0.69	0.489	-1.153369	2.411081
Johnholm	-.4998775	.7824147	-0.64	0.523	-2.033382	1.033627
Christineberg	-.2870811	.9627761	-0.30	0.766	-2.174088	1.599925
_cons	2.179062	.8488291	2.57	0.010	.5153879	3.842737
Athletic	(base outcome)					
Opera						
Millennial	-.6004926	1.189075	-0.51	0.614	-2.931036	1.730051
GenX	-.5612224	1.246762	-0.45	0.653	-3.004831	1.882386
Reg_Maurizio	.9324138	1.644018	0.57	0.571	-2.289803	4.154631
SanArco	.9208026	1.304812	0.71	0.480	-1.636582	3.478188
Johnholm	-.4795036	1.397699	-0.34	0.732	-3.218943	2.259936
Christineberg	1.327446	1.239449	1.07	0.284	-1.10183	3.756722
_cons	-.4395451	1.232001	-0.36	0.721	-2.854223	1.975133
Dance						
Millennial	-1.177744	.916271	-1.29	0.199	-2.973602	.6181143
GenX	-.5965134	.9364	-0.64	0.524	-2.431824	1.238797
Reg_Maurizio	.8487602	1.225059	0.69	0.488	-1.552311	3.249832
SanArco	-.7920205	1.140392	-0.69	0.487	-3.027148	1.443107
Johnholm	-.0081766	.8142739	-0.01	0.992	-1.604124	1.587771
Christineberg	.5937213	.9620556	0.62	0.537	-1.291873	2.479316
_cons	1.502627	.8905943	1.69	0.092	-.2429058	3.24816
Summer_Vac						
Millennial	-1.7199	.8749394	-1.97	0.049	-3.43475	-.0050508
GenX	-1.738418	.9222978	-1.88	0.059	-3.546089	.0692523
Reg_Maurizio	1.143128	1.177631	0.97	0.332	-1.164985	3.451242
SanArco	.3019285	.9477692	0.32	0.750	-1.555665	2.159522
Johnholm	-1.255392	.8900816	-1.41	0.158	-2.99992	.489136
Christineberg	.5081756	.9371825	0.54	0.588	-1.328668	2.345019
_cons	2.441767	.8491326	2.88	0.004	.7774973	4.106036

Reference categories are Baby Boomers for the generations and Sherianne and Raazpuram for labor markets.

```
. mlogit Q3_lifeis Millennial GenX Reg_Maurizio SanArco Johnholm
Christineberg if small_n==1, base(4);

note: sweeden omitted because of collinearity
Iteration 0:     log likelihood = -202.4449
Iteration 1:     log likelihood = -178.34673
Iteration 2:     log likelihood = -176.12816
Iteration 3:     log likelihood = -175.8169
Iteration 4:     log likelihood = -175.74595
Iteration 5:     log likelihood = -175.72892
Iteration 6:     log likelihood = -175.72535
Iteration 7:     log likelihood = -175.7246
Iteration 8:     log likelihood = -175.72443
Iteration 9:     log likelihood = -175.72439
Iteration 10:    log likelihood = -175.72438
```

Multinomial logistic regression

	Number of obs		149
	LR chi2(20)		53.44
	Prob > chi2		0.0001
Log likelihood = -175.72438	Pseudo R2		0.1320

Q3_lifeis	Coef.	Std. Err.	z	P>z	[95% Conf. Interval]	
Investigation						
Millennial	-.5918796	.991656	-0.60	0.551	-2.53549	1.35173
GenX	.125172	.9238305	0.14	0.892	-1.685502	1.935846
Reg_Maurizio	2.182691	1.168042	1.87	0.062	-.1066298	4.472012
SanArco	1.825633	1.2818	1.42	0.154	-.6866488	4.337915
Johnholm	0	(omitted)				
Christineberg	1.880146	1.202206	1.56	0.118	-.476134	4.236427
_cons	-3.259273	1.224803	-2.66	0.008	-5.659843	-.8587032
Pursuit						
Millennial	-.6097112	.6517632	-0.94	0.350	-1.887144	.6677213
GenX	-.6285726	.6670225	-0.94	0.346	-1.935913	.6787674
Reg_Maurizio	-15.13999	826.3475	-0.02	0.985	-1634.751	1604.471
SanArco	.2545522	.6488948	0.39	0.695	-1.017258	1.526363
Johnholm		0	(omitted)			
Christineberg	-.3330341	.6646738	-0.50	0.616	-1.635771	.9697027
_cons	-.4472649	.5528951	-0.81	0.419	-1.530919	.6363896
Difficult_ March						
Millennial	-2.147836	.5707415	-3.76	0.000	-3.266469	-1.029203
GenX	-1.603987	.5338946	-3.00	0.003	-2.650402	-.5575733
Reg_Maurizio	1.040227	.6011844	1.73	0.084	-.1380726	2.218527
SanArco	1.518029	.6154856	2.47	0.014	.3116993	2.724358
Johnholm		0	(omitted)			
Christineberg	.5321522	.6386917	0.83	0.405	-.7196606	1.783965
_cons	-.0547027	.4824385	-0.11	0.910	-1.000265	.8908594
Journey	(base outcome)					
Leisurely_ Walk						
Millennial	-2.94925	1.117991	-2.64	0.008	-5.140473	-.7580277
GenX	-2.146916	.8685388	-2.47	0.013	-3.849221	-.4446116
Reg_Maurizio	-1.083632	1.159204	-0.93	0.350	-3.355631	1.188367
SanArco	-.6709383	1.168069	-0.57	0.566	-2.960311	1.618435
Johnholm		0	(omitted)			
Christineberg	-.464884	.9138887	-0.51	0.611	-2.256073	1.326305
_cons	-.0957505	.5433423	-0.18	0.860	-1.160682	.9691808

Reference categories are Baby Boomers for the generations and Sherianne and Raazpuram for labor markets.

References

Aassve, A., Billari, F. C., Mazzuco, S., and Ongaro, F. (2002). Leaving home: A comparative analysis of ECHP data. *Journal of European Social Policy, 12*(4), 259–275.

Adler, N. J., and Gundersen, A. (2007). *International dimensions of organizational behavior*. Mason, OH: South-Western Cengage Learning.

Agell, J. (1999). On the benefits from rigid labour markets: Norms, market failures, and social insurance. *Economic Journal, 109*(1), 143–164.

Akerlof, G. A., and Yellen, J. A. (1990). The fair wage-effort hypothesis and unemployment. *Quarterly Journal of Economics, 105*(1), 255–283.

Albaek, K., Asplund, R., Barth, E., Lindahl, L., von Simson, K., and Vanhala, P. (2015). *Youth unemployment and inactivity: A comparison of school-to-work transitions and labour market outcomes in four Nordic countries.* Copenhagen, Denmark: Nordic Council of Ministers.

Allard, G. (2010, March 17). Rigid labour markets. *Forbes India.* Retrieved from https://forbesindia.com//article/ie/rigid-labour-markets/11362/1

American College Testing. (2017). *The condition of college and career readiness, 2017.* Retrieved from https://www.act.org/content/dam/act/unsecured/documents/cccr2017/CCCR_National_2017.pdf

Anderlini, L., and Terlizzese, D. (2017). Equilibrium trust. *Games and Economic Behavior,102*, 624–644.

Andreoni, J. (1990). Impure altruism and donations to public goods: A theory of warm glow giving. *Economic Journal, 100*, 464–477.

Angrist, J. D., and Pischke, J. S. (2015). *Mastering metrics.* Princeton, NJ: Princeton University Press.

Annie E. Casey Foundation. (2019, June 16). 2019 kids count data book. Retrieved from https://www.aecf.org/resources/2019-kids-count-data-book/

Askenazy, P. (2018). The changing of the French labor market, 2000–2017. *IZA World of Labor, 412.* https://doi.org/10.15185/izawol.412

Attanasio, O. P. (2015). The determinants of human capital formation during the early years of life: Theory, measurement, and policies. *Journal of the European Economic Association, 13*, 949–997. http://doi.org/10.1111/jeea.12159.

Audretsch, D. B., Bonte, W., and Tamvada, J. P. (2007). *Religion and entrepreneurship* (Jena Economic Research Papers, 2007-075). Jena, Germany: Friedrich-Schiller-University.

Banfield, E. C., and Fasano, L. F. (1958). *The moral basis of a backward society.* New York, NY: Free Press.

Baron, J. D., Cobb-Clark, D. A., and Erkal, N. (2008). Cultural transmission of work-welfare attitudes and intergenerational correlation in welfare receipt. *IZA Discussion Papers* (No. 3904). Retrieved from https://www.iza.org/publications/dp/3904/cultural-transmission-of-work-welfare-attitudes-and-the-intergenerational-correlation-in-welfare-receipt

Bartlett, D. L., and Steele, J. B. (1996). *America: Who stole the dream?* Kansas City, MO: Andrews and McMeel.

Baumol, W. J. (2010). *The microtheory of innovative entrepreneurship.* Princeton, NJ: Princeton University Press.

Becker, G. S. (1993). *Human capital: A theoretical and empirical analysis with special reference to education.* Chicago, IL: University of Chicago Press.

Becker, G. S. (1996). *Accounting for taste.* Cambridge, MA: Harvard University Press.Bell, L., Burtless, G., Gornick, J., and Smeeding, T. M. (2007). Failure to launch: Cross-national trends in the transition to economic independence. In S. Danzinger and C. E. Rouse (Eds.), *The price of independence: The economics of early adulthood* (pp. 27–55). New York, NY: Russell Sage Foundation.

Ben-Akiva, M., and Lerman, S. R. (1994). *Discrete choice analysis: Theory and application to travel demand.* Cambridge, MA: MIT Press.

Bennett, J. C. (2004). *The anglosphere challenge: Why the English-speaking nations will lead the way in the twenty-first century.* London, England: Rowman and Littlefield.

Berg, J., Dickhaut, J., and McCabe, K. (1995). Trust, reciprocity, and social history. *Games and Economic Behavior, 10*, 122–142.

Bergquist, T. (2016). The everyday life of young long-term unemployed in Sweden: Coping with limited participation and feelings of inferiority, experiencing long-term unemployment in Europe. In C. L. Lahusen and M. Guigni (Eds.), *Experiencing long term unemployment in Europe: Youth on the edge* (pp. 107–138). London, England: Palgrave Macmillan.

Bigoni, M., Bortolotti, S., Casari, M., and Gambetta, D. (2018). At the root of the north-south cooperation gap in Italy: Preferences or beliefs? *Economic Journal, 129*, 1139–1152. http://doi.org/10.1111/ecoj.12608.

Bigoni, M., Bortolotti, S., Casari, M., Gambetta, D., and Pancotto, F. (2016). Amoral familism, social capital, or trust? The behavioural foundations of the Italian north-south divide. *Economic Journal, 126*, 1318–1341. http://doi.org/10.1111/ecoj.12292.

Bilksy, W., Janik, M., and Schwartz, S. H. (2011). The structural organization of human values: Evidence from three rounds of the European social survey (ESS). *Journal of Cross Cultural Psychology, 42*(5), 759–776. http://doi.org/10.1177/0022022110362757

Bisin, A., and Verdier, T. (2011). The economics of cultural transmission and socialization. *Handbook of Social Economics, 1*, 339–416.

Blanchard, O. (2006). European unemployment: The evolution of facts and ideas, *Economic Policy, 21*, 5–59.

Borjas, G. (2008). *Labor economics.* New York, NY: McGraw Hill.

Boruch, R. (2005). Preface: Better evaluation for evidence-based policy: Place randomized trials in education, criminology, welfare, and health. *Annals of the American Academy of Political and Social Science, 599*, 6–18.

Bosma, N., and Kelley, D. (2018). *Global entrepreneurship monitor 2018/2019.* London, England: Global Entrepreneurship Research Association.

Boswell, J. (1934). *Boswell's life of Samuel Johnson* (Vol. 2). New York, NY: Oxford University Press. (Original work published 1791)

Bourdieu, P. (1986). The forms of capital. In J. G. Richardson (Ed.), *Handbook of theory and research for the sociology of education* (pp. 241–258). London, England: Greenwood Press.

Bourdieu, P. (1996). *The state of nobility: Elite schools in the field of power.* New York, NY: Policy Press.

Bourdieu, P. (2005). *The social structures of the economy*. New York, NY: Polity Press.Breen, R., and Buchmann, M. (2002). Institutional variation and the position of young people: A comparative perspective. *Annals of the American Academy of Political and Social Science, 580,* 288–305. https://doi.org/10.1177/000271620258000112

Brinton, C. (1965). *The anatomy of revolution*. New York, NY: Vintage Books.

Brooks, D. (2000). *Bobos in paradise: The new upper class and how they got there*. New York, NY: Simon and Schuster.

Brooks, D. (2010, May 4). The limits of policy. Retrieved from https://www.nytimes.com/2010/05/04/opinion/04brooks.html

Brooks, D. (2013, January 25). The Great Migration. *New York Times.* Retrieved from https://www.nytimes.com/2013/01/25/opinion/brooks-the-great-migration.html?searchResultPosition=3

Brunnschweiler, C. N., and Bulte, E. (2008). Linking natural resources to slow growth and more conflict. *Science, 320,* 616–617.

Bruno, G., Tanveer, M., Marelli, E., and Signorelli, M. (2017). The short- and long-run impacts of financial crises on youth unemployment in OECD countries. *Applied Economics, 49,* 3372–3394.

Burghardt, J., and Schochet, P. Z. (2001, June 1). National job corps study: Impacts by center characteristics. *Mathematica.* Retrieved from https://www.mathematica.org/our-publications-and-findings/publications/national-job-corps-study-impacts-by-center-characteristics

Burtless, G. (2007). What have we learned about poverty and inequality? Evidence from cross-national analysis. *Focus, 25*(1), 12–17.

Byambadorj, P. (2007). The youth unemployment situation in Sweden. *University of Goteborg, Department of Social Work.* Retrieved from https://gupea.ub.gu.se/bitstream/2077/4603/2/IMSSW%20degree%20report%20Byambadorj-%20after%20seminar.pdf

Cahuc, P., Carcillo, S., Rinne, U., and Zimmermann, K. F. (2013). Youth unemployment in old Europe: The polar cases of France and Germany. *IZA Journal of European Labor Studies, 2,* 18. https://doi.org/10.1186/2193-9012-2-18

Calhoun, C. (2007). *Nations matter: Culture, history, and the cosmopolitan dream*. London, England: Routledge.

Caliendo, M., and Schmidl, R. (2016). Youth unemployment and active labor market policies in Europe. *IZA Journal of Labor Policy, 5*(1), 1–30.

Calvino, C., Criscuolo, C., and Menon, C. (2016). No country for young firms? (Directorate for Science, Technology and Innovation Policy Note No. 29). Paris, France: OECD.

Camasso, M. J. (2007). *Family caps, abortion and women of color*. New York, NY: Oxford University Press.

Camasso, M. J., and Jagannathan, R. (2001). Flying personal planes: Modeling the airport choices of general aviation pilots using stated preference methodology. *Human Factors, 43*(3), 392–404. https://doi.org/10.1518/001872001775898232

Cappelen, A. W., Nygaard, K., Sørensen, E. O., and Tungodden, B. (2015). Social preferences in the lab: A comparison of students and a representative population. *Scandinavian Journal of Economics, 117,* 1306–1326.

Cappelli, P. H. (2015). Skill gaps, skill shortages, and skill mismatches: Evidence and arguments for the United States. *ILR Review, 68,* 251–290.

Caprar, D. V., Devinney, T. M., Kirkman, B. L., and Caligiuri, P. (2015). Conceptualizing and measuring culture in international business and amangement: From challenges to potential solutions. *Journal of Inernational Business Studies, 42,* 1011–1027.

Carcillo, S., Hyee, R., and Keane, C. (2016). *Investing in youth: Sweden.* Paris, France: OECD.

Card, D., Kluve, J., and Weber, A. (2017). What works? A meta-analysis of recent active labor market program evaluations. *Journal of the European Economic Association, 16*(3), 894–931.

Card, D., and Krueger, A. B. (1995). *Myth and measurement: The new economics of the minimum wage.* Princeton, NJ: Princeton University Press.

Carneiro, P., and Heckman, J. (2003). Human capital policy. In J. Heckman and A. Krueger (Eds.) *Inequality in America: What role for human capital policy?* (pp. 77–239). Cambridge, MA: MIT Press.

Caroleo, F. E., and Pastore, F. (2016). Overeducation: A disease of the school-to-work transition system. In G. Coppola and N. O'Higgins (Eds), *Youth and the crisis: Unemployment, education and health in Europe* (pp. 36–56). London, England: Routledge.

Casson, M. (2003). *The entrepreneur: An economic theory* (2nd ed.). Cheltenham, England: Edward Elgar.

Casson, M. (2006). Culture and economic performance. In V. A. Ginsburgh and D. Throsby (Eds.), *Handbook of the economics of art and culture* (pp. 359–397). London, England: Elsevier.

Causa, O., de Serres, A., and Ruiz, N. (2015). Can pro-growth policies lift all boats?: An analysis based on household disposable income. *OECD Journal: Economic Studies, 2015*, 227–268. https://doi.org/10.1787/eco_studies-2015-5jrqhbb1t5jb.

CEDEFOP. (2018a). *Apprenticeship schemes in European countries: A cross-nation overview.* Luxembourg: Office of European Union. Retrieved from http://data.europa.eu/doi/10.2801/722857

CEDEFOP. (2018b). *Insights into skill strategies and skill mismatch: Learning from CEDEFOP's European skills and jobs survey.* Luxembourg: Office of European Union. Retrieved from http://data.europa.eu/doi/10.2801/645011

Charlemagne. (2019, March 21). The difference between Italy and Spain. *The Economist.* Retrieved from https://www.economist.com/europe/2019/03/21/the-difference-between-italy-and-spain

Chua, A., and Rubenfeld, J. (2014). *The triple package: How three unlikely traits explain the rise and fall of cultural groups in America.* New York, NY: Penguin Press.

Coates, K. S., and Morrison, B. (2016). *Dream factories: Why universities won't solve the youth jobs crisis.* Toronto, ON: Tap Books.

Cohen, P. (2010, October 17). "Culture of poverty" makes a comeback. *New York Times.* Retrieved from https://www.nytimes.com/2010/10/18/us/18poverty.html

Coleman, J. S. (1958). Relational analysis: The study of organizations with survey methods. *Human Organization, 17*, 28–36.

Coleman, J. S. (1967). Research chronicles: The adolescent society. In P. E. Hammond (Ed.), *Sociologists at work* (pp. 213–243). New York, NY: Doubleday.

Coleman, J. S. (1990). *Foundations of social theory.* Cambridge, MA: Harvard University Press.Coleman, J. S., Katz, E., and Menzel, H. (1966). *Medical innovation: A diffusion study.* Indianapolis, IN: Bobbs-Merrill.

Collins, C. J., Hanges, P. J., and Locke, E. A. (2004). The relationship of achievement motivation to entrepreneurial behavior: a meta-analysis. *Human Performance, 17*(1), 95–117. https://doi.org/10.1207/S15327043HUP1701_5.

Cook, T. D., and Furstenberg, F. F. (2002). Explaining aspects of the transition to adulthood in Italy, Sweden, Germany, and the United States: A cross-disciplinary, case synthesis approach. *Annals of the American Academy of Political and Social Science, 580*(1), 257–287. https://doi.org/10.1177/000271620258000111

Council of Economic Advisors. (2016, October). Labor market monopsony: Trends, consequences, and policy responses (Issue brief). Retrieved from https://obamawhitehouse.archives.gov/sites/default/files/page/files/20161025_monopsony_labor_mrkt_cea.pdf

Crisp, R., and Powell, R. (2017). Young people and UK labour market policy: A critique of employability as a tool for understanding youth unemployment. *Urban Studies, 54*, 1784–1807.

Cunha, F., Heckman, J. J., and Schennach, S. M. (2010). Estimating the technology of cognitive and noncognitive skill formation. *Econometrica, 78*, 883–931. https://doi.org/10.3982/ECTA6551 Danziger, S., and Rouse, C. (2007). *The price of independence: The economics of early adulthood.* New York, NY: Russel Sage Foundation.

Dasgupta, I., and Kar, S. (2018, March) The labor market in India since the 1990s. *IZA World of Labor, 425.* https://doi.org/10.15185/izawol.425

David, Q., Janiak, A., and Wasmer, E. (2010). Local social capital and geographical mobility. *Journal of Urban Economics, 68*(2), 191–204. https://doi.org/10.1016/j.jue.2010.04.003 Deaton, A. (2013). *The great escape: Health, wealth, and the origins of inequality.* Princeton, NJ: Princeton University Press.

Deaton, A. (2018, January 24). The U.S. can no longer hide from its deep poverty problem. *New York Times.* Retrieved from https://www.nytimes.com/2018/01/24/opinion/poverty-united-states.html

De Bekker-Grob, E. W., Ryan, M., and Gerard, K. (2012). Discrete choice experiments in health economics: A review of the literature. *Health Economics, 21*, 145–172. https://doi.org/10.1002/hec.1697

Deci, E., and Ryan, R. M. (2000). The "what" and "why" of goals: Human needs and the self-determination of behavior. *Psychological Inquiry, 11*, 227–268. https://doi.org/10.1207/S15327965PLI1104_01

Denzin, N. (1978). The research act. New York, NY: McGraw-Hill.

Dertouzos, M., Lester, R. K., and Solow, R. (1989). *Made in America: Regaining the productive edge.* Cambridge, MA: MIT Press.

Desilver, D. (2017). U.S Student academic achievements still lags that of their peers in many other countries. *Pew Research Center.* Retrieved from https://www.pewresearch.org/fact-tank/2017/02/15/u-s-students-internationally-math-science/

De Tocqueville, A. (1945). *Democracy in America (Volume II).* New York, NY: Vintage Books. (Work originally published 1840) Dietrich, H., and Moeller, J. (2016). Youth unemployment in Europe: Business cycle and institutional effects. *International Economics and Economic Policy, 13*, 5–25.

Di Lampedusa, G. (1960). *Il gattopardo.* New York, NY: Pantheon Books.

Dillman, D. A. (2000). *Mail and internet surveys: The tailored design method* (2nd ed). Hoboken, NJ: Wiley.

Dilworth, T. K. (1996). The crippling flaws in the New Jersey fast food study. *Employment Policies Institute.* Retrieved from https://www.epionline.org/wp-content/studies/epi_njfastfood_04-1996.pdf

D'Iribarne, P. (2009). National cultures and organizations in search of a theory: An interpretative approach. *International Journal of Cross Cultural Management, 9*(3), 309–321. https://doi.org/10.1177/1470595809346601

Donohue, J. J., and Levitt, S. D. (2001). The impact of legalized abortion on crime. *Quarterly Journal of Economics, 116*, 379–420.

Douglas, M., and Wildavsky, A. (1982). *Risk and culture: An essay on the selection of technological and environmental dangers.* Berkeley, CA: University of California Press.

Duesenberry, J. (1960). An economic analysis of fertility: Comment. In G. B. Roberts (Ed.), *Demographic change and economic change in developed countries* (p. 233). Princeton, NJ: Princeton University Press.

Dukas, H., and Hoffmann, B. (1979). *Albert Einstein: The human side.* Princeton, NJ: Princeton University Press.

Durant, W. (1939). *The life of Greece: The story of civilization (#2).* New York, NY: Simon and Schuster.

Durant, W., and Durant, A. (1963). *The age of Louis XIV: The story of civilization* (Vol. 8). New York, NY: Simon and Schuster.Dutta-Gupta, I., Grant, K., Eckel, M., and Edelman, P. (2016). Lessons learned from 40 years of subsidized employment programs. *Georgetown Center on Poverty and Inequality.* Retrieved from https://www.georgetownpoverty.org/wp-content/uploads/2016/07/GCPI-Subsidized-Employment-Paper-20160413.pdf

Easterly, W. (2006). *The White man's burden: Why the West's efforts to aid the rest have done so much ill and so little good.* London, England: Penguin Books.

Eberts, R. W. (2017). An example of a low-cost intervention to target services to participants of a local welfare-to-work program. In S. A. Wander (Ed.) *Lessons learned from public workforce program experiments* (pp. 41–59). Kalamazoo, MI: Upjohn Institute for Employment Research.

Economic Policy Institute. (2019, January 16). Why America needs a $15 minimum wage. *National Employment Law Project.* Retrieved from https://www.nelp.org/publication/america-needs-15-minimum-wage-2/

The Economist Intelligence Unit. (2014, May 8). The learning curve 2014. *The Economist.* Retrieved from https://eiuperspectives.economist.com/talent-education/learning-curve-2014

Eichhorst, W., and Rinne, U. (2016). Promoting youth employment in Europe: Evidence-based policy lessons (IZA Policy Papers 119). *Institute of Labor Economics.* Retrieved from http://ftp.iza.org/pp119.pdf

Eichhorst, W., Rodríguez-Planas, N., Schmidl, R., and Zimmermann, K. F. (2015). A road map to vocational education and training in industrialized countries. *ILR Review, 68*(2), 314–337. https://doi.org/10.1177/0019793914564963

Embery, P. (2019, December 13). Is this the end for Labour? *UnHerd.* Retrieved from https://unherd.com/2019/12/is-this-the-end-for-labour/

Esping-Andersen, G. (1985). *Politics against markets: The social democratic road to power.* Princeton, NJ: Princeton University Press.

Esping-Andersen, G. (1990). *The three worlds of welfare capitalism.* Princeton, NJ: Princeton University Press.

Esping-Andersen, G. (2002). Towards the good society, once again?. In G. Esping-Andersen (Ed.), *Why we need a new welfare state* (pp. 1–25). New York, NY: Oxford University Press.

Esser, H. (2008). The two meanings of social capital. In D. Castiglione, J. W. van Deth, and G. Wolleb (Eds.), *The handbook of social capitol* (pp. 22–49). New York, NY: Oxford University Press.

Esser, I., and Lindh, A. (2018). Job preferences in comparative perspective 1989–2015: A multidimensional evaluation of individual and contextual influences. *International Journal of Sociology, 48*(2), 142–169. https://doi.org/10.1080/00207659.2018.1446118

Fadulu, L. (2018, January 4). Why is the U.S. so bad at worker retraining? *The Atlantic.* Retrieved from https://www.theatlantic.com/education/archive/2018/01/why-is-the-us-so-bad-at-protecting-workers-from-automation/549185/

Fayer, S., Lacey, A., and Watson, A. (2017, January). STEM occupations: Past, present, and future. *U.S. Bureau of Labor Statistics.* Retrieved from https://www.bls.gov/spotlight/2017/science-technology-engineering-and-mathematics-stem-occupations-past-present-and-future/pdf/science-technology-engineering-and-mathematics-stem-occupations-past-present-and-future.pdf

Fazekas, M., and Field, S. (2013). *A skills beyond school review of Germany, OECD reviews of vocational education and training.* Paris, France: OECD. https://doi.org/10.1787/9789264202146-en

Fernández, R. (2008). Culture and economics. In S. Durlauf and L. E. Blume (Eds.), *The new Palgrave dictionary of economics* (pp. 1229–1236). London, England: Palgrave Macmillan.

Fernandez, R., and Fogli, A. (2006). Fertility: The role of culture and family experience. *Journal of the European Economic Association, 4,* 552–561.

Fernandez-Villaverde, J., and Ohanian, L. E. (2019, January 9). How Sweden overcame socialism. *Wall Street Journal.* Retrieved from https://www.wsj.com/articles/how-sweden-overcame-socialism-11547078767

Fishbein, M., and Ajzen, I. (1975). *Belief, attitude, intention and behaviour: An introduction to theory and research.* Reading, MA: Addison Wesley.

Fiske, A. P. (1991). *Structures of social life: The four elementary forms of human relations: communal sharing, authority ranking, equality matching, market pricing; with a new epilogue.* New York, NY: Free Press.

Franke, R. H., Hofstede, G., and Bond, M. H. (2002). National culture and economic growth. In M. J. Gannon and K. I. Newman (Eds.), *The Blackwell handbook of cross cultural management* (pp. 5–15). London, England: Blackwell.

Freeman, R. B., and Wise, D. A. (1982). *The youth labor market problem: Its nature, causes, and consequences.* Chicago, IL: University of Chicago Press.

Freitag, M., and Buhlmann, M. (2009). Crafting trust: The role of political institutions in a comparative perspective. *Comparative Political Studies, 42*(12), 1537–1566.

Freud, S. (1930). *Civilization and its discontents.* New York, NY: Norton.

Friedman, M. (1962). *Capitalism and freedom.* Chicago, IL: University of Chicago Press.

Furstenberg, J. R., Cook, T. D., Sampson, R., and Slap, G. (2002). Preface. *Annals of the American Academy of Political and Social Science, 580,* 6–15. https://doi.org/10.1177/0002716202580001001

Gabel, S. G., and Kamerman, S. B. (2006, June). Investing in children: Public commitment in twenty-one industrialized countries. *Social Service Review, 2006,* 239–263.

Galbraith, J. K. (1973). *Economics and the public purpose.* Boston, MA: Houghton Mifflin.

Gallie, D. (2019). Research on work values in a changing economic and social context. *Annals of the American Academy of Political and Social Science, 682*(1), 26–42. https://doi.org/10.1177/0002716219826038

Galston, W. (n.d.). William Galston quotes. *AZ Quotes.* Retrieved from https://www.azquotes.com/author/24614-William_GalstonGannon, M. J. (2009). The cultural metaphoric method: Description, analysis, and critique. *International Journal of Cross Cultural Management, 9*(3), 275–287. https://doi.org/10.1177/1470595809346604.

Gannon, M. J., Locke, E. A., Gupta, A., Audia, P., and Kristof-Brown, L. (2006). Cultural metaphors as frames of reference for nations: A six country study. *International Studies of Management and Organization, 35*(4), 37–47.

Gannon, M. J., and Pillai, R. (2016). *Understanding global cultures: Metaphorical journeys through 34 nations, clusters of nations, continents, and diversity*. Los Angeles, CA: SAGE.

Geertz, C. (1973). *Interpretation of cultures: Selected essays*. New York: Basic Books.

Geertz, C. (1991). On ethnography and social construction: Interview by GA Olson. *Journal of Advanced Composition, 11,* 245–268.

German Center for Research and Innovation. (2019, July 24). Germany to strengthen 11 universities to elite states. Retrieved from https://www.dwih-newyork.org/en/2019/07/24/excellence-universities/.

German Federal Ministry of Education and Research. (2014). One stop international cooperation in vocational training. Retrieved from https://www.bmbf.de/upload_filestore/pub/One_stop_International_Cooperation_in_Vocational_Training.pdf

Gibson, D. (2007). *The rule of Benedict: Pope Benedict XVI and his battle with the modern world*. New York, NY: Harper Collins.

Giuliano, P. (2007). Living arrangements in western Europe: Does cultural origin matter? *Journal of the European Economic Association, 5*(5), 927–952.

Glaeser, E. L., Laibson, D. I., Scheinkman, J. A., and Soutter, C. L. (2000). Measuring trust. *Quarterly Journal of Economics, 115,* 811–846. https://doi.org/10.1162/003355300554926

Glaser, B., and Strauss, A. L. (1967). *The discovery of grounded theory*. Chicago, IL: Aldine.

Glenn, N. D. (1977). *Cohort analysis*. Thousand Oaks, CA: SAGE.

Goethe, J. W. von. (1963). *Faust: Part One and sections from Part Two* (W. Kaufmann, Trans.). Garden City, NY: Anchor Books.

Gorodnichenko, Y., and Roland, G. (2013, September). *Culture, institutions and the wealth of nations* (NBER working paper no. 16368). Cambridge, MA: NBER. https://doi.org/10.3386/w16368

Gottfries, N. (2018). The labor market in Sweden since the 1990s. *IZA World of Labor, 411.* https://doi.org/10.15185/izawol.411

Griliches, Z., and Ringstad, V. (1971). *Economies of scale and the form of the production function: An economic study of Norwegian manufacturing establishment data*. Amsterdam, The Netherlands: North-Holland.

Grimmer, B. (2016). Being long-term unemployment in Germany: Social contacts, finances and stigma. In C. Lahusen and M. Giugni (Eds.), *Experiencing long-term unemployment in Europe: Youth on the edge* (pp. 39–72). London, England: Palgrave Macmillan.

Guillaud, E. (2013). Preferences for redistribution: An empirical analysis over 33 countries. *Journal of Economic Inequality, 11,* 57–78.

Guiso, L., Sapienza, P., and Zingales, L. (2004). The role of social capital in financial development. *American Economic Review, 94*(3), 526–556. https://doi.org/10.1257/0002828041464498

Guiso, L., Sapienza, P., and Zingales, L. (2006). Does culture affect economic outcomes? *Journal of Economic Perspectives, 20,* 23–48.

Guiso, L., Sapienza, P., and Zingales, L.(2008). Social capital as good culture" Marshall Lecture. *Journal of European Economics Association, 6,* 295–320.

Gujarati, D. N., and Porter, D. C. (2010). *Essentials of economics* (4th ed.) New York, NY: McGraw-Hill.

Gupta, B. S. (1997). India in the twenty-first century. *International Affairs, 73,* 297–314.

Hahn, G. J., and Shapiro, S. S. (1966). *A catalog and computer program for the design and analysis of orthogonal symmetric and asymmetric fractional factorial experiments*. Schenectady, NY: General Electric, Research and Development Center.

Hall, P. A. (2007). The evolution of varieties of capitalism in Europe. In B. Hancke, M. Rhodes, and M. Thatcher (Eds.), *Beyond varieties of capitalism: Conflict, contradictions, and complementarities in the European economy* (pp. 39–85). New York, NY: Oxford University Press.

Hall, P. A., and Soskice, D. (2001). An introduction to varieties of capitalism. In P. A. Hall and D. Soskice (Eds.), *Varieties of capitalism: The institutional foundations of comparative advantage* (pp. 1–68). New York, NY: Oxford University Press.Hamermesh, D. S. (2017). The labor market in the US, 2000–2016. *IZA World of Labor, 361.* https://doi.org/10.15185/izawol.361

Hancke, B., Rhodes, M., and Thatcher, M. (2007). Introduction: Beyond varieties of capitalism. In B. Hancke, M. Rhodes, and M. Thatcher (Eds.), *Beyond varieties of capitalism: Conflict, contradictions, and complementarities in the European economy* (pp. 3–38). New York, NY: Oxford University Press.

Hannon, P. (2019, February 8). Experiment in Finland with guaranteed income creates less stress but no jobs. *Wall Street Journal.* Retrieved from https://www.wsj.com/articles/experiment-in-finland-with-guaranteed-income-creates-less-stress-but-no-jobs-11549650636

Hardy, Q. (2005, November 14). Google thinks small. *Forbes.* Retrieved from https://www.forbes.com/forbes/2005/1114/198.html#45f067d3341

Haskins, R. (2009). Moynihan was right: Now what? *Annals of the American Academy of Political and Social Science, 621*(1), 281–314. https://doi.org/10.1177/0002716208324793

Hauff, S., and Kirchner, S. (2015). Identifying work value patterns: Cross-national comparison and historical dynamics. *International Journal of Manpower, 36*(2), 151–168. https://doi.org/10.1108/ijm-05-2013-0101

Hayek, F. A. (1967). *The road to serfdom.* Chicago, IL: University of Chicago Press.

Hessler, U. (2004, August 6). Germany to spend €1.9 billion to develop elite universities. *DW.* Retrieved from https://www.dw.com/en/germany-to-spend-19-billion-to-develop-elite-universities/a-1230174

Hill, H. C. (2017). The Coleman report, 50 years on: What do we know about the role of schools in academic inequality? *Annals of the American Academy of Political and Social Science, 674*(1), 9–26. https://doi.org/10.1177/0002716217727510

Hirsch, B. Jahn, E. J., and Schnabel, C. (2018). Do employers have more monopsony power in slack labor markets? *ILR Review, 71*, 676–704.

Hoeckel, K., and Schwartz, R. (2010). *OECD reviews of vocational education and training: A learning for jobs review of Germany 2010.* Paris, France: OECD.

Hoffman, S. D., and Duncan, G. (1988, September). Multinomial and conditional logit discrete-choice models in demography. *Demography, 25*(3), 414–427. https://doi.org/10.2307/2061541

Hofstede, G. (1977). *Lion's cultures and foxes' culture and the feasibility of self-management* (Working paper 77-26). Brussels, Belgium: European Institute for Advanced Studies in Management.

Hofstede, G. (1978). *Organization-related value systems in forty countries* (Working paper 78-22). Brussels, Belgium: European Institute for Advanced Studies in Management.

Hofstede, G. (2001). *Culture's consequences: Company values, behaviors, institutions and organizations across nations* (2nd ed). Thousand Oaks, CA: SAGE.

Hofstede, G. (2006). What did GLOBE really measure? Researchers' minds versus respondents' minds. *Journal of International Business Studies, 37*, 882–896.

Hofstede, G. H., Hofstede, G. J., and Minkov, M. (2010). *Cultures and organizations: Software of the mind* (3rd ed.). New York, NY: McGraw-Hill.

Hofstede, G., Noorderhaven, N., Thurik, R., Uhlaner, L., Alexander, R. M., Wennekers, L. M., and Wildeman, R. E. (2004). Culture's role in entrepreneurship: Self-employment out of dissatisfaction. In T. Brown and J. M. Ulijn (Eds.). *Innovation, entrepreneurship and culture* (pp. 162–204). Cheltenham, England: Edward Elgar.Hollenbeck, K. (2009, November). *Workforce Investment Act (WIA) net impact estimates and rates of return.* Paper presented at European Commission. What the European Social Fund Can Learn From the WIA Experience, Washington, DC. Retrieved from https://research.upjohn.org/confpapers/2/

Hosmer, D. W., and Lemeshow, S. (2000). *Applied logistic regression.* Hoboken, NJ: Wiley.

House, R. J., Hanges, P. J., Javidan, M., Dorfman, P. W., and Gupta, V. (2004). *Culture, leadership, and organizations: The GLOBE study of 62 societies* (1st ed.). Thousand Oaks, CA: SAGE.

Human Rights Council, United Nations General Assembly. (2018). Report of the Special Rapporteur on Extreme Poverty and Human Rights on his mission to the United States of America (A_HRC_38_33_Add-1). Retrieved from https://digitallibrary.un.org/record/1629536?ln=en

Iacovou, M. (2002). Regional differences in the transition to adulthood. *Annals of the American Academy of Political and Social Science, 580*(1), 40–69.

Ibarraran, P., Ripani, L., Taboada, B., Villa, J. M., and Garcia, B. (2014). Life skills, employability and training for disadvantaged youth: Evidence from a randomized evaluation design. *IZA Journal of Labor and Development, 3*, 1–24. https://doi.org/10.1186/2193-9020-3-10

INAPP. (2016). Vocational education and training in Europe: Italy. *Cedefop ReferNet VET in Europe reports.* Retrieved from https://www.refernet.de/dokumente/pdf/2016_CR_IT.pdfJardim, E., Long, M. C., Plotnick, R., van Inwegn, E., Vigdor, J., and Wething, H. (2017). *Minimum wage increases, wages, and low-income employment: Evidence from Seattle* (NBER working paper series 23532). Cambridge, MA: NBER.

Javidan, M., House, R. J., Dorfman, P. W., Hanges, P. J., and Sully de Luque, M. (2006). Conceptualizing and measuring cultures and their consequences: A comparative review of GLOBE's and Hofstede's approaches. *Journal of International Business Studies, 37*(6), 897–914. https://doi.org/10.1057/palgrave.jibs.8400234

Joyce, T. (2004). Did legalized abortion lower crime?. *Journal of Human Resources, 39*, 1–28. http://jhr.uwpress.org/content/XXXIX/1/1.abstract

Jung, C. G. (1945, 1957). Nach der katastrophe. In G. Adler and R. F. C. Hull (Eds.), *Civilization in transition: The collected works of C. G. Jung* (Vol. 10, pp. 194–217). Princeton, NJ: Princeton University Press.

Jussim, L., Cain, T. R., Crawford, J. T., Harber, K., and Cohen, F. (2009). The unbearable accuracy of stereotypes. In T. D. Nelson (Ed.), *Handbook of prejudice, stereotyping, and discrimination* (pp. 199–227). New York, NY: Psychology Press.

Kahneman, D., Ritov, I., and Schkade, D. (1999). Economic preferences or attitude expressions?: An analysis of dollar responses to public issues. *Journal of Risk and Uncertainty, 19*, 203–235. https://doi.org/10.1023/A:1007835629236

Kahneman, D., and Tversky, A. (1979). Prospect theory: An analysis of decision under risk. *Econometrica, 47*(2), 263–291.

Kalleberg, A. L., and Marsden, P. V. (2013). Work values in the United States, 1973–2006. *Social Science Research, 42*, 255–270.

Kalleberg, A. L., and Marsden, P. V. (2019). Work values in the United States: Age, period, and generational differences. *Annals of the American Academy of Political and Social Science, 682*(1), 43–59. https://doi.org/10.1177/0002716218822291

Kamerman, S. B., and Gatenio Gabel, S. (2006). Social protection for children and families: A global overview. *Social Service Review, 80*, 239–263.

Kautsky, K. (1959). *Communism in central Europe in the time of reformation*. New York, NY: Russell and Russell.

Kennedy, P. (1989). *The rise and fall of the great powers*. New York, NY: Vintage Books.

Keynes, J. M. (1936). *The general theory of employment, interest and money*. New York, NY: Harcourt, Brace and World.

Killingsworth, M. (1994). *Labor Supply*. New York: Cambridge University Press.

Kim, J., and Muller, C. W. (1978). *Factor analysis: Statistical methods and practical issues*. Beverly Hills, CA: SAGE.

Kincheloe, J. L. (2018). *How do we tell the workers*. New York, NY: Routledge.

Kissinger, H. (1986, June 29). Soccer imitates life. *The Washington Post*, C8. Retrieved from https://www.washingtonpost.com/archive/opinions/1986/06/29/soccer-imitates-life/9458bd3c-4c43-4db0-9497-a0135e62988d/

Kittel, B., Kalleitner, F., and Tsakloglou, P. (2019). The transmission of work centrality within the family in a cross-regional perspective. *Annals of the American Academy of Political and Social Science, 628*(1), 106–124.

Kluckhohn, C. (1951). Values and value-orientations in the theory of action: An exploration in definition and classification. In T. Parsons and E. Shils (Eds.), *Toward a general theory of action* (pp. 388–433). Cambridge, MA: Harvard University Press.

Kluckhohn, F. R., and Strodtbeck, F. L. (1961). *Variations in value orientations*. Evanston, IL: Row, Peterson.

Komisar, E. (2018, July 11). The human cost of Sweden's welfare state. *Wall Street Journal*. Retrieved from https://www.wsj.com/articles/the-human-cost-of-swedens-welfare-state-1531346908

Kosanovich, K., and Theodossiou Sherman, E. (2019). Trends in long-term unemployment. Spotlight on Statistics. *US Bureau of Labor Statistics*. Retrieved from https://www.bls.gov/spotlight/2015/long-term-unemployment/pdf/long-term-unemployment.pdf

Kraaykamp, G., Cemalcilar, Z., and Tosun, J. (2019). Transmission of work attitudes and values: Comparisons, consequences, and implications. *Annals of the American Academy of Political and Social Science, 682*(1), 8–24. https://journals.sagepub.com/doi/full/10.1177/0002716219831947

Kroeber, A. L., and Kluckhohn, C. (1952). *Culture: a critical review of concepts and definitions* (Papers, Peabody Museum of Archaeology and Ethnology). Cambridge, MA: Harvard University.

Kruskal, J. B., and Wish, M. (1978). *Multidimensional scaling*. Thousand Oaks, CA: SAGE.

Kuczera, M., Field, S., Hoffman, N., and Wolter, S. (2008, April). *Learning for jobs OECD reviews of education and training: Sweden*. Paris, France: OECD.

Kuczera, M., and Field, S. (2013). *A skills beyond school review of the United States*. Paris: OECD Publishing.

Kuczera, M., and Jeon, S. (2019). *Vocational education and training in Sweden* (OECD Reviews of Vocational Education and Training). Paris, France: OECD. https://doi.org/10.1787/g2g9fac5-enKumar, R. (2004). Brahmanical idealism, anarchical individualism, and the dynamics of Indian negotiation behavior. *International Journal of Cross Cultural Management, 4*, 39–58.

Kuttner, R., and Stone, K. (2020, April 8). The rise of neo-feudalism: The private capture of entire legal systems by corporate America goes far beyond neoliberalism, it evokes the private fiefdoms of the Middle Ages. *Prospect.* Retrieved from https://prospect.org/economy/rise-of-neo-feudalism/

Lahusen, C., and Giugni, M. (2016). Experiencing long-term unemployment in Europe: An introduction. In C. Lahusen and M. Giugni (Eds.), *Experiencing long-term unemployment in Europe: Youth on the edge* (pp. 1–16). London, England: Palgrave Macmillan.

Lakoff, G., and Johnson, M. (1980). *Metaphors we live by.* Chicago, IL: University of Chicago Press.

Lakoff, G., and Johnson, M. (1999). *Philosophy in the flesh.* New York, NY: Basic Books.

LaLonde, R. J. (1995). The promise of public sector sponsored training programs. *The Journal of Economic Perspectives, 9*(2), 149–168.

Landes, D. (2000). *Culture makes almost all the difference.* In L. E. Harrison and S. P. Huntington (Eds.), *Culture matters: How values shape human progress* (pp. 1–13). New York, NY: Basic Books.

Layard, R. (1982). Youth unemployment in Britain and United States compared. In R. B. Freeman and O. A. Wise (Eds.), *The youth labor market: Its nature, causes and consequences* (pp. 499–542). Chicago, IL: University of Chicago Press.

Lefebvre, G. (1962). *The coming of the French Revolution, 1789.* London, England: Routledge and Kegan Paul.

Legrand, P. (1996). European legal systems are not converging. *International and Comparative Law Quarterly, 45*(1), 52–81.

Lemieux, T., and MacLeod, W. B. (2000). Supply side hysteresis: The case of the Canadian unemployment insurance system. *Journal of Public Economics, 74,* 139–170.

Lerman, R. (2017). Why firms do and don't offer apprenticeships. In M. Pilz (Ed.), *Vocational education and training in times of economic crisis* (pp. 305–320). Cham, Switzerland: Springer Nature.

Levin, J. S., Lopez-Damian, A. I., Martin, M. C., and Hoggatt, M. J. (2017). The US community college after globalization. In L. Tran and K. Dempsey (Eds.), *Internationalization in vocational education and training. technical and vocational education and training: Issues, concerns and prospects* (Vol. 25, pp. 19–40. Cham, Switzerland: Springer.

Lewis, M. (2011). *Boomerang: Travels in the new Third World.* New York, NY: W. W. Norton.

Leyda, J. (1951). *The Melville log: A documentary life of Herman Melville (1819–1891).* New York, NY: Harcourt, Brace.

Lindsay, S. (2000). Culture, mental models, and national prosperity. In L. E. Harrisonand S. P. Huntington (Eds.), *Culture matters: How values shape human progress.* New York, NY: Basic Books.

Lipset, S. M. (1967). *The first new nation: The United States in historical and comparative perspective.* New York, NY: Anchor Books.

Ljunge, M. (2011). Increasing demands on the welfare state? Trends in behavior and attitudes. *CESifo Economic Studies, 57,* 605–622.

Long, J. S. (1983). *Confirmatory factor analysis.* Beverly Hills, CA: SAGE.

Lopez-Fogues, A. (2017). Addressing mismatch in Spain: A concern and proposal beyond the economic sphere. In M. Pilz.(Ed.), *Vocational education and training in times of economic crisis* (pp. 355–368). Cham, Switzerland: Springer Nature.

Louviere, J. J., Hensher, D. A., and Swait, J. D. (2000). *Stated choice methods*. New York, NY: Cambridge University Press.

Lowe, S. (2014). *Fear and loathing in La Liga: Barcelona vs Real Madrid*. New York, NY: Nation Books.

Lucas, R. E. (2002). *Lectures on economic growth*. Cambridge, MA: Harvard University Press.

Machiavelli, N. (1975). *The prince*. London, England: Penguin Books. (Original work published 1513)

Majumdar, S. (2016). Forward: Reflections on opportunities and challenges of skills development in India. In M. Pilz (Ed.), *India: Preparation for the world of work: Education system and school to work transition* (pp. 7–13). Wiesbaden, Germany: Springer VS.

Manacorda, M., and Moretti, E. (2006). Why do most Italian youths live with their parents? Intergenerational transfers and household structure. *Journal of European Economic Association, 4*(4), 800–829.

Manca, F., Quintini, G., and Keese, M. (2017). *Getting skills right in Italy*. Paris, France: OECD. https://dx.doi.org/10.1787/9789264278639-en

Mandrone, E. Landi, R. Marocco, M., and Radicchia, D. (2016). I canali di intermediazione e i Servizi per il lavoro. *Collana ISFOL Research Paper No. 32*. Retrieved from http://www.bollettinoadapt.it/wp-content/uploads/2016/06/2276.pdf

Marino, F., and Nunziata, L. (2017). The labor market in Italy, 2000–2016. *IZA World of Labor, 407*. https://www.doi.org/10.15185/izawol.407

Marx, K. (1967). *The process of capitalist production as a whole*. New York, NY: International Publishers. (Original work published 1894)

Mas, A., and Pallais, A. (2016). *Valuing alternative work arrangements* (NBER Working Paper No. 22708). Cambridge, MA: NBER.

Massey, D. S., and Sampson, R. J. (2009). Moynihan redux: Legacies and lessons. *Annals of the American Academy of Political and Social Science, 621*(1), 6–27. doi.org/10.1177/0002716208325122.

Maynard, R. (1995). Subsidized employment and non-labor market alternatives for welfare recipients. In D. S. Nightingale and R. H. Haveman (Eds.), *The work alternative: Welfare reform and the realities of the job market* (pp. 109–136). Washington, DC: Urban Institute.

Mazur, A., and Rosa, E. (1977). An empirical test of McClelland's "achieving society" theory. *Social Forces, 55*, 769–774. https://doi.org/10.1093/sf/55.3.769

McClelland, D. C. (1961). *The achieving society*. Princeton, NJ: Van Nostrand.

McClelland, D. C. (1964). *The roots of consciousness*. Princeton, NJ: Van Nostrand.McCloskey, D. N. (2006). *The bourgeois virtues: Ethics for an age of commerce*. Chicago, IL: University of Chicago Press.

McFadden, D. (1986). The choice theory approach to market research. *Marketing Science, 5*(4), 275–299.

McFadden, D. (1975). The revealed preferences of a government bureaucracy: Theory. *Bell Journal of Economics, 6*, 401–416.

McGuinness, S., Pouliakas, K., and Redmond, P. (2017, May). How useful is the concept of skills mismatch? Background notes of the ILO International conference on jobs and skill mismatch. Geneva, Switzerland.

McKinney, J. (1966). *Constructive typology and social theory*. New York, NY: Appleton-Century-Crofts.

McSweeney, B. (2002). Hofstede's model of national cultural differences and their consequences: A triumph of faith, a failure of analysis. *Human Relations. 55*(1), 89–118.

Metabolically different. (2019, March 23). *The Economist.*

Michau, J. (2008). Unemployment insurance and cultural transmission: Theory and application to European unemployment (CEP Discussion Papers dp0936, Center for Economic Performance, LSE). Retrieved fromhttps://ideas.repec.org/p/cep/cepdps/dp0936.html

Michau, J. (2013). Unemployment insurance and cultural transmission: Theory and application to European unemployment. *Journal of European Economic Association, 11,* 1320–1347.

Mokyr, J. (2019). *A culture of growth: The origins of the modern economy.* Princeton, NJ: Princeton University Press.

Molina, O., and Rhodes, M. (2007). The political economy of adjustment in mixed market economies: A study of Spain and Italy. In B. Hancké, M. Rhodes, and M. Thatcher (Eds.), *Beyond varieties of capitalism, conflict, contradictions, and complementarities in the European economy* (pp. 223–252). New York, NY: Oxford University Press.

Monticelli, L., Baglioni, S., and Bassoli, M. (2016). Youth Long-term unemployment and its social consequences in Italy: In a world that does not belong to Me. In C. Lahusen and M. Giugni (Eds.), *Experiencing long term unemployment in Europe: Youth on the edge* (pp. 139–169). London, England: Palgrave Macmillan.

Morath, E. (2019, October 8). Germany's apprentice challenge: Finding young applicants. *Wall Street Journal.* Retrieved from https://www.wsj.com/articles/germanys-apprentice-challenge-finding-young-applicants-11570527003

Morris, J. (2008). *Spain.* London: Faber and Faber.

Mosca, G. (1959). *Ruling class.* New York. McGraw-Hill. (Work originally published 1939)

Mosteller, F., and Moynihan, D. P. (1972). *On equality of educational opportunity.* New York, NY: Vintage Books.

Muehlemann, S., Ryan, P., and Wolter, S. C. (2013). *Monopsony power, pay structure, and training.* Bonn, Germany: Forschungsinstitut zur Zukunft der Arbeit GmbH.

Mueller, T. (2012). *Extra virginity: The sublime and scandalous world of olive oil.* New York, NY: W. W. Norton.

Mullock, K., Quintini, G., and Keese, M. (2017). Getting skills right: Spain. Paris, France: OECD. https://doi.org/10.1787/9789264282346-en

Murphy, J. P. (2017). *Yearning to labor. Youth, unemployment, and social destiny in urban France.* Lincoln, NE: University of Nebraska Press.

Murray, C. A. (2012). *Coming apart: The state of White America, 1960–2010.* New York, NY: Crown.

Musick, K., and Bumpass, L. (1999). How do prior experiences in the family affect transitions to adulthood? In A. Booth, A. Crouter, and M. J. Shanahan (Eds.), *Transitions to adulthood in a changing economy* (pp. 69–102). Westport, CT: Praeger.

Naguib, C. (2015). The relationship between inequality and GDP growth: An empirical approach. *Swiss Journal of Economics and Statistics, 153,* 183–225.

Neumark, D., and Wascher, W. (2000). Minimum wages and employment: A case study of the fast-food industry in New Jersey and Pennsylvania. *American Economic Review. 90*(5), 1362–1396.

Newman, K., and Aptekar, S. (2007). Sticking around: Delayed departure from the parental nest in western Europe. In S. Danziger and C. E. Rouse (Eds.) *The price of independence: The economics of early adulthood* (pp. 207–230). New York, NY: Russell Sage Foundation.

Nuti, V. (2018, December 7). Cenis: Italiani Incattiviti e in preda al "sovranesmo psichico." *Il Sole 24,* 1.OECD. (1984). *Youth unemployment in France: Recent strategies.* Paris, France. Author.

OECD. (2011). The economic significance of natural resources: Key points for reformers in eastern Europe, Caucasus and central Asia. *OECD Environmentalist Performance and Information Directorate.* Retrieved fromhttp://www.oecd.org/env/outreach/2011_AB_Economic%20significance%20of%20NR%20in%20EECCA_ENG.pdf

OECD. (2016). Job creation and local economic development 2016. Paris, France: Author. https://dx.doi.org/10.1787/978964261976-enOECD.   (2017a).   Getting   skills right: France. Paris, France: Author. https://dx.doi.org/10.1787/9789264284456-en.

OECD. (2017b). Program for international student assessment: PISA 2015. *National Center for Educational Statistics.* Retrieved from https://nces.ed.gov/pubsearch/pubsinfo.asp?pubid=2017120

OECD (2017c). *Strictness of employment protection legislation: Regular employment.* Paris, France: Author. https://doi.org/10.1787/LFS-data-en.OECD. (2019a), OECD Compendium of Productivity Indicators 2019. Paris, France: Author. https://doi.org/10.1787/b2774f97-en.

OECD. (2019b), Under pressure: The squeezed middle class. Paris, France: Author. https://doi.org/10.1787/689afed1-en

OECD. (2019c). What characterizes upper secondary vocational education and training?. *Education Indicators in Focus, 68.* https://doi.org/10.1787/a1a7e2f1-en

O'Leary, C. J. (2017). Incentive experiments in unemployment insurance. In S. A. Wandner (Ed.), *Lessons learned from public workforce program experiments* (pp. 85–110). Kalamazoo, MI: W. E. Upjohn Institute for Employment Research.

Oops-onomics. (2005, December 1). *The Economist.* Retrieved from https://www.economist.com/finance-and-economics/2005/12/01/oops-onomics

O'Reilly, J., Eichhorst, W., Gabos, A., Hadjivassiliou, K., Lain, D., Leschke, J., . . . Villa, P. (2015). Five characteristics of youth unemployment in Europe: Flexibility, education, migration, family legacies, and EU policy. *Sage Open, 5*(1). https://doi.org/10.1177/2158244015574962

Ortony, A. (2001). Why metaphors are necessary and not just nice. In M. J. Gannon (Ed.), *Cultural metaphors: Readings, research translations, and commentary* (pp. 9–21). Thousand Oaks, CA: SAGE.

Ostry, J. D., Berg, A., and Tsangarides, C. G. (2014). Redistribution, inequality, and growth. *International Monetary Fund: IMF Staff Discussion Note.* Retrieved from https://www.imf.org/external/pubs/ft/sdn/2014/sdn1402.pdf

Pareto, V. (1963). *The mind and society. a treatise of general sociology* (A. Livingston, Ed.). New York, NY: Harcourt, Brace. (Work originally published 1935)

Pastore, F. (2018). *Why is youth unemployment so high and different across countries? IZA World of Labor, 420.* https://doi.org/10.15185/izawol.420

Payer, L. (1988). *Medicine and culture: varieties of treatment in the United States, England, West Germany, and France.* New York, NY: Henry Holt.

Peet, J. R. (2012, November 17). Special report: France: So much to do, so little time. *The Economist.* Retrieved from https://www.economist.com/special-report/2012/11/17/so-much-to-do-so-little-time

Perloff, J. M. (2001). *Microeconomics* (2nd ed.). Boston, MA: Addison-Wesley.

Pew Research Center. (2017, September 8). Indians in the US fact sheet. Retrieved from https://www.pewsocialtrends.org/fact-sheet/asian-americans-indians-in-the-u-s/

PewResearchCenter.(2018,June13).Theagegapinreligionaroundtheworld.Retrievedfrom https://www.pewforum.org/2018/06/13/the-age-gap-in-religion-around-the-world/

Phillips, K. A., Johnson, F. R., and Maddala, T. (2002). Measuring what people value: A comparison of "attitude" and "preference" surveys. *Health Services Research, 37*(6), 1659–1679. https://doi.org/10.1111/1475-6773.01116

Phillips, K. A., Maddala, T., and Johnson, F. R. (2002). Measuring preferences for health care interventions using conjoint analysis: An application to HIV testing. *Health Services Research, 37*, 1681–1705.

Piketty, T. (2014). *Capitol in the twenty-first century*. Cambridge, MA: Harvard University Press.

Prieto, A. M. (2014). Social protection and youth unemployment in Spain. In M Gunderson and F. Fazio (Eds.), *Tackling youth unemployment* (pp. 169–184). Newcastle, England: Cambridge Scholars.Putnam, R. D. (1995). Bowling alone: America's declining social capital. *Journal of Democracy, 6*, 65–78.

Putnam, R. D. (2000). *Bowling alone: The collapse and revival of American community*. New York, NY: Simon and Schuster.

Putnam, R. D. (2007). *E. pluribus unum*: Diversity and community in the twenty-first century. The 2006 Johan Skytte Prize lecture. *Scandinavian Political Studies, 30*, 137–174.

Putnam, R. D., Leonardi, R., and Nanetti, R. (1993). *Making democracy work: Civic traditions in modern Italy*. Princeton, NJ: Princeton University Press.

Rainsford, E., Maloney, W. A., and Adrian Popa, S. (2019). The effect of unemployment and low-quality work conditions on work values: Exploring the experiences of young Europeans. *Annals of the American Academy of Political and Social Science, 682(1)*, 172–185. Retrieved fromhttps://journals.sagepub.com/doi/abs/10.1177/0002716219830378

Rainwater, L., and Yancey, W. L. (1967). *The Moynihan report and the politics of controversy*. Cambridge, MA: MIT Press.

Ransom, M. R., and Sims, D. P. (2010). Estimating the firm's labor supply curve in a "new monopsony" framework: School teachers in Missouri. *Journal of Labor Economics, 28*(2), 331–335.

Rawls, J. (1999). *A theory of justice* (Rev. ed.). Cambridge, MA: Harvard University Press.

Reamer, A. (2017). Federal efforts in support of entrepreneurship: A reference guide. *George Washington University Institute of Public Policy*. Retrieved from https://gwipp. gwu.edu/federal-efforts-support-entrepreneurship-reference-guide-working-draft

Reiff, M. (2015). *On unemployment, Vol. 1: A micro-theory of economic justice*. London, England: Palgrave Macmillan.

Richardson, K., and van den Berg, G. (2006, September). Swedish labor market training and the duration of unemployment (IZA Discussion Papers, No. 2314). *IZA*. Retrieved from http://ftp.iza.org/dp2314.pdf

Ricucci, R. (2017). *The new southern European diaspora: Youth, unemployment, and migration*. Lanham, MD: Lexington Books.

Riley, J. L. (2019, March 26). Culture explains Asians' educational success. *Wall Street Journal*. Retrieved from https://www.wsj.com/articles/culture-explains-asians-educational-success-11553640350

Rinne, U. (2017). The labor market in Germany, 2000–2016. *IZA World of Labor, 379*. https://doi.org/10-15.185/ijawol.379

Ryan, P. (2016). Monopsony power and work-based training. In G. Coppola and N. O'Higgins (Eds.), *Youth and the crisis: Unemployment, education and health in Europe* (pp. 13–35) London, England: Routledge.Saad, L. (2019, November 25). Socialism as popular as capitalism among young adults in U.S. Gallup. Retrieved from https://news. gallup.com/poll/268766/socialism-popular-capitalism-among-young-adults.aspx

Sachs, J. D., and Warner, A. M. (2001). The curse of natural resources. *European Economic Review, 45*, 827–838.

Samuelson, P. A., and Nordhaus, W. D. (2010). *Economics* (19th ed.). New York, NY: McGraw-Hill.

Sanz-de-Galdeano, A., and Terskaya, A. (2017). The labor market in Spain, 2002–2016: Youth and long term unemployment, which skyrocketed during the Great Recession, were still very high in 2016. *ISA World of Labor, 403.* https://doi.org/10.15185/izawol.403

Sateesh, G. M., and Sekher, T. V. (2014). Factors leading to school dropouts in India: An analysis of national family health survey- 3 data. *International Journal of Research and Methods in Education, 4,* 75–83.

Scheiber, N. (2017, June 15). Trump move on job training brings "skills gap" debate to the fore. *New York Times.* Retrieved from https://www.nytimes.com/2017/06/15/business/economy/trump-job-training-skills-gap.html

Schein, E. H. (1984). Coming to a new awareness of organizational culture. *Sloan Management Review, 25*(2), 3–16.

Schmid, G. (2015). Youth unemployment in India: From a European and transitional labour market point of view (IZA Policy Paper no. 95). *IZA.* Retrieved from https://www.iza.org/en/publications/pp/95/youth-unemployment-in-india-from-a-european-and-transitional-labour-market-point-of-view

Schuck, B., and Shore. J. (2019). How intergenerational mobility shapes attitudes toward work and welfare. *Annals of the American Academy of Political and Social Science, 682,* 139–154.

Schumpeter, J. A. (1962). *Capitalism, socialism, and democracy.* New York, NY: Harper and Row.

Schumpeter, J. A. (1939, 1964). *Business Cycles.* New York: McGraw-Hill.

Schumpeter, J. A. (1966). *History of economic analysis.* Oxford, England: Oxford University Press.

Schwartz, S. (1994). Beyond individualism-collectivism: New cultural dimensions of values. In U. Kim, H. C. Triandis, C. Kagitcibasi, S-C. Choi, and G. Yoon (Eds.), *Individualism and collectivism: Theory, method, and applications* (pp. 85–122). Newbury Park, CA: SAGE.

Schwartz, S. H. (2012). An overview of the Schwartz theory of basic values. *Online Readings in Psychology and Culture, 2*(1). https://doi.org/10.9707/2307-0919.1116

Scott, R. E. (2017, January 31). Growth in U.S.–China trade deficit between 2001 and 2015 cost 3.4 million jobs: Here's how to rebalance trade and rebuild American manufacturing. *Economic Policy Institute.* Retrieved from https://www.epi.org/publication/growth-in-u-s-china-trade-deficit-between-2001-and-2015-cost-3-4-million-jobs-heres-how-to-rebalance-trade-and-rebuild-american-manufacturing/

Selltiz, C., Wrightsman, L. S., and Cook, S. W. (1976). *Research methods in social relations* (3rd ed.). New York, NY: Holt, Rienhart, and Wilson.

Semuels, A. (2017, September 28). Why does Sweden have so many startups?. *The Atlantic.* Retrieved fromhttps://www.theatlantic.com/business/archive/2017/09/sweden-startups/541413/

Settersten, R. A., Jr., Furstenberg, F. F., and Rumbaut, R. G. (2008). *On the frontier of adulthood: Theory, research, and public policy.* Chicago, IL: University of Chicago.

Simpson, G. E., and Yinger, J. M. (1985). *Racial and cultural minorities: An analysis of prejudice and discrimination.* New York, NY: Springer US.

Singer, M. (1966). Religion and social change in India: The Max Weber thesis phase Three. *Economic Development and Cultural Change, 14,* 497–505.

Singh, D. P. (2011). Framework for undertaking Indian cultural knowledge and its managerial implications. *International Journal of Business Management, Economics and Information Technology, 3*, 127–136.

Slovic, P., Flynn, J., Mertz, C. K., Poumadere, M., and Mays, C. (2000). Nuclear power and the public. In B. Rohrmann and O. Renn (Eds.), *Cross cultural risk perception* (pp. 55–102). Boston, MA: Springer.

Small, M. L., Harding, D. J., and Lamont, M. (2010). Reconsidering culture and poverty. *Annals of the American Academy of Political and Social Science, 629*, 6–27. https://doi.org/100.1177/0002716210362077

Smith, A. (2000). *The wealth of nations* (E. Connan, Ed.). New York, NY: Modern Library. (Original work published 1776)

Solow, R. M. (1970, Fall). Science and ideology in economics. *National Affairs: The Public Interest, 21*, 94–107. Retrieved from https://www.nationalaffairs.com/public_interest/detail/science-and-ideology-in-economics

Sombart, W. (1951). *The Jews and modern capitalism.* New York, NY: Collier Books. (Original work published 1911)

Sowell, T. (1994). *Race and culture: A world view.* New York, NY: Basic Books.

Sowell, T. (1996). *Migrations and cultures: a world view.* New York, NY: Basic Books.

Spolaore, E., and Wacziarg, R. (2009). The diffusion of development. *Quarterly Journal of Economics, 124*(2), 469–529.

Spolaore, E., and Wacziarg, R. (2018). Ancestry and development: New evidence. *Journal of Applied Econometrics, 33*, 748–762.

Stake, R. E. (1995). *The art of case study research.* Thousand Oaks, CA: SAGE.

Stake, R. E. (2006). *Multiple case study analysis.* New York, NY: Guilford Press.

Stam, E., and Van Stel, A. (2011). Types of entrepreneurship and economic growth. In A. Szirmai, W. Naude, and M. Goedhuys (Eds.), *Entrepreneurship, innovation, and economic development* (pp. 78–95). New York, NY: Oxford University Press.

Steinberg, P. (2015). Can we generalize from case studies. *Global Environmental Politics. 15*(3), 152–175.

Steinberg, S. (2011, January 13). Poor reason: Culture still doesn't explain poverty. *Boston Review Magazine.* Retrieved from http://bostonreview.net/steinberg.php

Stigler, G., and Becker, G. (1977). De Gustibus Non Est Disputandum. *American Economic Review, 67*(2), 76–90.

Svendsen, G. L., and Svendsen, G. T. (2004). *The creation and destruction of social capital: Entrepreneurship, co-operative movements and institutions.* Cheltenham, England. Edward Elgar.

Sweezy, P. M. (1972). *Modern capitalism and other essays.* New York, NY: Monthly Review Press.

Tabellini, G. (2008a). Presidential address: Institutions and Culture. *Journal of the European Association, 6*, 255–294. https://doi.org/10.1162/JEEA.2008.6.2-3.255

Tabellini, G. (2008b). The scope of cooperation: Values and incentives. *The Quarterly Journal of Economics, 123*(3), 905–950. https://doi.org/10.1162/qjec.2008.123.3.905Tara, S., and Kumar, N. (2017). Initiatives in skill upgrading: The case of centres of excellence (COE) in industrial training institutes (ITI) in Karnataka, India. In M. Pilz (Ed.), *Vocational education and training in times of economic crisis: Lessons from around the world.* (pp. 151–170). Cham, Switzerland: Springer Nature.

Tasci, M., and Zenker, M. (2011). Labor market rigidity, unemployment, and the great depression. (Economic Commentary. No. 2011-11). *Federal Reserve Bank of Cleveland.* Retrieved from https://www.clevelandfed.org/en/newsroom-and-events/publications/economic-commentary/economic-commentary-archives/2011-economic-commentaries/ec-201111-labor-market-rigidity-unemployment-and-the-great-recession.aspx

Tawney, R. H. (1922). *Religion and the rise of capitalism*. New York, NY: Penguin Books.

Teubner, G. (2001). Legal irritants: How unifying law ends up in new divergences. In P. A. Hall and D. Soskice (Eds.), *Varieties of capitalism: The institutional foundations of comparative advantage*. (pp. 417–444). New York, NY: Oxford University Press.

Thakur, Y. (2016, November 16). In India entrepreneurship is at an all-time high. *CNBC*. Retrieved from http:www.cnbc/2016/11/16/indian-entrepreneurship

The White House, Office of the Press Secretary (2017). Presidential executive order expanding apprenticeships in America. (June 2015). Retrieved from: https://www.whitehouse.gov/presidential-actions/3245/

Thrush, G. (2018, August 26). $1.7 billion federal job training programs "failing the students." *The New York Times*. Retrieved fromhttps://www.nytimes.com/2018/08/26/us/politics/job-corps-training-program.html

Tosun, J., Arco-Tirado, J., Caserta, M., Cemalcilar, Z., Freitag, M., Horisch, F., . . . Vegetti, F. (2019). Perceived economic self-sufficiency: A country-and generation-comparative approach. *European Political Science, 18*, 510–531. https://doi.org/10.1057/s41304-018-0193-4

Treglown, J. (2013). *Franco's crypt: Spanish culture and memory since 1936*. New York, NY: Farrar, Straus, and Gioux.

Triandis, H. C. (1971). *Attitude and Attitude Change*. New York, NY: Wiley.

Triandis, H. C. (2002). Generic individualism and collectivism. In M. Gannon and K. L. Newman (Eds.), *Handbook of cross-cultural management* (pp. 16–45). Oxford, England: Blackwell.

Twenge, J. M., Campbell, S. M., Hoffman, B. J., and Lance, C. E. (2010). Generational differences in work values: Leisure and extrinsic values increasing, social and intrinsic values decreasing. *Journal of Management, 36*(5), 1117–1142. https://doi.org/10.1177/0149206309352246Ulijn, J., and Fayolle, A. (2004). Towards cooperation between European start-ups: The position of the French, Dutch, and German entrepreneurial and innovative engineer. In T. E. Brown and J. M. Ulijn (Eds.), *Entrepreneurship, innovation and culture: The interaction between technology, progress and economic growth* (pp. 204–232). Cheltenham, England: Edward Elgar.

The uncultured science. (2019, July 27). *The Economist*. Retrieved from https://www.economist.com/printedition/2019-07-27

UNICEF Innocenti Research Center. (2000, June). *A league table of child poverty in rich nations* (Innocenti report card no. 1). Retrieved from https://www.unicef-irc.org/publications/226-a-league-table-of-child-poverty-in-rich-nations.html

UNICEF Innocenti Research Center. (2005). Child poverty in rich countries, 2005 (Innocenti report card 6). Retrieved from https://www.unicef-irc.org/publications/pdf/repcard6e.pdf

UNICEF Innocenti Research Center. (2012). *Measuring child poverty in the world's rich countries* (Innocenti report card no. 10). Retrieved from https://www.unicef-irc.org/publications/pdf/rc10_eng.pdf

UNICEF Innocenti Research Center. (2016). Child poverty in rich countries. Innocenti Report Card 14. UNICEF Innocenti Research Center, Florence.

U.S. Bureau of Labor Statistics. (2020, April 15). Employment projections: Occupations with the most job growth. Retrieved from https://www.bls.gov/emp/tables/occupations-most-job-growth.htm/Valiente, O., and Scandurra, R. (2017). Challenges to the implementation of dual apprenticeships in OECD countries: A literature review. In M. Pilz (Ed.), *Vocational education and training in times of economic crisis* (pp. 41–58). Cham, Switzerland: Springer Nature.

Van Den Broeck, A., Schreurs, B., Proost, K., Vanderstukken, A., and Vansteenkiste, M. (2019). I want to be a billionaire: How do extrinsic and intrinsic values influence youngsters' well-being? *Annals of the American Academy of Political and Social Science, 622,* 204–219.

Veblen, T. (1990). *The place of science in modern civilization.* Boca Raton, FL: CRC Press. (Original work published 1919)

Vogel, P. (2015). *Generation jobless?* London, England: Palgrave Macmillan.

Voltaire. (1979). *Candide: Or optimism.* London, England: Penguin Classics. (Original work published 1759)

Walras, L. (1900). *Elements of theoretical economics* (D. A. Walker and J. Van Daal, Eds.). Cambridge, England: Cambridge University Press.

Wang, D., and Evans, J. A.(2019, February 21). Research: When small teams are better than big ones. *Harvard Business Review.* Retrieved from https://hbr.org/2019/02/research-when-small-teams-are-better-than-big-ones

Wealth distribution and income inequality by country: 2018. (2018, November 26). *Global Finance Magazine.* Retrieved from https://www.gfmag.com/global-data/economic-data/wealth-distribution-income-inequality

Weber, E. U., Hsee, C. K., and Sokolowska, J. (1998). What folklore tells us about risk and risk taking: Cross-cultural comparisons of American, German, and Chinese proverbs. *Organizational Behavior and Human Decision Processes 75*(2), 170–186.

Weber, M. (1958). *The protestant ethic and spirit of capitalism.* New York, NY: Charles Scribner's Sons. (Work originally published 1904)

White House Office of the Press Secretary. (2014, April 16). Remarks by the president and vice president on skills training. Retrieved from https://obamawhitehouse.archives.gov/the-press-office/2014/04/16/remarks-president-and-vice-president-skills-training.

Wildeman, R. E., Hofstede, G., and Noorderhaven, N. (1999). *Self-employment in 23 OECD Countries: The Role of Cultural and Economic Factors.* Zoetermeer, The Netherlands: EIM Small Business Research and Consultancy.

Wilson, W. J. (2009). *More than just race: Being black and poor in the inner city.* New York, NY: Norton.

World Health Organization. (2012). How to conduct a discrete choice experiment for health workforce recruitment and retention in remote and rural areas: A user guide with case studies. Retrieved from https://www.who.int/hrh/resources/dceguide/en/

Wu, L., Wang, D., and Evans, J. A. (2019). Large teams develop and small teams disrupt. *Science and Technology: Nature, 566,* 378–382.

Yang, Y., and Land, K. C. (2013). *Age-period-cohort analysis: New models, methods, and empirical applications.* New York, NY: CRC Press.

Zimmermann, K. F., Biavaschi, C., Eichhorst, W., Giulietti, C., Kendzia, M. J., Muravyev, A., . . . Schmidl, R. (2013). Youth unemployment and vocational training. *Foundations and trends in Microeconomics, 9,* 1–157.

Zirkle, C. (2017). A qualitative analysis of high school level vocational education in the United States: Three decades of positive change. In M. Pilz (Ed.), *Vocational education and training in times of economic crisis* (pp. 321–337). Cham, Switzerland: Springer Nature.

Index

Figures and tables are indicated by *f* and *t* following the page number.